Online Belongings

Debra Ferreday

Online Belongings

Fantasy, Affect and Web Communities

PETER LANG
Oxford • Bern • Berlin • Bruxelles • Frankfurt am Main • New York • Wien

Bibliographic information published by Die Deutsche Bibliothek
Die Deutsche Bibliothek lists this publication in the Deutsche Nationalbibliografie; detailed bibliographic data is available on the Internet at <http://dnb.ddb.de>.

A catalogue record for this book is available from The British Library.

Library of Congress Cataloging-in-Publication Data:

Ferreday, Debra, 1972-
Online belongings : fantasy, affect and web communities / Debra Ferreday.
p. cm.
Includes bibliographical references and index.
ISBN 978-3-03911-529-7 (alk. paper)
1. Online social networks. 2. Communities. 3. Virtual reality--Social aspects. 4. Cyberspace--Social aspects. 5. Internet--Social aspects. I. Title.
HM742.F47 2008
303.48'33--dc22
2009007542

Cover image: Garden spider web with dew drops © Frank Krahmer/Getty images
Cover design: Mette Bundgaard, Peter Lang Ltd

ISBN 978-3-03911-529-7

Hochfeldstrasse 32, CH-3012 Bern, Switzerland
info@peterlang.com, www.peterlang.com, www.peterlang.net

Printed in Germany

Contents

Acknowledgements

My thanks first of all go to Alison Easton and Sara Ahmed: although they will think I am exaggerating, without their wisdom, generosity and encouragement, I don't think I would have written a word. Parts of this project were carried out with funding from the Arts and Humanities Research Council, for which I am deeply grateful. I am indebted as well to colleagues in the Centre for Gender and Women's Studies, Department of Sociology and Institute for Cultural Research, and others at Lancaster and beyond who read and commented on various bits of this book: Jackie Stacey, Anne-Marie Fortier, Claudia Castañeda, Imogen Tyler, Simon Lock, Madeleine Chatterjee, Bela Chatterjee, Vivien Hodgson, Chris Jones, and Lucy Suchman, are all among those whose thoughtful suggestions have influenced me in ways too subtle and mysterious to list. Sarah Kember's trenchant insights improved the text beyond measure. Thanks too to family and friends, RL and virtual, who provided tea and sympathy when I needed it most: you know who you are, and a special mention for Winnie Mitchell who believed it but didn't get to see it. Adi Kuntsman deserves special thanks for sticking up for the project at times when my own enthusiasm flagged. Thanks also to friends and colleagues in the ICR, especially Fiona Summers, Gary Bettinson, Charlie Gere, and special thanks to Beckie Coleman for the incredibly inspiring and illuminating conversations. A big thank you to Simone Gristwood and to all the students on the MA module, Critical Media Practice, who shared stories of their own experiences and showed me new things to do on Facebook. My thanks also to the editorial team at Peter Lang: Alexis Kirschbaum for supporting this project in its early stages, and Nick Reynolds for being patient with an anxious newbie. Finally, words cannot express my love, admiration and gratitude for my husband, David Leedal: this book is for you.

Parts of Chapters 2 and 5 previously appeared as 'Unspeakable Bodies: Erasure, Embodiment and the Pro-Ana Community' in the *International Journal of Cultural Studies*. A much shorter version of Chapter 2 appeared as 'Bad Community' in *M/C Online*.

INTRODUCTION

Desiring Community

> Obsession is the most durable form of intellectual capital.
> — EVE KOSOFSKY SEDGWICK, 2003: 2

I began using the Internet in the early 1990s. As for many women workers at this time, my interest in online communities began as a side-effect of the office temping, the dull 'day job' that funded my academic studies: as a result, my access to the Internet was heavily monitored and proscribed. Computers, or 'word processors' as they were still widely known, were a tool for typing memos and doing the books, as well as a convenient scapegoat when something went wrong; the relationship between computer and user being less widely understood than it is today, we would attempt to soothe enraged clients by ensuring them that the error in their monthly bill was simply due to a 'computer error'. The Internet existed as something tantalising, forbidden; at work by the watchful eyes of supervisors and managers, and at home by the exigencies of a primitive dial-up connection and soaring phone bills. As I sat trapped in a stuffy office, the Netscape icon on my desktop, with its distinctive ship's wheel motif (it was that long ago) seemed to represent the potential for travel: a voyage out of my constrained life of graduate student shabby gentility, to a wider world beyond. As the focus of my research shifted, I returned to my original desire to have greater access to the Web. As a 'newbie' who had read a great deal of theory about virtual reality, but had only very limited experience of actually participating in the chat rooms, bulletin boards and Usenet groups described there, I began to be more interested in the Web, traditionally the flashy, vacuous, commercialised younger sister of 'true' online communities: to wonder how taken-for-granted, everyday online activities might in themselves raise questions of community, belonging and subjectivity. I became increasingly interested in the Web as an area of the Internet that is less widely theorised. I wanted to ask how community might also be at stake in those technologies that require less technical skill on the part of the user: the online shopping sites, institutional and personal homepages, and information sources that I used every day but did not at first consider significant or important.

I am including this brief autobiographical detail to illustrate the main question that informs this book: how to think through our capacity to be affected by and through technologies, and the stories, interactions and debates that surround them? By posing this question, it is my intention to examine the relationship between technology, belonging, and desire (and I am using desire as a subset of the positive affective response that Silvan Tomkins calls interest: an important distinction, of which more later). I began researching online communities in 1998, at a time when the World Wide Web still felt like a 'new' phenomenon (although it is generally agreed to have originated in 1993, and five years is, as we are constantly reminded, a long time in computing). As a result, my fantasy of a wide world of knowledge on the Web resulted in my being plunged into a set of debates in which just such fantasies were called into question. In the early 1990s, a love of computers was limited to Turkle's hackers, ubergeeks who alone were capable of 'loving the machine for itself' (1984: 196). Cyberculture theory, meanwhile, was polarised between a utopian position which sought to align itself with the geeks, and more critical, feminist and postcolonial accounts of cyberspace which were highly suspicious of technocentrism. It might seem strange, then, that this book aligns itself firmly with feminist and postcolonial theory, but also with an affective attachment to the everyday technologies of the Internet: especially since, as Jonathan Sterne has argued, 'the technophilic position is at least somewhat less acceptable in serious scholarship than it was five years ago' (2006: 17). What I am arguing for in this book, then, is not a return to a technophilic position, but a position which acknowledges our attachment to not just computers, but what they can do: the attachments, relationships and subjectivities that are made possible by digital technologies.

This book is hence inspired by affect: affect in the sense, not only of my own experience of 'loving the machine' (and what it can do), but of my own ongoing, passionate engagement with scholarly work on emotion, particularly that of Eve Kosofsky Sedgwick. In relation to Silvan Tomkins' work, Sedgwick poses the crucial question: what does it mean to fall in love with a writer (2003: 117)? This book at least partly charts my own falling in love: with the Internet, with Sedgwick's own work and, through her interest, her enthusiasm, with the theory of affect outlined by the psychologist Silvan Tomkins. As a result, it is Tomkins' version of affect that structures this book. Although there are plenty of exceptions, it is fair to say that the critical literature on affect has two main strands, the Deleuzian, and what I think of as the 'queer theory version' based on Tomkins. Whilst I am now in the process of falling in love with the former, too late for this book, it is the latter that first engaged my interest, not least in that the notion of interest itself seems to speak eloquently of the experience of positive affect in a way that does not insist on lack as a motivating factor and hence need not involve a reading of desire as a drive to incorporate the other. Aspects of Tomkins' work, particularly his deterministic view of affect as biological are problematic.[1] Perhaps it is even the resulting sense of annoyance, of 'yes, but', that motivates my ongoing engagement with his work: my love, unlike Sedgwick's, is not a pure one. But, problematic as the experience of reading Tomkins can be, his ideas map elegantly onto the cyberculture research: as a beautifully

1 To say the least. There is a wonderful section in Sedgwick's book where she reproduces a passage from his work, in order to explain why his version of affect has been overlooked within cultural theory (and, I would argue, still is: in the index to Clough and Halley's *The Affective Turn*, for instance, there are only two references to Tomkins). In the short paragraph she cites, the word 'innate' or 'innately' appears five times, while 'neural firing' appears four times. These terms, she says, are likely to produce 'fear, distress and anger' in theory-minded readers, as well as laughter from scientists (2003: 102). As she sums up, 'you don't have to be long out of theory kindergarten to make mincemeat of, let's say, a psychology that depends on ... affects hardwired into the human biological system' (1993: 94).

simple theory that imagines affect in terms of movements across lines of connection, Tomkins' theory seems to anticipate the process of making connections that, as I will argue, underpins research in general and online research in particular. The notion that 'any affect may have any object' (cited in Sedgwick and Frank 2003: 99), in particular, seems to account for the complex webs of feeling that inform users' experience of technology: we may love the machine 'for itself' as well as the others we encounter through the machine, and indeed the possibility of such encounters itself. Tomkins presents affect as a process: suggesting, for example, that identification might begin with a highly determined moment of recognition, but that it continues not only through the repetition of particular practices, but, crucially, through a process of storytelling. The recognition of affect as a process is, therefore, a crucial part of my argument, since it is precisely this that links community and fantasy (which is concerned first and foremost with stories, as we shall see). However, my argument diverges from Tomkins' theory of affect in its account of why one might experience that initial moment of recognition that comes to be articulated as a sense of belonging. Indeed, the word 'sense' is indicative here since it suggests that such an identification might be so strong as to feel biological, even if it is in fact culturally constructed.

If the following chapter is structured around those theorists with whose work I have fallen in love, I must also mention Lisa Nakamura, whose analysis of the 'post-Internet' age in which we are living suggests a new way of looking at the Web. For Nakamura, the term 'Internet' is itself so loaded with theoretical baggage that it is no longer relevant to users' experience: as she argues, 'it is safe to say that we live in a post-Internet age', if 'the Internet' is understood to mean the text-based Internet together with the constellation of grand theoretical claims associated with it (2007a: 2). However, I am not only concerned with what she calls the 'post-2000 popular graphical Internet' (2007a: 4) as a replacement for old, elitist values which privileged textual sites and early experiments in virtual reality as the only authentic sites of online belonging. Instead, I would question whether those values were ever as dangerous as they seemed. The starting point for this book is to suggest that the notion of 'cyberspace' that so enraged feminists, myself included, in the mid-1990s, bears re-examination in the light of more recent developments in both Internet practice, and critical theory. This is not to deny the difficulties experienced by feminist and postcolonial theorists (though certainly the field has moved on from Zoe Sophia's satirical account of the reaction of virtual reality experts to her research as follows: 'since I am "one of Those" ... (i.e. one who hasn't donned the data glove), I cannot write as an experienced or expert user of VR technology' (1992: 11–12).

As Nakamura points out, virtual reality technologies are no longer considered the benchmark for authority in writing about cyberspace, since 'the Internet is a daily technology, but virtual reality isn't' (2007b: 35). Whether it refers to VR or not, though, the idea of 'immersion' is central in defining who has the right to speak about new technologies. Historically, 'immersion' has been used almost interchangeably with 'disembodiment' (see for example Dibbell 1993, 1998) in ways that implicitly construct a hierarchy between those whose experience of digital cultures is immersive (and hence authentic) and those others who fail at the work of immersion. Most frequently, discussion of offline lived experience, especially of racial or gendered identities, is presented as the moment at which immersion fails: and I discuss this distinction, and the ways in which it works to police some subjects' access to 'authentic' online experience, in Chapter 2 below. Nakamura's invocation of her own sense of immersion is hence a political act. Her argument is a passionate call for a cyberculture studies that is not only aware of difference, but that constitutes 'rigorous academic analysis [of] ... popular cultural forms that established academic disciplines wouldn't address but that people actually used and related to in their daily lives' (2007b: 34–5). Nevertheless, she articulates her own immersion in cyberspace through her experiences as a 'MUD addict':

> People deep in the throes of gaming addiction are maybe not the people you'd expect to find writing meticulously researched, theoretically inclusive academic articles, but ... the kind of personal engagement and detailed knowledge of the interface and interactivity that comes from personal use cannot be feigned. I was a MUD addict for years, and there was no way I could have done my work without that experience (2007b: 35).

Whilst one might argue whether MUDs can truly be opposed to VR as 'everyday technologies' – in retrospect the MUD and the VR helmet seem like the twin pillars that defined the utopian tendency in cyberculture studies[2] – it is instructive to see the notion of 'immersion' transposed from often rather elitist narratives of 'cyberspace' to the more banal and taken-for-granted technologies that increasingly structure our day-to-day experience. In this book, I too am interested in the everyday things that computers can do. Many of these things take place on the Web. Email, blogging and commenting on blogs, shopping, reviewing, homepages, web communities, networking sites and so on are not somehow inferior to, or less immersive than, VR, although the Web has not often been written about in these terms. For example as I show in Chapter 4, shopping for clothes online is not simply a matter of see, point and click: it may involve deep immersion in a number of sites: the practice of finding a particular pair of shoes (and in coming to want those particular shoes in the first place) may involve a level of concentration, tenacity and interest – a central term for this book, and one I shall examine more closely – that renders it indistinguishable, in practical and affective terms, from the preliminary stages of academic research. I do not make this comparison frivolously. What the devoted clothes addict has in common with the academic is a willingness to concentrate, an interest, which is really all that is meant by 'immersion'. Immersion is not a property of certain technologies, but a relation between technologies and users: hence the absurdity of claiming that some activities or technologies are more immersive than others. Taking Nakamura's model to its logical conclusion, we can see that the Web itself is not only an immersive technology, but one that threatens the boundaries of scholarship itself: anyone who 'Googles', as the popular

2 To be fair, Nakamura's point is that gaming is an everyday technology, and one that is still undertheorised. In this sense one could argue for a re-situating of MUDs in a tradition that leads to hugely popular contemporary games such as the Grand Theft Auto series which, however, do not involve interaction between a global network of players: once again, the movement is away from the textual and networked, to the visual and commercial. Certainly, in my experience, games are immersive whether they involve outside interaction or not.

verb has it, is after all engaged in the work of making connections that underpins all research practice.[3]

Nakamura, then, posits a reading of the Web that is grounded in immersion in online texts, which she sees as part of a longer tradition of studying the popular: her approach is hence grounded in cultural studies, and this book shares a concern with, as it were, putting the 'culture' back into cyberculture studies. For Nakamura, this approach stands in contrast to that of 'critics of postmodernity and technology' (she mentions Baudrillard, Guattari and Žižek among others). Reading these theorists, she says, 'you rarely get the feeling that [they] have been truly immersed in the Internet' (2007b: 35). Certainly I recognise her account of the nightmare of trying to teach students to analyse web pages, using the work of writers who 'appear never to have used the Web, much less stooped to including screenshots in their work to illustrate their points' (2007b: 30).[4] She emphasises the desirability of 'enshrining exercises in form and

3 A colleague recently joked that, unlike other academics who are engaged in empirical and archival research, we in cultural studies 'just Google things and make stuff up'. This (and my enthusiastic agreement) were motivated by false modesty, but this joke hints at a deeper truth. There is a resonance between the act of navigating hypertext, and the work of cultural studies: both are intertextual; both are immersive; both involve the 'making up' of a body of knowledge and experience through the making of connections which may be determined, to some extent, by a pre-existing canon (whether of key theoretical texts or sponsored links) but are also structured through the subject's affective responses to canonical texts. Hence, I suspect, my love of the Web, which is partly a narcissistic projection invoked by the pleasure of – it sometimes seems – seeing one's own worldview as a post-disciplinary cultural studies scholar, writ large.

4 This polarisation between 'cultural studies' (as something that needs 'illustrating') and 'theory' (which is assumed to speak for itself) is in itself problematic. Although this book is located in the same tradition as Nakamura's, there are no screen grabs in this book. This decision resulted precisely from my suspicion of using images of web pages to 'illustrate one's points'. Partly this arose from my research on trans identity (see Ferreday and Lock 2007). Whilst writing up our research on transvestite homepages for a conference presentation, Simon Lock and I felt that it would be unhelpful to show images of our research participants, thus potentially reproducing the moment of passing (that is, allowing the audience to

obscurity that students can't relate to and that you can't make popular arguments about' (34) will make sense to many who have taught courses in 'cyberculture studies', 'digital culture', and so on. Nevertheless, one of my objectives in this book is to call into question the idea that 'theory' necessarily implies an elitist and utopian reading of cyberculture. Indeed it is by drawing on recent developments in cultural theory, particularly theories of affect, that I argue it is possible to read beyond the impasse in cyberculture studies. The test of theory ought not to be whether it can be 'applied' to web pages or any other media, but where it can take us. This may not always be to a place that feels comfortable. If theory does not 'fit into' an existing political position or worldview, then we need to at least consider whether it is the position, not the theory, that needs to be rethought. Thinking through affect can be a way of doing this: to use Sedgwick and Frank's evocative phrase, affect has the power to disrupt and question 'what theory knows' (2003: 93).

As well as asking what it might mean to read the Web through affect, this book examines how and why the Web came to be excluded from other readings of online community. My argument suggests that it is possible, indeed necessary, to read the Web as a site of community. This is less controversial now that theory has moved on from the distinction between what used to be seen as 'authentically' virtual texts, and those which are considered simply 'commercial' (and hence unworthy of attention). Historically, the theoretical commentaries that accompanied the growth of 'new' technologies and media and which privileged fantasy

---

judge the 'authenticity' of online identity performances according to how closely the subjects resembled biological women). This is not to claim that all audiences would have made such a judgment, nor is it perfect as a means of reproducing our online encounters with subjects; nevertheless, it felt important to ask listeners and readers to think through the ways in which we encounter others through research. A static image does not in any way recreate the experience of looking at that page online, let alone the intensity and immersion – or, paradoxically, the banality and casualness – of the activity formerly known as 'surfing the web'. By giving web addresses but excluding screen grabs, this book becomes connected to a network of other sites and other media, but does not attempt to incorporate them as mere 'source material'.

and text-based web communities such as text-based multi user domains (MUDs) and UseNet communities as a site for the creation of 'virtual' selves. This is exemplified in Sherry Turkle's ironic description of online spaces as a 'through the looking glass' world (1995: 9). This led to much critical emphasis being placed on the notion of 'the virtual' as 'different from' the real: from this, much debate ensued about whether such an alternative reality might result in the formation of utopian or dystopian forms of community.

Early theories focussed on two privileged sites of virtual reality: one highly visual (the early experiments in virtual reality environments, which are bearing fruit today in the form of sites like Second Life), and the other entirely textual. In practice, user experience of online spaces has been dominated, not by participation in these over-determined online spaces, but by the World Wide Web. As Nakamura illustrates, the 'text-based Internet' not only no longer dominates theory, but often no longer exists, since many of the textual communities that so preoccupied theorists in the mid-90s have since disappeared (although we should note that some of the most celebrated communities, notably Lambdamoo and the Well, have continued to survive and thrive). As we have seen, for Nakamura, their passing has also meant the end of the Internet as a niche interest or subculture dominated by 'an elite and largely male digerati' (2007a: 1). The increasing commercialisation of online space, together with constant developments in interactive and visual technologies, has led to the Internet increasingly becoming synonymous with the Web (Gill 2002: cited in O'Riordan and Phillips 2007: 5). At the same time, the upsurge in blogging culture, which postdates much of the canonical work on virtual reality, challenges the notion that the potential of online communities lies precisely in their detachment from 'real life'. Indeed, the upsurge in blogging culture, with its integration between online and offline life, calls into question the very notion of the need for a field called 'cyberstudies', since it radically problematises the notion of a discrete, privileged 'cyberculture'. Some have suggested that these changes may suggest the possibility of new critical insights: for example O'Riordan and Phillips argue that 'we can expect different analytic approaches as well as different empirical insights' to arise from these shifts' (2007: 5).

Others argue that in practice, whilst the field has expanded to incorporate a wide range of theoretical insights from various disciplines, it has generated few new theoretical approaches of its own: these are still to come (Silver 2006: 5).

Whilst not wishing to detract from the importance of these studies, we might want to question why, as scholars familiar with the exigencies as well as the excitement of interdisciplinarity, we in the field of cyberstudies are so committed to the idea of a 'new theory' (or at least a new theoretical canon). What is at stake in the desire, the longing, for 'a canon'? In a sense, the *imprimateur* of interdisciplinary scholarship has always been its ability to generate new formations, new insights, by *using* existing theory, by bringing together existing theories and practices in unexpected ways. As for Freud's child who dreams of angels (1991: 168), it is the juxtaposition of familiar elements in unexpected ways (human body + wings), that is uncanny, and it is this uncanniness that unsettles the subject and that (potentially) generates new ways of seeing. Theory, like the unconscious, cannot imagine an entirely new thought, though, perhaps haunted by the grand 'discoveries' of science, it may dream of such a possibility. Instead, newness lies in the making of connections, the juxtaposition of elements in uncanny and unsettling ways. The Internet, that vast and expanding field of knowledge, stories, exchanges, arguments, revelations and lies, constantly being re-constituted through pathways of desire, is inherently concerned with the making of just such connections. The Internet calls into question the relative status of researcher and subject, since often new formations, new connections are already being made. New theoretical insights are not 'made' by scholars: instead, they surface through the reader's relationship with the text, coming into being through textual encounters.

I use the terms 'text' and 'reading' deliberately, here. Although some (but not all) studies of cyberculture have privileged the notion of online experience as encounter, in this book I am sceptical of the notion of encountering the Other in online 'space', for reasons that will become clear. Instead of thinking of the Web simply 'as' a space, I want to pay attention to the practices and politics of reading in structuring notions of online encounters. If as I have suggested interdisciplinarity is the outcome of a kind of scholarly restlessness, a fascination for what lies beyond disciplinary boundaries, then it intrinsically mirrors the practice of wide and voracious reading which, for many of us, is what got us into this profession in the first place. Interdisciplinary thus arguably finds its ideal archive in cyberspace. It is perhaps unfashionable, at this point in the field's history, to sing the praises of hypertext, but nevertheless there is something about the process of finding one's way through the overwhelming mass of data that constitutes the Internet, guided only by one's own concerns and curiosities, one's capacity to be affected and 'interested' (or not), that speaks particularly powerfully to practices of interdisciplinary scholarship. The ability to make connections, arbitrarily, serendipitously and on the spot, is what matters. Researchers have always worked in this way, making connections between ideas, theories, subjects, hopefully in new and startling ways to create new constellations of knowledge. The broad and diverse field known as 'cyberstudies' is such a new formation, yet as scholars we long for more, for a 'new theory' which cannot presently be imagined. Before we berate ourselves for not having achieved this, I am suggesting that Internet scholars might rethink this question of 'the new' in two ways. One is to think about what cyberculture studies might gain by engaging with wider debates in cultural theory (an strategy of which the approach I take in this book, which draws on theories of fantasy and affect, is only one possible interpretation). This would avoid the fault line that ran through earlier attempts to form a canon, namely that some of the debates that were 'live' and generating the most exciting theoretical development of the time – especially in feminist and postcolonial theory – were seen as 'not new enough' and even as actively outmoded, although the critical interventions of feminist and postcolonial scholars, as well as the gulf between theory and actual Internet practice that quickly became evident, means that this has begun to change in recent years (Silver 2006: 3). It needs to be recognised, then, that the call for new theoretical insights does not mean that cyberculture studies needs to stand alone, or that it cannot work with existing theory.

A different approach might be to question why the idea of 'the new' is so central, and so affecting, for Internet scholarship. In early theories of cyberculture, there was much debate about whether the Internet could be studied using the tools of existing disciplines, or whether 'cyberculture studies' constituted a new field. In an interview given in 2002, David Silver recalls a keen desire to establish a 'canon' for cyberculture studies:

> There was this professor in Maryland, and I love this guy, but he said, 'You can't have a field, you don't have a canon. You can't have a canon when you don't have any books. I turned around and this was in 1996 when maybe there were only two shelves of books in my office. Now there's this,' Silver said, pointing to no less than 10 shelves packed side to side and up and down with books. 'This is all cyberculture studies ...' (Silver cited in Hill 2002).

The interviewer goes on to note that Silver's longing for a 'canon' was not only motivated by visions of academic respectability, but also out of a feeling of isolation as an Internet scholar: as he puts it, 'I wanted a community' (Hill 2002). This longing to be part of a community of scholars, and the anxiety about whether this can be achieved, underpins much early writing in the field. I wonder now whether this anxiety was perhaps heightened by the very experience of studying online communities, particularly the text-based communities and multi-user games that formed the basis for much (though not all) research at that time. Certainly there was a sense of a vast, complex communities already forming, at such a pace that academic research could not keep up. At the same time, an academic community was beginning to form, but this community often seemed to be in schism: divided between researchers and practitioners; between those with technological and humanities backgrounds; and (especially) between theorists who took a positive, optimistic view of the potentialities of new media, and those who took a more cautious and critical position. With the exception of the various positions inspired by the germinal work of Donna Haraway and generally grouped together as 'cyberfeminist', some of whom argued for what Faith Wilding calls a 'utopian vision' as well as 'a repudiation of old-style feminism' (Haraway 1991, 1995, 1997, Wilding 1998: 6), the latter position was often associated with feminism. A familiar story thus began to emerge: of a cyber-theory presented as masculine, exploratory and daring, versus the constraining maternal voices counselling caution. The field felt polarised, especially between those theorists who were invested in the Internet as a site of liberation from fixed identity categories, and those who argued that this position would only lead to offline power relations becoming reified in cyberspace, increasing the marginalisation of already marginalised subjects.

Whilst this book is concerned with these issues, it does not seek to argue definitively for one position. Instead, it argues that cyberculture studies needs to pay attention to the importance of power, as well as the continuities and connections between online and offline life (and indeed, this is the direction the field appears to be taking in the early twenty-first century, as we shall see). However, by paying attention to the affectivity of texts and examining the ways in which online texts work to produce a sense of belonging, my argument goes beyond this, intervening in debates around virtual community by challenging the hegemony of the term 'virtual reality' itself. I use the concept of fantasy to examine how 'the virtual' has come to be accepted as the dominant theoretical concept for thinking through the ways in which new technologies are used to create a sense of community. I ask to what extent theories of virtuality work to constitute a fantasy community: I also ask what it might mean to question that dominant status. So, whilst my argument suggests that the category of virtual community be extended to include the Web, it goes on to propose that, if a text can be read as virtual, it can also be read as fantastic. In a sense, virtuality works in a similar way to fantasy in that it represents a means of making connections that bridge the gaps between 'the real' and 'the imagined'.[5] However, in the following chapter, I ask what it might mean to read 'the virtual' as a fantasy, and to ask what fantasies are at stake in theories of virtual reality. Such a reading, I argue, allows us to account for the ways in which 'virtuality' works to reproduce an oppositional relationship between the real and the imagined, and how such a relationship conceals the extent to which they are mutually constitutive. Further, by reading online community through fantasy, my research pays attention

5 For helping me to clarify the notion of 'connections' and 'gaps', as for much else in this chapter, I am indebted to conversations with Rebecca Coleman. For a much more articulate account of the notion of 'gaps', see her book, *The Becoming of Bodies*, forthcoming from Manchester University Press.

to the process by which theories of virtuality have worked to construct 'the virtual' as inherently liberating and have hence tended to obscure the ways in which online communities may exclude some subjects. What is more, it asks how such exclusions work in practice: how do websites and associated texts work to produce and maintain boundaries, and how do these boundaries marginalise some users whilst simultaneously producing a sense of belonging in others?

However, fantasy is not a fixed category which simply provides the theoretical background for my research. Instead, I take advantage of the fact that fantasy is itself a contested term, using fantasy in a number of ways, as a thread that runs through my reading of online communities. In Chapter 2, I go on to look more closely at some of the concerns I have raised in this section, by asking how theories of virtual community have tended to reproduce a particular fantasy of liberation through creating new identities. Whilst this question is central, subsequent chapters continue to problematise the term 'fantasy' by reading the ways in which different websites use fantasy in a variety of ways to create a sense of belonging.

Conclusion and Guide to Chapters

Whilst my desire to read the Internet reflexively stems from an earlier engagement with feminist methodology and epistemology, I have stated that it is also informed by my early experiences of engaging with online communities as a 'newbie', that is a novice or amateur. What does it mean to be a 'newbie'? Traditionally, this term represents a use of language to reinforce a sense of community: hence it may be read as a form of resistance, a deliberate attempt to resist comprehension by the dominant culture. The term 'newbie', besides simply describing a state of being at a certain point in time, has an implied pejorative import:

> Newbie
>
> Think adolescent: awkward, clueless, even annoying. That's what you feel like when you're new to the Web. It can be quite overwhelming at first. Certain online environments are more tolerant of newbies – like America Online, for example. If you're a newbie, be patient with yourself. Even the most notorious hacker and the most eloquent nethead were newbies once! (Young 1998)

The newbie is thus constructed as a figure to be tolerated at best. Such attitudes of grudging 'tolerance' construct a power relationship between newcomers and long-time users which threatens to become oppressive. Despite the designation of her glossary as 'Kinder, Gentler' – (in itself an ironic play on the language of advertising and thus, perhaps, implying an acknowledgement of the Internet's place within consumerism, as a by-product of global capitalism) – Young's insider's view of the newbie as a barely tolerated annoyance positions the new user as vulnerable and powerless. This powerlessness of the individual is, in fact, a recurring trope in the language of the Internet. For example, the expression 'to surf the Web' tends to naturalise the idea of the Internet as a place, drawing upon the perception of the sea as a massive and only partially knowable force of nature. The image of the surfer calls to mind the frailty of the human subject, and especially the unreliability of human technologies in establishing mastery over the forces of nature; it also makes all too clear the distinction between the skilled subject who avoids dangerous immersions, and the novice who places herself in constant danger. As Sherry Turkle has pointed out, one of the most persistent arguments against the liberating value of digital culture is the insistence upon the belief in an autonomous ego which implies investment in the post-Enlightenment model of the self as capable of, and defined through, such acts of mastery (Turkle 1995: 178). In this discourse, the Internet's constant refusal to be mastered, is experienced as threatening. The condition of being a newbie, then, is always presented as precarious and even dangerous, and in this respect it is related to the position of newcomers or outsiders in other types of community. In cyberspace, the technologies for excluding strangers take new forms, principally because the identification of the outsiders occurs through a reading of text rather than by means of visual acts of (mis)recognition. Boundaries do not simply exist in a fixed form: rather, they are formed through reading.

In choosing to become a newbie, a greater personal investment is clearly implied than in (for example) simply learning to use a new software package or play an interactive computer game, and this investment is problematic for the researcher. Although many academics have experience of using the Internet as a tool or series of tools (for personal and professional e-mail, for looking up books in library catalogues, for registering for conferences, or as a news service, and so on) without ever coming across terms such as 'newbie', what is at stake here is the right of entry into the paradigm of Internet-as-space, the virtual community of cyberpunk fiction (and postmodern theory). Like all new users, the researcher is positioned within a self-development trope, inscribed in the language of self-help culture, in which use of the Web becomes a personal progression from newbie to nethead, in the process becoming set apart from 'the masses' whose grasp of Internet culture and language is supposed to be inaccurate and inauthentic. For example, the glossary cited above defines the term 'cyberpunk' as 'somewhat out-dated', concluding that 'Hollywood hasn't figured out the term ... and continues to pedal it to the masses in ridiculous movies about cyberspace' (Young 1998).

Whilst I do not want to under-emphasise my own privilege when reflecting on my relationship with the online texts I read here, this prevalence of an exclusionary rhetoric of authenticity raised interesting questions concerning the role of the researcher. Although there is no single feminist methodology, one of the concerns shared by many feminist epistemologists is the importance of reflexivity. Yet, as I will explain further in the following chapter, my argument hinges on a reading of online interaction as reading: I engage with websites not as spaces of encounter, but as texts. Although the online text may be autobiographical and may allow the self to be made intelligible in various ways (as in the case of blogs), my engagement with that text is primarily as a reader. To reflect on the role of the researcher is hence to open up a wider reflection on what it means to read and how reading might be performative. Reflexivity in feminist research has often been discussed in terms of a need to 'put oneself in the text', in order partially to deconstruct the traditional power relation between subject (researcher) and object (researched) (Skeggs 1995, Reinharz 1992, Fonow and Cook 1991, Stanley and Wise 1990). Of course, not all Internet researchers are newbies. However, when the researcher does approach the Web as a beginner, the traditional power relationship between researcher and subject is already implicitly deconstructed to a certain extent, since the researcher may be in a position of vulnerability in relation to her subject. This tension between deliberately making oneself accountable – for example, by attempting to make the finished research available to the subject – and the vulnerability associated with being a newbie, constitutes both a source of anxiety and an opportunity to work through ethical questions which would otherwise, perhaps, be consigned (in the finished book) to the relatively safe text of the methodology chapter and assumed to have been resolved and stabilised. The study of the Internet rejects such a fantasy of stability. The 'self' that the researcher 'puts into' the text becomes decentred as a result of the tension between the privileged role of academic, and the subordinate positioning of the 'newbie'.

However, as I write this I am aware that I can no longer be said to occupy such a position. This movement between earlier and present reality is, again, a point at which fantasies of the researcher's relationship with her material come into play. By thinking back to my experiences as a newbie, I am aware that I may seem to be claiming a marginality that no longer speaks to my real position as an experienced researcher. By claiming in some sense to speak for the newbie, I am attempting to take up a position that implies certain privileges (not least of which is the privilege of making mistakes), as well as disadvantages. For many feminist theorists, the Internet has great potential to transform lives in a positive way. This potential is often represented as an almost mystical sense of liberation, particularly in relation to gender. So, for example, Sadie Plant has stated that there is a long-standing link between information technology and women's liberation, to the extent that, 'Just as machines get more intelligent, so women get more liberated' (quoted in Cross 1996), whilst other feminist theorists have more cautiously embraced the potential offered by the Web as a means of forming feminist communities (Spender 1995, Smith and Balka 1988).

I have attempted to show here how my argument, which is concerned with mapping the ways in which boundary policing works in the context of online communities, was informed by my early experiences as a new user feeling excluded from communities, and how my original resistance came to be modified through a growing affective attachment to those communities based on an increasing familiarity. However, this is not to claim that such processes are unique to virtual cultures. What is more, it is important to note that the FAQs and glossaries I cite here are provided with the intention of easing the user's progress from the marginality of 'newbie' status to full participation. However, it should also be noted that just as one ideally becomes inducted into the community through the reiteration of certain acts (such as logging on, reading posts, and so on), those very processes might also work to reinforce a sense of not-belonging, of exclusion. An example of this would be where the FAQ pages for a particular community were worded so as to produce a narrative of whiteness or heterosexuality as the norm: this is an ongoing problem of online communities and one that generates activism and resistance.[6] It is important, then, to distinguish between the sense of marginality that derives simply from being a newbie (and which gradually dissipates as one comes to develop a 'sense of belonging') from that occurs as a result of conditions that constantly perpetuate the inclusion of some subjects at the expense of others: indeed, the need to identify specific practices of inclusion and exclusion is a crucial aspect of my argument. Whilst it was my experiences as a newbie that first made me aware of the ways in which a 'sense of belonging' might fail, it is with less contingent and temporary forms of marginality that this book is concerned.

6 For example, there is currently a campaign to protest against Facebook's policy of forcing users to select 'male' or 'female' gender identities. At the time of writing, the petition launched by the group Campaign for Facebook to have other gender options (and to use the word 'gender' rather than 'sex'), has over 9,000 members: see http://www.facebook.com/home.php#/group.php?gid=2247153069&ref=mf, accessed 28 November 2008. This is only one of a growing number of groups calling for Facebook and other social networking groups to adopt more inclusive and queer-positive membership policies.

Further, a concern with the politics of reading shows us that the Web does not exist in isolation, and one of the ways in which my argument does this is by reading websites alongside other texts including theory, advertisements, fantasy fiction, and writings about the Web. Indeed the object of my argument is often not simply the website plus its associated community of users; rather, I also take into account the relationships between the various Web communities, and other associated texts that might shape the ways in which one engages with those communities. This involves reading responses to particular websites both in the mass media and in other sections of the Web, as well as the ways in which theory informs practice to influence the forms taken by Web communities. These concerns are contained within the structure of the book, which begins with a reading of an early article that attempts to prescribe what an online community should do, and then progresses through readings of multiple texts to end with a reading of critical responses to a community, the pro-ana subculture, which is at the centre of contemporary debates about gender, embodiment and the digital.

The readings I present here cover a variety of websites, some of which are addressed as representative of particular categories or types that I think support my claim that a sense of community can be constructed through a reading of the Web, and some as more specific sub-genres or individual sites that speak to my concerns about fantasy and community. Whilst the choice of websites is necessarily highly subjective, all the sites I discuss here have one feature in common: that is, they all seem to address the reader directly. Whilst I surveyed thousands of websites in the course of my research, then, I have selected those that I felt attempted to interpolate the reader into a community. Often, I found that the pages of hypertext links included in the sites useful in tracking the boundaries of particular communities: as a result that the sites within each chapter are usually linked in this way. These links do not always refer to 'like-minded' communities: for example, the two sites discussed in Chapter 2 are connected by an unwanted link, in which homophobic communities provide the Web address of the virtual Aids quilt (and other gay-identified sites) so that their members can visit in order make hostile interventions. Similarly, the pro-ana sites in Chapter 5 are hypertextually linked to hostile journalistic accounts on other servers. On the other hand, a careful tracking of the links can also reveal much about the political allegiances of particular communities, and the ways in which they link into everyday experience, working to structure and delimit users' offline lives as well as opening up new connections and possibilities.

Guide to Chapters

In the following introductory chapter, 'Webs of Affect: Fantasy, Virtuality and Belonging', I pose the questions: what is at stake in theories of virtual community, and what does it mean to re-position online communities as fantastic? Fantasy, virtuality and community are contested terms: by carrying out close readings of academic texts, his chapter tracks the development of notion of 'the virtual' within studies of online sociality, paying close attention to the ways in which it has been taken up across a range of disciplinary and theoretical contexts. This chapter prepares the ground for the case studies, by explaining how my account of online belonging uses fantasy to interrogate existing models of virtual community, and introduces my method of reading websites as fantastic communities.

Chapter 2, '(Un)deleted Subjects: Mourning, Violence and Community', goes on to interrogate the question of what 'a sense of belonging' means in the context of online spaces. I begin by posing the question: if one desires 'a sense of belonging', what must one do in order to achieve it? For many commentators, a crucial aspect of virtual community is its potential to produce social spaces in which 'unfreedoms' such as gender, race, ethnicity and class are left behind (Seidler 1998). In other words, some subjects/bodies are imagined as 'having' unfreedom. Since virtual communities are imagined primarily as a site of liberation, I argue, it is through becoming separated from one's inherent unfreedoms that one comes to belong. Online belonging is hence dependent upon one's ability to produce an 'unmarked' self. Therefore, I argue that it is necessary to pay attention not only to the ways in which online belongings may obscure offline identity and preclude discussion of lived experience, but also to the ways in which 'belonging' itself may involve invisible forms of labour that demand more from some subjects than others, thus reproducing inequality rather than challenging it. I propose the term 'deletion' as a means of articulating the norms, practices and technologies through which this model of community, far from liberating subjects from their racially marked and gendered identities, requires that they constantly engage in technologically mediated practices of self-censorship. Through a reading of the Virtual Aids Quilt as a site which produces a sense of belonging through the invocation of an affective response on the part of the reader, I argue that such practices, in that they involve constant awareness of oneself as Other, mean that it is impossible for some subjects, and some bodies, to belong. Belonging itself, therefore, becomes the object of a desire whose gratification is constantly deferred; the community is split between those who belong (and can hence move on to full participation in the community), and those who are caught in an eternal longing-to-belong.

In Chapter 3, 'At-home in Cyberspace: Home, Belonging and Subjectivity', I return to the question of erasure, asking how subjects come to feel at-home in online communities. This chapter brings together theories of fantasy, community and virtuality, but focuses on the status of 'the self' in relation to the community. By paying attention to the question of subjectivity in this way, I am able to explore further the importance of notions of subjectivity both in determining the ways in which Web communities come to be read and imagined, and in defining the limits of communities themselves. I continue to explore the relationship between self and community, between the psychic and the social, arguing that being 'at-home' in cyberspace is imagined as involving an element of self-erasure. I begin by examining two different approaches to imagining the relationship of the self to a site of online community. The first section draws on a close reading of two online subcultures: the 'virtual vampires' webrings and domestic webcams, to demonstrate how the online reproduction of everyday lived experience alongside fantasy narratives of the self works to destabilise oppositional models of the virtual and the real.

The second section examines the ways in which web communities, such as the 'identity testing' site Emode offer the fantasy that it is possible to produce an identity that is 'at-home' in cyberspace precisely in that it is marked not by race, class, gender or ability, but by forms of subcultural identification and consumer preference. However, by reading the Emode quizzes alongside the site's banner advertising for antidepressant medication, I suggest that these 'new, improved' selves are haunted by practices of deletion that extend into offline bodily experience.

Chapter 4, 'Cyberconsumption: Pleasure, Fantasy and Online Shopping', opens up the notion of transcendence first raised in Chapter 2, by exploring how online shopping sites have been informed by theories of virtuality in constructing a model of 'shopping in comfort'. It draws on close readings of the online designer clothes store Net-A-Porter and online supermarkets alongside 'virtual' gift sites, especially from which users can send 'virtual' goods (that is, goods that do not exist except as on-screen images). The chapter suggests that theories of online belonging are appropriated in order to interpolate the user, using fantasy to produce an investment in the role of cyber-consumer: a trend which gained intensity in the aftermath of September 11 2001 and the subsequent terrorist attacks in Madrid and London, through the production of online shopping as a 'safe' way to fulfil one's 'patriotic' role as consumer. I go on to analyze the ways in which commercial sites create fantasies and sell them to the user by encouraging her to share them. This in a sense reverses the process outlined in the previous chapter by which users use their own homepages to create highly situated and unique fantasy narratives. Finally, the chapter provides a reading of British online supermarkets which examines the shifting role of community in these websites. Whilst supermarkets do not construct a Web community as such, I argue that they work to produce a sense of belonging which, in its limiting of interactive function to the shopping software itself, recalls Žižek's (1998, 2007) notion of 'interpassivity', a phenomenon which he argues constitutes the 'uncanny double' of interactivity (2007: 23). In this case, a fantasy of 'being interactive' itself becomes central to the work of identification. The chapter goes on to examine how supermarkets further encourage the reader to identify as a member of an existing community of Western consumers which is assumed to share common fantasies both of 'the Orient', and of 'the local' as an object of classed desire. For example, the images and texts used to promote 'exotic' foods works alongside the notion of virtuality to construct online shopping as a privileged (and implicitly classed) activity. I suggest a reading that brings together feminist accounts of consumption, drawing on bell hooks' notion of 'Eating the Other' (hooks 1992) together with theories of foodism (Probyn 2000), and commodity racism (McClintock 1995). Such a reading allows for an awareness of the ways in which these sites construct a fantasy of consuming the Other.

The fifth and final chapter, 'Pro-Ana: Writing the Virtual Body', returns to my concern with erasure, specifically with the question of what happens to the body if online belonging is imagined as dependent upon self-erasure. As I have described above, this chapter looks at pro-eating disorder communities in order to argue that it is precisely their performance of a refusal to become disembodied that causes some sites to become the object of censorship. What is more, the controversy surrounding pro-ana allows for an insight into the ways in which the 'newness' of 'new media' has been mobilised in the emergence of a number of moral panics that centre on the impossibility of fixing 'real' identity in online spaces. This chapter suggests that by seeing self-erasure as liberating, theories of online belonging conceal the fact that if such an erasure is not undertaken willingly, it may be imposed by the dominant culture within which these sites are situated. Censorship can, therefore, be seen as the indirect result of an economy of difference which privileges a fantasy of becoming unmarked and which implicitly positions the body, and by extension certain experiences and fantasies, as unspeakable.

In the conclusion, I think critically about the argument of this book, and to reflect on the ways in which my analysis of online and offline textual materials might build on existing debates on community, belonging and identity within studies of online media, and in feminist theory and cultural studies more generally. What does a model of fantastic community and identity make possible for studies of the relation between the virtual and the real? In keeping with the exploratory approach of *Online*

Belongings, this conclusion, rather than proposing a simplistic answer to this question, examines the ways in which my case studies work to challenge historic notions of 'the virtual', asking how the debate might be opened up by a reading that pays attention to the role of fantasy in producing offline, as well as online identities.

CHAPTER 1

Webs of Affect: Fantasy, Virtuality and Belonging

In this book I am centrally concerned with questions of community. However, this is not to assume the existence of 'the Web community' (or indeed 'Web communities') as a given, something that simply exists 'out there' and can be investigated. Community is not a given but a process, an achievement: to borrow Stuart Hall's well-known formulation, it suggests that cultural identity is 'a matter of "becoming" as well as "being"' (1994: 225). This is true of online communities: not only in that subjects 'become' participants in a community (in making the transition from newbie status to full membership, for example), but also that communities themselves are constantly in a process of becoming. Communities are open to transformation as members join or leave, and as values and rules change. Whilst communities themselves are unfixed, however, the term itself has currency within popular and political discourse as a means of describing 'minority' groups, as in 'the black community' or 'the gay community'. It is this model of society as composed of diverse tribal groups (which, however, simultaneously works to reinforce a white, middle-class norm: one seldom hears about the 'white middle-class male community', except in satire) that most often underpins the notion of 'online communities'. This use of the term suggests a certain fixity: for example, the notion of community policing might suggest that 'the black community' is inextricably linked to a particular geographic space, which traditionally excludes the police but which can be visited and hence incorporated into a multicultural society. There is therefore a slippage between the notion of many separate, 'tribal' communities, and 'the' community in which difference becomes submerged in favour of a more generalised rhetoric of belonging. As Andre Lemos points out, this reading of 'community' tends to depoliticise questions of social collectively, a function which can be seen in its gradual displacement of the term 'society'. Hence, Lemos argues,

> [Community] now signifies a social collectivity ... in which the contract, institutionalisation, a common project, a certain utopian optimism, the appearance of proximity, a physical territoriality and form of communication which are direct or almost unmediated, prevail (1996: 43).

This model is certainly applicable to some imaginings of online community, as we shall see. However, I want to focus here on an important characteristic of this version of community: that is it insists that community is founded on (physical) proximity, as well as communication and shared beliefs and practices. In this sense, Lemos' model of community is similar to that found in the work of Benedict Anderson's theory of the imagined community. Famously, Anderson argues that cultural identity is constructed by means of imagination: 'the fellow members of even the smallest nation will never know most of their fellow-members, meet them, or even hear of them, yet in the minds of each lives the image of their communion' (1991: 6). Clearly, this model does not entail communication between members of the community, although it does depend on the dissemination of ideas about nationality by literature and the media. However, it does require physical proximity: following on from his analysis of the national as imagined, Anderson argues that it is also limited. That is, it has boundaries that distinguish it from other nations (1991: 7), and the formation and maintenance of these boundaries is central to the imagining of the nation.

Therefore, whilst the imagined community is conceived of as a 'deep, horizontal comradeship' and as a 'fraternity' (1991: 7), it also implies geographic proximity as well as shared interests: and it is for this reason that Anderson has specifically rejected the notion of the Internet as a site of imagined community, stating that 'you don't have to talk to anybody you don't want to talk to, and in that sense it is the exact opposite of a bar or newspapers' (cited in Smith and Kelemen 1999: 12). Other commentators have expanded on this argument, suggesting that virtual communities are inauthentic precisely because they do not require face to face interaction: for example, Clifford Stoll writes, '[much] of what happens over the networks is a metaphor-we chat without speaking, smile without grinning, and hug without touching ... How sad – to dwell in a metaphor without living the experience. The only sensations are a glowing screen, the touch of a keyboard, and the sound of an occasional bleep. All synthetic' (1995: 43–4). In a sense, then, the virtual community is seen as problematic precisely in that it is too imagined: the virtual threatens to displace material reality.

In theories of cyberculture, as well as debates on community more generally, the comradeship described by Anderson is most often articulated in terms of 'a sense of belonging'. For example, as early as the 1980s McMillan and Chavis described a sense of community as 'a feeling that members have of belonging, a feeling that members matter to one another and to the group, and a shared faith the members' needs will be met through their commitment to be together' (1986: 9). In his article on cyberculture, Shaun Wilbur also evokes the notion of belonging as evidence of a shift from the notion of geographic space as the grounds of cultural identity:

> Community seems to refer primarily to relations of commonality between persons and objects, and only rather imprecisely to the site of such community. What is important is a holding-in-common of qualities, properties, identities or ideas (Wilbur 2000: 47).

This 'holding-in-common' is central to the notion of a 'sense of belonging'. This trope appears repeatedly in early writings on online community. For example, in *Life on the Screen*, Sherry Turkle argues that the shift from using machines as a tool, to full participation in a virtual community occurs when 'a new kind of conversational space opens up', so that '[t]he particular mix of spatial metaphors and the dynamics of instantaneous communication ... build a sense of belonging' (1995: 34). She compares this sense of belonging to that traditionally associated with 'the good place' or 'third place'. She illustrates her argument by using an analogy between online cafés, and the local bars and cafes of geophysical communities. Hence, an online community is imagined as a place in which one feels comfortable and where one can enjoy easy conversations with what David Gauntlett terms 'like-minded people' (2000: 13–14). This would suggest that a sense of belonging derives from an identification resulting from feeling comfortable within a community of shared interests which is, crucially, based on likeness. Whilst computer technology is valued for its ability to bring the user into contact with others, they are others with whom one is able to identify, whose minds are like one's own, rather than different and hence potentially threatening.

Early accounts of text-based virtual communities used the term 'a sense of belonging' to describe how a shared responsibility for building and helping to develop the online environment leads to an enhanced identification with the community (Bruckman 1997; Roberts, Smith and Pollock 1996). However, this 'sense of belonging' does not simply result from entry into a pre-existing, fixed community in which one shifts from newbie status to full participation. Rather, such identifications are crucial in the surfacing and emergence of community. Despite multiple examples of how specific online communities work, accounts such as Turkle's leave the question of what actually constitutes a 'sense of belonging' somewhat vague. In the texts on computer-mediated cultures discussed above, the term 'sense of belonging' is not fully present: whilst it is taken for granted that such a sense is a necessary factor in engaging with online communities, the term itself is rarely interrogated or explained. It is precisely this taken-for-grantedness that feminist studies of belonging have attempted, in other contexts, to address. The imperative to challenge the notion that one simply 'belongs' to particular groups or categories can be rethought in relation to Butler's well-known theory of performativity.

In *Gender Trouble*, Butler seeks to problematise the idea that one simply belongs to one of two oppositional genders: instead, she argues, gender is produced through the reiteration of particular actions (Butler 1990). However, the performative nature of identity is obscured by the very credibility of those performances, with the result that gender is 'a construction that conceals its genesis' (1990: 140). Following Bell, it is possible to extend Butler's model of gender performativity to account for 'belongings' more generally. For Bell, a less explored aspect of Butler's work is that it allows us to see that 'one does not simply or ontologically "belong" to the world or any group within it', rather 'belonging is an achievement at many levels of abstraction' (1999: 3). Like gender identity, belonging itself is citational: 'the performativity of belonging "cites" the norms that constitute or make present the "community" or group as such' (Bell 1999: 3). It is this citational model of belonging that informs my argument. We might want to question how the repetition of particular acts – such as the clicking of a mouse – allow identifications and belongings to surface.

In addition to this focus on belonging as performative, we might also want to think critically about the notion of belonging as 'having in common' or 'like-mindedness'. As Elspeth Probyn points out, the term 'belonging' suggests both identification and a sense of shared imaginary possessions or 'belongings'. Her account represents a shift from the notion of group identity as fixed: instead, she suggests the term 'belonging' as a basis for thinking about how one identifies with a group or community. For Probyn, the term 'belonging'

> [Captures] ... the desire for some sort of attachment, be it to other people, places, or modes of being, and the ways in which individuals and groups are caught within wanting to belong, wanting to become, a process that is fuelled by yearning rather than the positing of identity as a stable state (1996: 19).

Belonging thus comes about through cultural practices that aim to fill an affective longing which Anne-Marie Fortier has termed the 'longing to belong' (Fortier 1999). What is more, these practices come to constitute a shared set of cultural practices ('belongings'), which are held in common. Communities are therefore based through the repetition of cultural practices that construct a group identity, through the accumulation of 'the imaginary possessions that are created in the name of an identity project' (Probyn 1996: 68).

By paying attention to the ways in which specific online communities create norms, and provide spaces in which their members are able to 'cite' those norms, it should become possible to explain how those communities work to produce a sense of identification in the user. It should further be possible to provide a fuller account of the ways in which they naturalise these identifications, creating the impression that a sense of belonging is somehow unaccountable, that it 'just happens'.

What is more, by demystifying belonging in this way, it becomes possible to ask why belonging sometimes fails, and to make visible the processes by which some subjects might feel excluded or rejected by particular communities.

Affect, Fantasy and Belonging: The Fantastic Community

So far, I have outlined the ways in which my argument juxtaposes the notion of community with that of belonging. However, I have stated that my theoretical framework in this book centres on the notion of 'fantasy community' as a formulation which attempts to adapt theories of belonging and community to the particular problems and question posed by online spaces, and which problematises discourses of 'virtual community'. Here, I want to argue that what links community, belonging and fantasy is the notion of affect; that it is the capacity of bodies and texts to affect and be affected that structures online belongings. One of the most interesting things about online experience is its capacity to surprise: hence the emphasis on 'newness' in both theoretical and popular storytelling about the Internet. Importantly, affective readings are open to the possibility of unpredictable effects. Elizabeth Wissinger, writing in a different context, sums this up:

> Tomkins understood affect in terms of specific physiological responses that then give rise to various effects, which may or may not translate into emotions. Affect therefore precedes emotions; affect is not conscious, but it has a dynamism, a sociality or social productivity. The effects of affect, however, are not predictable: affective change from passivity to activity, from inertia to motivation, for example, is not reducible to a single stimulus (2007: 232).

To illustrate the final point, she refers to Tomkins' 'circus of affective responses' that can result from a single stimulus (2007: 232). The notion of a 'circus', suggesting a spectacular carnival of affective responses in between different subjects, but also within the same subject – whether at different moments or simultaneously – is hence inscribed with diversity, with proliferation. In this it speaks to the contingent and shifting relationships between reader, author/creator and text, that abound in cyberspace. In particular, it problematises the notion of subjection, suggesting that the effects of seeing, hearing or reading are always unpredictable: for example, as a reader approaching the hate speech sites I examine in the following chapter – assuming I do not agree with the aims of the site and am not simply reading to have existing prejudices confirmed and amplified (a practice that is certainly not limited to homophobic religious bigots) may experience a number of affects: rage, anxiety, repulsion, but also boredom, scorn, even a hatred of my own so powerful he or she may feel the site's excess of that emotion to be contagious. In fact, hatred creates an attachment as strong, arguably, as that of love: both create lines of movement between subject and object. My responses to such a site might be various. I might joke about the site's atrocious spelling and grammar as a way of managing my fear. I might become a responsible citizen, petitioning for the site to be closed down, for the common good, as a way of 'channelling' my rage. I might suggest that we 'just ignore them', even construct sophisticated arguments about freedom of speech, yet the vileness and violence of their comments may haunt my dreams.

My response to theoretical work is also affective: in the introduction I described how I, like Sedgwick, find Tomkins' work profoundly engaging. Tomkins claimed that affect consists of an automatic biological response to a stimulus, and that it is in the process of interpreting these responses, by applying 'scripts' based on past experiences, cultural 'knowledge' and so on – that emotions come into being (Tomkins 1962, Sedgwick and Frank 1996). Tomkins identified nine primary affects. These are: interest/excitement and enjoyment/joy (the positive affects), surprise/startle (the neutral affect), and fear/terror, distress/anguish, anger/rage, dissmell, disgust and shame/humiliation (the negative affects) (Tomkins 1962 cited in Sedgwick and Frank 2003: 115–17, Moore 1994: 11–12). Each of these affects represents a response to an object. Most obviously, the positive affects suggest a movement toward the object. Similarly, the negative affects may suggest either a turning away (as in the case of 'dissmell', or revulsion, which implies an absolute rejection of the other, as though they smelled unpleasant). However, crucially, negative affect may also entail desire to move towards the object: for example, one could argue that shame suggests a feeling of rejection by the other, which is bound up with a desire to return. In each case, however, desire is a crucial and primary characteristic of the affective relationship between subject and object, whether this takes the form of an unambiguous desire for the object, or a desire to move away from or return to proximity with the object. 'Attachment' results from affect, suggesting multiple invisible channels between subject and object, trajectories of desire which imply constant movement. One is constantly held in a web of movement, both in being moved and in moving towards and away from objects of desire and revulsion. This returns us to the work of Probyn, who argues that belongings are grounded in the desire to belong, a desire which results from a perceived lack or absence. When she states that 'desire is productive' (1996: 13), this can be read as an assertion that all belongings are produced through affect. Furthermore, affects are produced within and through communities: as Elizabeth Wissinger argues, affect is intrinsically social in that it 'constitutes a contagious energy ... that can be whipped up or dampened in the course of interaction' (2007: 232). For me the most interesting thing about affect is that it de-privileges lack as the drive motivating all engagements. For Tomkins, it is possible to have positive affect that does not arise from lack. Affective responses may be culturally constructed, and in particular that they can be constructed through engagement with a text; but they are not pre-determined. By re-reading Tomkins in a way that rejects the explanation of affect as something that 'just is', it becomes possible to track the ways in which particular texts work to produce a sense of identification in some readers, whilst also excluding others or leaving them indifferent.[1]

1 Here, I am following Ann Cvetkovich's (1992) claim that affect is discursively constituted. Sedgwick herself is rather unfairly dismissive of Cvetkovich's position, which she sees as unreflexively anti-biological. But a reading of Butler (1993) suggests that it is absurd to make a distinction between the material and the discursive in this way: if the body itself is culturally produced, then so are the 'neural firings' that constitute affects.

This re-reading of Tomkins' work draws on recent debates within feminist and postcolonial theory, where his model of affect has been used, with the caveats I have outlined, to describe the strong emotional attachments that underpin and perpetuate the practices of reiteration that constitute identity. In particular, feminist theorists have brought together theories of affect with Judith Butler's notion of performativity (Butler 1990, 1993) in order to show how emotional attachments play a crucial role in shaping the relationship between the subject and the community (Probyn 1996, Campbell and Rew 1999, Ahmed 2002, 2004). In particular, the discussions of identification cited in the previous section draw out the affective and emotive character of belonging. Probyn's argument, that the notion of belonging 'captures the desire for some sort of attachment' (1996: 19) represents an important link in my discussion of Web community, since it suggests that affect plays a key role in the creation of communities.

Throughout this book, I attempt to draw out the ways in which different websites work to construct a sense of identification with an online community, through the mobilisation of fantastic tropes centring around notions of community, home and belonging. Hence, the terms of my argument are drawn from feminist and postcolonial theories of home, identity and community, as well as literary and psychoanalytic writings on fantasy. In a sense, then, whilst my argument seeks to intervene in theories concerning cyberculture and online community, its 'field' is broad and interdisciplinary: this intervention is animated by the desire to interrogate debates on cyberculture by bringing them into proximity with feminist, postcolonial and literary theory. Nevertheless, in order to intervene in debates on virtual community it is necessary to examine the development of those debates, and the visions of community they have constructed. In the Introduction, I explained how accounts of virtual culture overlap with, and differ from, pre-existing models of community; here, I look in more detail at the ways in which specific texts have accounted for these differences and similarities.

As I have noted, the term 'community' suggests communication: indeed, the work derives from the Latin *communicare*, which, as Peter Gould explains, 'originally meant to share, to join and to unite' (Gould

1991: 3), and from which is also derived the verb 'to communicate'. Hence, accounts of online culture draw on this definition of community, suggesting that computer technology brings people together by allowing them to communicate: such a proximity is therefore privileged over geophysical location (Rheingold 1993, Turkle 1988, Turkle 1995, Jones 1997). In recent debates on cyberculture, definitions of online community tend to share two characteristics. Firstly, they define community through the concept of 'shared interests'; and secondly, they tend to present online community as 'virtual', a term I shall go on to interrogate in the following section. What is more, some accounts of cyberculture share a certain view of online community as inherently liberating (Turkle 1984, Turkle 1995, Rheingold 1993, Jones 1997, Gauntlett 2000). Therefore, I shall also examine how the debate has tended to polarise, with critics often representing computer technologies as dystopian and oppressive, and even by invoking a narrative of 'neo-Luddism' (Robins and Webster 1999).

Since the earliest online communities were largely text-based, they tend to foreground communication to a greater extent than geophysical location, nationality, race, gender and so on (although these continue to be significant, as we shall see). However, for communication to be effective, it is necessary for members to have something to talk about: whilst it is possible to imagine that that 'something' may involve discussions of difference, in practice it is more often discussed in terms of similarity: 'shared interests'. These may consist of pre-existing interests and hobbies – 'the banal and the everyday' according to Lemos (1996: 43–4) – or they may be more loosely defined as a shared interest in the development of the community and adherence to a shared set of ideals. In his germinal work *The Virtual Community*, for example, Howard Rheingold writes that virtual communities like the WELL fulfil the prediction that 'life will be happier for the on-line individual because the people with whom one interacts most strongly will be selected more by commonality of interests and goals than by accidents of proximity' (Rheingold 1993).

The notion of 'shared interests and goals' suggests a shift from a model of community based on geographic space, to one based on communication. David Gauntlett sums up this shift as follows:

> [Before] the internet, communities were people who lived or worked close to each other. If you were lucky, you might have a community of like-minded people, although it was unlikely that you would get a very compatible bunch all in the same place. The global internet transforms this ... because it enables like-minded people to form communities regardless of where they are located in the physical world (Gauntlett 2000: 13).

Hence, cyberculture is presented as representing an advance over pre-existing types of community. For Gauntlett, it is via communication that one comes into proximity with 'like-minded others', and it is this proximity that constitutes the community. This process of community formation is presented as only happening in the non-virtual world 'if you are lucky', resulting in a rather unproblematic model of online culture.

As some theorists have pointed out, this liberal and optimistic model of virtual community is grounded in the privileging of 'communication' as the basis of belonging. As Robins and Webster point out, 'communication' is a politically loaded term, since it has come to be associated with transparency and hence with understanding. As a result, community, through its association with communication, has utopian as well as political implications: 'the utopia or ideology of communication is about "bringing people together," and this bringing together, it is assumed, will consolidate the bonds of community' (1999: 228). Whilst Robins and Webster are rather pessimistic about the ability of computer-mediated communication technologies to maintain this commitment to a shared social project, however, others have pointed out the ways in which online spaces might be used by socially excluded groups not only as a place to talk, but also as a base from which to bring about social change (Jones 1997, Miller and Slater 2000, Mitra 1997, Shaw 1997).

Since much of the literature on online communities stresses the sharing of interests, and communication about those interests, it can be seen that communication, not location, is what members of the virtual community hold in common. A sense of belonging is derived from a participation in a 'new kind of conversational space' where subjects can talk about interests they have in common, and which becomes in itself something in common (Turkle 1995: 234). This results in a community that is perceived as liberating in that it rejects traditional forms of authority and hierarchy in favour of self-regulation deriving from a sense of belonging (Turkle 1995: 232–54). Hence, this sense of belonging is rooted in a feeling of having a stake in the creation and maintenance of the community. For Turkle, this inherent liberalism (offering liberation from the boundaries of geographic space as well as cultural institutions) is reflected in, and to some extent derives from, a culture of personal liberation in which one is able to transcend the boundaries of lived experience by experimenting with different online personae. David Bell expresses this destabilising of identity as 'making ourselves over in cyberspace, rather than being made over' (2000: 4): that is, as a process that is potentially threatening, but one over which the user has control.

Following on from Turkle and Rheingold, other postmodern theorists have seized on the utopian and liberal possibilities of online community. For example, Heather Bromberg writes that MUDs and chat networks can

> offer an antidote to loneliness and malaise, allow the exploration of alternate identities and personae, offer the promise of connectivity and allow users to experience the feeling of mastery over their environments (Bromberg 1996: 146).

Hence, she argues, they function as a means of responding to a sense of loneliness and lack of meaning in the exterior world (1996: 146–7). Whilst this may be true of some users' experience of virtual community, however, it is problematic in that it suggests an oppositional relationship between virtual and non-virtual communities, in which the former are clearly constructed as superior. This represents a shift from the reciprocal version of online belonging suggested by Rheingold (1993), in which the 'shared interests' that form the basis of the community might be firmly rooted in the non-virtual world, to a model in which the user's sense of his or her own identity is privileged over their ability to communicate with others. Community is hence formed through networks of intersubjectivity, in which what is at stake is a shared interest which may be external to the community, or may be an interest *in* the community itself as a shared project: a shared longing to belong.

As Elspeth Probyn's play on words has it, belonging is affective, since consists of 'be-ing and longing' (Probyn 1993, 1996: 35). Following on from Probyn's work, Vikki Bell asks us to consider that the very idea of belonging implies an affective dimension to social identifications. In order to understand how subjectivity is formed in relation to communities, she says, we must attempt to understand 'ourselves, our politics, our desires and our passions': as she rhetorically asks, 'what is identity without that affect implied more strongly by the term identification?' (1999: 1). Similarly, Sara Ahmed argues that affect is crucial to the formation of collective as well as personal identity: 'emotions play a crucial role in the "surfacing" of individual and collective bodies' (2002: 414); what is more, she says, such a claim challenges the notion that emotions are individual and private (and hence apolitical). Instead, she argues that 'emotions are crucial to politics, in the sense that subjects must become "invested" in and attached to the forms of power in order to consent to that power' (2002: 414). Thus, a reading of community and belonging through theories of affect should allow for a deconstruction of the oppositional model of the public and the private, and hence to a reading of community based on the understanding that the personal is political (and vice versa).

I want to suggest, then, that the notion of affect is present, if not fully articulated, in some theories concerning online communities; indeed, one way in which 'affect' appears is through the invocation of a 'sense of community', as I have outlined above. It is this implicit acknowledgement of the role played by affect which motivated me to wonder whether literary theory, specifically theories of fantasy, might be used in juxtaposition with 'community' and 'belonging' as a means of reading online communities. My argument, then, suggests that affect and fantasy are linked: that the yearning for a 'sense of belonging' represents a fantasy of community that permeates not only scholarly texts on virtual community, but also the processes by which particular communities are constructed. I have argued that plays a key role in forming attachments to, and identification with, a community, and that this is a relationship that is characterised by desire ('longing' or yearning). If desire is implicit in all affective relationships, it is also a key component in theories of fantasy.

The term fantasy, in the sense in which I use it here, is derived from psychoanalysis, and in particular from Freud, notably in *The Interpretation of Dreams*. Freud introduces the term to describe how dreams are not simply unreal 'phantasmagoria', but texts which can be interpreted and decoded (Freud 1991 cited in Ahmed 1999: 52). Thus, Freud does not define the term 'fantasy': rather, the term materialises as a means of questioning the assumption that dreams and stories are opposed to material 'reality' (Freud 1991). Indeed, as the feminist literary scholar Rosemary Jackson has noted, fantasy seems to resist definition, she claims (and I would agree) that the value of the term itself seems to reside precisely in this resistance to easy summarisation, in what she calls its 'free-floating and escapist qualities' (1981: 1). Jackson does suggest a provisional definition of fantasy as those stories that '[attempt] to compensate for a lack resulting from cultural constraints' (1981: 3). Whilst I will examine this claim below, since it constitutes an unignorably powerful narrative of what fantasy does, I am not using the term in this sense here. In the section on reading, below, I explain how a theory of online experience as reading overturns the notion of lack as central to positive affective relations or movements-towards. Nevertheless, the notion of fantasy as escapism is useful if we consider online reading, not as escape-from (the 'real world') but as escape-into or engagement-with (the text). Whilst not accepting lack as the founding principle of fantasy, however, I use the term because it embraces unspoken stories, such as daydreams, as well as literary (or online) texts: that is, it allows us to recognise the ways in which affect is produced and experienced through texts (Jackson 1981: 3–4), but it also accounts for the fact that affect precedes the text itself and indeed is instrumental in its production. Thus, by reading through fantasy, it ought to be possible to account for the precise ways in which affect plays a productive role in the formation of communities.

Further, such a reading can, I argue, be used to question the idea that online communities are 'virtual'. Such a reading challenges the narratives through which digital culture is constructed as the site of 'the virtual', which is then seen as separate from, and opposed to material 'reality', suggesting a binary opposition between the imaginary and the real. Such an account fails to pay attention to the complex relationship between the subject, the community or communities to which they belong, and the desires and imaginings that connect the two (and indeed that constitute interrelationships between the members of the community). In Freud's work on fantasy, in contrast, no such opposition exists. As LaPlanche and Pontalis show Freud's use of the term 'fantasy' precludes any simple opposition between the imaginary and the real (LaPlanche and Pontalis 1986). Instead, through the notion of 'psychical reality', Freud implies both that the relationship between the fantastic and the material is unstable and undecided, and that the two are inseparably intertwined (Freud cited in LaPlanche and Pontalis 1986: 7–9). Thus, it is possible to see how the notion of 'online belonging', for example, is a fantasy, not in the colloquial sense that belongings are unreal or inauthentic, but in that the idea of belonging has material effects in the reproduction of particular social identities and power structures within online communities.

In order to understand how belongings are produced through online texts, we need to pay attention to the role fantasy plays in making online belongings possible. In order to do this, I pay attention the stories they tell about the desirability of forming, maintaining and joining a community and experiencing an affective attachment to that community (a 'sense of belonging'). Following Jackson, I suggest that these stories construct and express a yearning to belong (rather than a simple, practical guide to joining a community that already exists). In their attempts to articulate a yearning to belong, Web communities can therefore be read as fantasy texts, but so can the academic commentaries, the 'canon' – of theoretical texts, but also of metaphors, stories and desires that give those texts life. This book, too, is a fantasy text, one that originates from the desire to tell stories in order to compensate for perceived lacunae in existing accounts of cyberculture, one that originates from a moment of interest, of being or not-being seduced by dominant accounts of the virtual.

This brings me back to the question of why the term 'virtual reality' was so seductive in the first place. As Shaun P. Wilbur has argued, the term 'virtual' is commonly used to mean 'as-good-as' (2000: 54). This colloquial usage, he argues, suggests that 'seeming and being might be confused, and that the confusion might not matter in the end'; it suggests 'that which appears to be (but is not) real, authentic or proper' (2000:

47). Crucially, then, whilst virtuality might suggest that seeming and being are to some extent capable of being confused, it still suggests an oppositional relationship between the two categories. As Patricia Wise summarises, the term 'virtual' suggests 'almost but not quite' but also potency and potential (1997: 179–80). The more optimistic theories of virtual reality are hence constantly engaged in playing with the boundaries between the real and the fantastic, between what is possible and the sense of incompleteness, of 'not-quite'. One the one hand, 'virtuality' suggests something that is wholly new and that is opposed to the real. In this model, entry into a virtual community is liberating because it means leaving behind the constraints of the body in order to experience new forms of subjectivity. This vision is central to the project of virtual community. In addition, 'virtual' has the connotation of 'almost real', meaning that experiences one has in virtual reality can be claimed as practically real; that is, they are not 'just' fantasies, they have an authority which would not apply to overtly 'fantastic' activities such as day-dreaming. This is the aspect of virtual reality that critics have found most disturbing, since it seems to suggest that, for example, a white man pretending to be a black woman can 'as good as' experience how it feels to be a black woman (Nakamura 1995). Indeed, in this fantasy, affect is central to this fantasy of 'as-good-as' becoming the Other. Emotion, the sense of 'feeling like' another, is imagined as the sign that one has (virtually) become them. On the other hand, when activities in cyberspace become problematic they can be dismissed as 'only' virtual: since they are not 'real', they can be imagined as without consequences and the complaints of those who feel threatened can be dismissed. What is more, the sense of being 'as good as' real or virtually the same as 'the real' offers a feeling of safety even as one is allowing oneself to be seduced; it is for this reason, perhaps, that early experiments with whole-body immersion in virtual environments situated the user not in some fantastic landscape, but in a suburban living-room.

Whilst 'virtual' is used to suggest wholly new experiences of self and community, its parallel meanings of 'almost' and 'not quite' suggest that virtual reality may be envisaged as a safe space in which to try out these experiences. These experiences can be imagined as authentic, since they take place in a space that is not so different from the real world, after all. Crucially, however, the 'not-quite' represents a kind of safety net. If the virtual experience becomes threatening, it can be dismissed as not 'really' real. Nevertheless, theories of virtual reality have privileged the idea of the almost-real, for example by comparing VR to other forms of technology. For example, David Holmes has pointed out that the problems and themes associated with virtual reality may not be 'as new as we think' (1997: 3), and that reactions to these 'new' technologies often mirror responses to previous technological developments: he lists cars, television and shopping malls as examples of technologies which already embody virtual realities, because of the ways in which they construct a spatial reality which bears no relation to the subject's outside experiences.[2]

In theories of the virtual, the comforting promise of a retreat back to reality suggests the existence of an originary state of 'truth' whilst simultaneously fixing contemporary Western culture as the embodiment of 'the real'. This closes off the possibilities for transformation supposedly offered by virtual reality, since it suggests both that the changes one might make in cyberspace are 'not quite real', and that the conditions of real life as they are experienced by those who have access to virtual technology are identical with the notion of 'the real', and hence are neither in need of, nor open to change. In other words, the 'as-good-as' produces a sense of danger, subversion, or adventure. The 'not-quite', in contrast, offers a comforting sense of familiarity. It is hence possible to start out by seeing one's involvement in a virtual community as 'as-good-as' real, but then to retreat into the defence that it is 'not-quite' real when things become

2 The most convincing example of this 'primitive' form of virtuality is cinema. Holmes describes how similar claims were made for cinema by its originators as for VR now; citing Bazin's work on the myth of 'total cinema', he comments:

> [Cinema's] inventors shared the dream about the infinite simulation of the real that contemporary VR enthusiasts have now ... Before its recent decline as an immersive, not-quite-total world of representation, cinema, with its dominating screen and invisible audience, was probably the closest approximation to what is today marketed as virtual reality (Holmes 1997: 4–5).

threatening or overwhelming, or when the belief that one's experiences are 'real' throws up insoluble moral dilemmas.

I am not arguing, here, that we need simply substitute fantasy for virtuality, such that fantasy is similarly imagined as opposed to reality. Such a simple substitution would solve nothing, since 'fantasy' could be used in the same way as 'virtuality', and would hence be open to reproducing the same problems. Instead, it is possible to use fantasy to intervene in debates around virtual reality. The next section of my argument suggests that fantasy, and particularly Freud's theory of fantasy as psychical reality, can be used to problematise the dualistic model of virtual versus real, and to pay attention to some of the more problematic aspects of virtual community outlined above. Thinking of the relationship between reality, fantasy and the virtual changes the energies at work in a discussion of the Internet, avoiding the construction of different, but still restrictive binary categories. In order to ask whether the virtual comes to replace other pre-existing fantasies, it is first necessary to ask whether fantasy itself is the imaging of desire or a replacement of desire. This question opens up the field of fantasies and notions of self that users bring to the Web, allowing us to reflect on the ways in which fantasies may be repeated with a difference.

Whist the virtual has seldom been imagined as fantastic, theories of fantasy have engaged with the possibilities offered by the virtual. We need to read virtuality through theories of fantasy (Freud 1991, Jackson 1981, LaPlanche and Pontalis 1986) in order to account for the ways in which dreams, daydreams, desires and fantasies play a role in the formation of communities: and I have argued that such an account does not suppose an oppositional relationship between the imaginary and the real, but rather pays attention to the ways in which they constitute one another. As I have shown, theorists of the virtual have presented the imaginary as secondary; in the examples cited above, 'fantasy' is either implicit (as in David Silver's yearning for a cyberculture canon), or, in more critical readings, as a problematic element which must be 'exposed' and ultimately routed out. However, some literary theorists have been swift to engage with the challenges suggested by virtuality. This is particularly true of the work of Lucie Armitt. As Armitt acknowledges in the introduction to *Theorising the Fantastic*, psychoanalysis has been a valuable tool for feminist literary critics precisely because it recognises the importance of fantasy in relation to 'real' life. Psychoanalytic critics maintain that 'fantasy ... is central to all fictional work' since it 'fuels our dreams, our phobias and therefore our narrative fictions' (Armitt 1996: 1). This approach is used to greatest effect in Rosemary Jackson's 1981 study, *Fantasy: the Literature of Subversion*. Some of Jackson's ideas seem to pave the way for later writings on cyberculture. Jackson's project is to reclaim fantasy writing from its marginal status as 'genre fiction', exploring its position as (she argues) an inherently subversive fictional mode. Fantasy is 'produced within, and determined by, social context' and cannot be understood in isolation from the cultural parameters within which it is produced; 'the literary fantastic is never "free"' (Jackson 1981: 3). Its function is not simply to reproduce the dominant culture's vision of reality, but rather to engage with the taboo and forbidden within that society: as an extension of Bakhtin's menippea, '[it] tells of descents into underworlds of brothels, prisons, orgies, graves; it has no fear of the criminal, erotic, mad, or dead' (1981: 15). From this position it is able to disrupt and subvert these definitions. According to Jackson, the need for such subversive literature is founded in the need to compensate for a lack resulting from cultural constraints. Thus fantasy is a literature that allows for the expression of desire, and this expression takes two forms: it can tell of desire, or expel it 'when this desire is a disturbing element' (Jackson 1981: 3–4).

Despite the impact of postmodernism, the idea of fantasy as a conduit for the expulsion of unsavoury desires persists in the discourse of virtual reality today. For example, accounts of 'VR rapists' (Dibbell 1993) have drawn on the idea of a separation between fantasy and the real, as well as arguing for VR and the Internet as an 'outlet' for their desire to rape, as a means of defending their actions: as Slavoj Žižek has noted, one of the dangers of virtuality is precisely that its uncertain relation to reality means that 'in the guise of a fiction, of "it's just a game," a subject can articulate and stage – sadistic, "perverse," etc. – features of his symbolic identity that he would never be able to admit in his "real" inter-subjective contacts' (Žižek 1998). Although Jackson's faith in fantasy as a means of subversion is questionable, her work still has relevance to feminist researchers in the field of virtual reality. One of the major strengths of her work is its insistence that fantasy can never be independent of the dominant culture within which it is produced, a position which is taken to its logical conclusion in Donna Haraway's 'Manifesto for Cyborgs'. Here, feminists are urged to reclaim computer technology from its association with militarism, and to harness it for more subversive purposes (Haraway 1991).

Furthermore, Bakhtin's theory of the carnivalesque – which Jackson presents as a crucial stage in critics' understanding of the importance of fantasy as a mode – also seems to present a prescient image of the communal enactment of fantasies on the Internet (Jackson 1981, Bakhtin 1981). (Post) modern ideas about free speech, together with the impossibility of policing the Web, mean that as in carnival, all is permitted. Whilst it is not quite true to say that the online community 'has no fear of the criminal, erotic, mad, or dead', it is possible to identify sites on the Web that open up the possibility for subjects who have traditionally been relegated to these categories, to find a place to speak. Jackson states that 'modern fantasy is severed from its roots in carnivalesque art: it is no longer a communal form' (1981: 16); the ascendancy of the Internet – a communal space where fantasies are produced and reproduced – seems to overturn this judgement. Indeed, it is possible to argue that all texts produce a community of readers, a process that simply becomes more visible in cyberspace. Yet the Internet also seems to embody some of the characteristics which set 'less festive modern fantasies' apart from the carnivalesque.

Theories of cyber-culture such as that espoused by Victor Seidler (1998) draw on Baudrillard's notion of simulation and on the theory of the carnivalesque to construct a composite picture of the ideal community (Baudrillard 1981). This is precisely Seidler's view of a society where 'unfreedoms' are left behind, where problematic aspects of subjectivity are denied for the sake of avoiding conflict in the community. One of my central concerns is to engage critically with this view of online community. Instead, I suggest that what is 'left behind' is not the unfreedom itself, but the body; in order for the community to come into being, some subjects are implicitly required to desist from discussing aspects of their lived experience (that is, of their experience of embodiment) that might constitute an unpleasant reminder that 'unfreedoms' exist. According to this model, the reward for this sacrifice is to build a community that transgresses the racist, sexist and classed codes of real-life society. Such a focus is limited because it tends to conceal the extent to which different subjects participate on unequal terms. My argument, then, suggests that the 'transgressive' community has its own boundaries, and its own ways of punishing or excluding those subjects who transgress them. In a sense, then, my argument is informed by critiques of Bakhtin's theory. As Terry Eagleton has noted, carnival is a licensed form of transgression and as such lacks true subversive power: 'there is no slander in an allowed fool' (cited in Stallybrass and White 1986: 13). It is possible to apply the same reading to virtual communities. As Stallybrass and White go on to note, it is not enough simply to argue that carnival is not, therefore, transgressive; rather, whilst it may be little more than a ritual with no real transformative effects, 'it may often act as catalyst and site of actual and symbolic struggle' (1986: 14). The same, I think, can be said of virtual communities, but it is the object of this project to identify those acts of boundary policing which may not be fully visible to the community itself, and which prevent it from becoming a site for some forms of struggle.

By reading the Web alongside other texts, this book seeks to examine how this most commercial and everyday of digital spaces might be read as a space of transgression. Partly, it does this by drawing attention to the intertextual relations that are inherent in Web communities, a reading informed by Donna Haraway's cyborg visions. Whilst Haraway rejects the label 'post-modernist', her theory also involves a challenge to an oppositional model of nature and culture, but not to the extent that the real becomes subordinated to culture (or bodies reduced to language). Rather, as Lucie Armitt points out, 'Haraway's theory is intrinsically corporeal and the body a site of full articulation'. The project of Haraway's 'feminist world view' is hence to deconstruct break down those 'restrictive dualistic hierarchies of thought'. Whilst Armitt's particular interest is in the dualistic gendered narratives that construct woman as 'natural' and man as 'cultured', this clearly has important implications for research (Armitt 1996: 75). A questioning of boundaries might be important in feminist research, since it enables a critical reflection on the relations of privilege that structure academic readings. However, whilst Armitt rightly suggests that Haraway's theory calls into question the assumption that that the questioning of boundaries implied by becoming cyborg necessarily leads to a liberating transcendence of those boundaries. The readings I offer here, then, might be seen as cyborg readings in that they pay close attention to the relationship between subject and text, and to the relationship between an online text, and the cultural context in which it is produced. Such a reading is able to account for the fact that 'virtual' communities do not simply appear fully formed, but are shaped by the desires of the author.

Cyborg identity might simply mean any engagement between an embodied subject and a machine; hence, for the purposes of my research, the act of creating a personal homepage is an act of cyborg belonging, since it involves using technology to construct an identity which is always, as I shall argue in Chapter 3, a fantastic identity. As I shall demonstrate, such cyborg identities might position themselves as subversive: indeed, in doing so they are drawing on the liberal ideal of online community as a site of escape from the 'unfreedoms' of geophysical communities, the norms of virtual community as well as those of real-life society. However, whilst this ideal might be read as implying a fantasy of subversion, communities that position themselves as subversive in the wrong way tend to attract criticism. So, for example, personal homepages often become the object of criticism, and this criticism is precisely focussed on the notion that they represent an exercise in attention-seeking; that is, they are seen as excessive, as transgressing the boundaries of 'normal' behaviour as well as that of a virtual community in which belonging is contingent on an element of self-erasure. The tension between differing fantasies of subversion can be seen most clearly in the case of the pro-anorexic homepages I examine in this book, which have become the object not only of censure, but also of censorship. Here, I argue that the attempted expulsion of these sites occurs as a result of a clash between, on the one hand, a utopian fantasy of 'the Web community as a whole', and on the other a fantasy of subversion that imagines itself as challenging the conventions of both online and offline communities.

Psychical Reality: the Fantastic and the Real

So far, I have identified a number of points of connection between the virtual and the fantastic. This book investigates the many ways in which websites engage with this connection, either explicitly in using the conventions of the fantastic to create communities that are imagined as transgressive, or implicitly, as when online shopping sites appear to invite their users to share the longing for an ideal, utopian society. Yet this is only half the story. My account is not limited simply to assuming that websites are fantastic, for to do so would be to assume that the virtual contains the fantastic, that fantasy is something that exists within websites and that can be identified, or in Wise's terms, 'exposed' (if it is understood to have dangerous or problematic implications). It is not enough simply to 'out' some websites as indicative of (masculine) fantasies, with the implication that there may be others that are not fantastic. Rather, my approach proposes that all online communities are fantastic communities. Indeed, it suggests that the fantastic contains the virtual, that the notion of virtuality is itself a fantasy, and that reading through fantasy allows for a more complex understanding of the relationship between the virtual and the real.

As we have seen, Rosemary Jackson (1981) uses the metaphor of fantasy as the 'underside' of the real as a means of describing its association with the repressed. This model is reproduced in those theories of virtuality I outline in Chapter 2, which insist that virtuality is inherently transgressive or that it is analogous with what has been called, in other media, the 'underground'. Such a model is problematic not only in that it tends to normalise such a model of transgression, and hence blinds us to the more normative and conservative aspects of virtual community, but also in that it still suggests a hierarchical relationship between fantasy and 'reality'. It is important, if difficult, to avoid this, if one is to avoid ending up with virtuality by another name. Importantly, though, the notion of fantasy is not hindered, as virtuality is, by the suggestion of a hierarchical relationship inherent in the word itself, by the suggestion that it is only 'almost' real. Indeed, there is a tradition in psychoanalytic theory that the fantastic does have the status of reality.

LaPlanche and Pontalis (1986) describe how the term 'psychical reality' was coined by Freud in an attempt precisely to think through the relationship between material reality, and the world of imagination, and as a direct challenge to the idea that the two are necessarily in opposition (1986: 6). Unlike virtual reality, psychical reality does not simply exist in an imagined space between the real (that is, the material, real life or 'RL' as it is sometimes known) and the symbolic or imagined, although as LaPlanche and Pontalis point out, Freud's own work reveals an anxiety that this may be the case. They argue that 'even the term itself, "psychical reality," shows that Freud felt he could confer the dignity of object on psychical phenomena only by reference to a material reality', and that this is borne out in his statement that 'they too possess reality of a sort' (1986: 7). I do not think this anxiety need imply a weakness in the term itself, of the kind I have identified in the term 'virtual reality'. Rather, I would suggest that Freud's anxiety results from a reluctance to deny the importance of material reality. In the case of Freud's theory, such an unwillingness to discount the importance of 'reality testing', (that is, checking whether the analysand's account of her experience has any basis in lived experience) would be spectacularly overturned, most notoriously in his assumption, later in his career, that accounts of childhood sexual abuse were mostly fantastic in character (Vincent 2002). Nevertheless, I think this anxiety can inform a reading of online community as fantastic, since it serves as a reminder of the ways in which lived and embodied experiences impact on, and are themselves affected by, the subject's position in the virtual community.

Anxieties apart, psychical reality is a useful model for reading virtual communities since it suggests the existence of a third category; the model is that of a triangle rather than of a line between two opposite points. My argument is based on the assumption that, just as the cyborg is simultaneously the result of an engagement between human and machine, and a third category in itself, so the fantastic community comes to inhabit its own category of reality as well as negotiating the space between material reality and the symbolic. Therefore, my readings resist the work of trying to distinguish which aspects of fantastic community are 'real', and which are 'mere' fantasy. Instead, it assumes that fantastic communities are real. As a result, it is attentive to the ways in which constraints and power relations operate in online communities. In other words, I claim that online communities involve the materialisation of psychical reality, a category that is not simply the opposite of material reality (RL). The work of Slavoj Žižek explains the status of psychical reality as follows:

> We can see, now, how the purely virtual, non-actual, universe of cyberspace can 'touch the Real': the Real we are talking about is not the 'raw' pre-symbolic real of 'nature in itself', but the spectral hard core of 'psychic reality' itself. When Lacan equates the Real with what Freud calls 'psychic reality', this 'psychic reality' is not simply the inner psychic life of dreams, wishes, etc., as opposed to the perceived external reality, but the hard core of the primordial 'passionate attachments', which are real in the precise sense of resisting the movement of symbolisation and/or dialectical mediation (Žižek: 1998).

The concept of psychical reality has much to offer cyberculture studies. We might argue that psychical reality is inextricably embedded in lived experience, but also that it operates less visibly in offline than in online communities. Cyberspace precisely offers the ability to make the psychic visible and intelligible through textual practices, that by writing the self online it is possible to create communities that are founded on the 'spectral hard core' described by Žižek. Further, I argue that a reading of the Internet as fantasy is freed from the shifting dualities implied by the term 'virtual reality', where positive aspects of virtual community are claimed as 'authentic' whilst undesirable effects are simultaneously dismissed as 'unreal', or in Žižek's terms, 'just a game'. It also allows us to question the notion of cyberspace as a site of liberation by resisting what he calls 'disidentification'. Žižek sums up this process as follows:

> Cyberspace can be used to counteract what one is tempted to call the ideological practice of disidentification ... ideology is effective precisely by way of constructing a space of false disidentification, of false distance towards the actual co-ordinates of the subject's social existence? Is this logic of disidentification not discernible from the most elementary case of 'I am not only an American (husband, worker, democrat, gay ...), but, beneath all these roles and masks, a human being, a complex

> unique personality' (where the very distance towards the symbolic feature that determines my social place guarantees the efficiency of this determination), up to the more complex case of cyberspace playing with one's multiple identities? (Žižek, 1998)

This passage has the potential to be profoundly important for cyberculture studies. Here, Žižek is identifying one of the most prevalent fantasies associated with virtual community. As I have noted, and as I will argue in Chapter 2, participation in online communities (or rather, in the kinds of online communities that are most likely to be recognised as such) is imagined as involving precisely such a process of identification. The fantasy of discovering the 'real' self that exists 'beneath all these roles and masks' is repeated over and over again in online spaces, as I shall demonstrate. I want to challenge this highly popular view of the benefits of virtual community over RL, and to propose that such identifications cannot be separated out from the 'true' self. Instead, identity positions can be read as having the status of reality; they cannot simply be left behind as part of a subject's linear and liberating progress from the constraints of real life, towards the ideal virtual community. Instead, the model of fantastic community reminds us that material reality, fantasy, and psychic reality are mutually constitutive, and this is true of 'virtual' as well as offline communities.

It is possible, then, to reading online communities as a space of fantasy that resists the disidentification that is central to interpellation by dominant ideologies of the self. The Web hence becomes a site of identification with the possible, with virtual selves and virtual communities. Fantasy and virtuality are thus intertwined: both carry a sense of the possibilities that arise when we negotiate the boundaries between the 'real' and the 'unreal'. By bringing the three terms, fantasy, virtual and real together into a more intimate relationship, it is possible to will make each term more porous to the others, demonstrating how fantasy has always been present in theories of the virtual, just as the virtual helps us to re-think existing constructions of fantasy and reality. I have suggested that by reading online communities as fantastic, it is possible to provide a fuller account of the constraints as well as the desires that are at stake in the formation of such communities, as well as opening up a broader definition of community and to think about how communities might be formed through intersubjective textual practices. The term I use here, 'fantastic community' evokes, deliberately, Benedict Anderson's model of the imagined community, but I do not wish simply to argue that online communities are a form of imagined community, but to open up the notion of 'community' itself and to examine the implications of feminist theories of belonging and community for a reading of the World Wide Web as a site of belonging. The notion of textuality, of reading, is central to this approach.

Getting Close to the Text

Throughout this chapter, I have used the term 'reading' over and over again, to describe what happens when we engage with online communities. Yet, as we will see in the course of this book, the act of reading (both textual and visual material) is not foregrounded in most popular and theoretical accounts of online experience. Some, though not all, studies of cyberspace construct the online encounter through narratives of spatiality; the idea of cyberculture studies as 'virtual ethnography', in particular, whilst it has generated important insights about the possibilities the Internet offers for new forms of proximity, has tended to obscure the extent to which the act of engaging with cyberculture is primarily one of reading.[3] In contrast, this book takes an approach to Web communities that pays involves reading websites as texts. Since this might seem an

3 One potential exception is the experience blind and partially sighted users. It is surely significant, though, that the technologies used to make the Internet accessible to visually impaired users are called 'text readers', a term which doubly invokes the inherent textuality of cyberculture. The question of whether cyberculture is encountered differently when it is read with the ears, instead of with the eyes, is one that requires further thought.

unusual approach to studying community, I would like to say a few words here about my methodological approach, and about the reasons behind my decision to approach Web communities in this way. Specifically, I wish to examine the ways in which my approach differs from accounts of online community based on 'virtual ethnography', a term which has been used to describe a variety of different research methods, but which has dominated studies of virtual community. In this book, I see the experience of cyberculture studies as contiguous with 'everyday' Internet use: both involve close reading. As I hope to show, these decisions are crucial in determining the shape of the project as a whole: methodology, practice and theoretical approach are mutually constitutive and are, furthermore, inseparable from the researcher's own lived experience.

This focus on textuality and reading might be seen as a retrogressive move; after all one of the key theorists whose work informed this book, Lisa Nakamura, includes 'hypertext' on her list of topics that are 'expired' as opposed to 'wired' (2007a: 32). However, I am not using textuality to refer simply to the hypertextual structures of cyberspace, but to call attention to the ways in which all encounters are always textual. It is a truism in cultural studies that we 'read' the body as a text of culture. Psychoanalysis likewise shows us that the intensely personal experience of dreaming can only be articulated as a text. Likewise, when we engage with others in online space, on the most basic level, we are simply reading: it is not possible, in a sense, to touch the other's body. Nevertheless, it is clear that bodies can and do retain the potential to affect and be affected. Reading hence need not imply a detached, disinterested perspective: instead, I am suggesting that reading is affective.

Sedgwick explores the act of reading in relation to Tomkins' notion of shame. For Sedgwick and Frank, all theory is motivated by shame, but shame is in constant tension with the positive affect variously known as enjoyment or (the term I prefer) interest. 'Without positive affect', they note, 'there can be no shame' and vice versa (Sedgwick and Frank 2003: 116), and both affect produce bodily knowledges. Reading reproduces the body language of shame – the lowered eyes, the hanging head – an association which is reinforced by a 'pernicious understanding of reading as escape', from the 'responsibility of acting or performing' in the 'real world' (114–15). But reading does not render the reader invisible to the 'real world': instead, it is both public and private, introverted and extroverted: as she notes, 'all a reader needs to do to transform this "inner life" experience to an audible performance is to begin reading aloud', and anyway the sight of somebody absorbed in reading is in itself theatrical, suggesting the primary narcissism of a child engaged in play (115). Sedgwick and Frank beautifully describe the intensity of being absorbed in reading:

> The additional skin shimmering as if shrink-wrapped around body-and-book, or body-and-playing/working environment, sharply and sheerly delineates the conjunction or composition, making figural not escape or detachment but attention, interest (2003: 115).

It should be clear, here, why I find the notion of 'reading' so important for considering the relationship between, not body-and-book, but body-and-computer. There is a powerful resonance between the desire to overturn the 'pernicious understanding of reading as escape', and debates about whether excessive Internet use destroys the subject's engagement with 'real life'. I am not sure that the notion of escape can be dispensed with altogether: instead, the question becomes what one escapes to, rather than what one escapes from (and in any case, when one 'finds' a community of others with similar experiences, the sense of belonging that results may precisely be grounded in relief at being able to shut out a 'real life' community that does not understand). But what is important here is the way that Sedgwick's argument allows us to perceive the sheer affective intensity of reading. Reading is imagined, not as a 'second best' activity that is distinct from and inferior to 'real life', but as intensity/enjoyment.[4] Reading is not being detached, but 'being in the moment', engaged in an attachment or orientation towards an object of pleasure

4 Think, for example, of the shame experienced in childhood when one was asked to fill in a form that included the dreaded 'hobbies' section, and having nothing to say but 'reading'. No matter how much pleasure and intensity one found in immersing oneself in the virtual world of a book, there was always a suspicion that this was being read as 'doing nothing' – as though one spent one's free time simply switched off, like a machine or indeed a cyborg.

which, unlike desire, is not imagined as motivated by lack, nor as seeking fulfilment, but simply *is*.

To see cyberculture as an act of reading is hence not a move backwards, but a way of theorising the constantly reiterated moves towards that characterise online engagement. Such a critical attention to reading does not rule out the notion of online experience as encounter/touch. Indeed, my methods are informed, at least in part, by a desire to question the distinction Bev Skeggs has identified between 'the neat and tidy world of theory' and 'the messy world of real lives' (1995: 191). Like real life, texts (and particularly online texts) are messy: that they produce strong affective responses that draw the reader in: that they inspire, challenge, threaten, in ways that not only influence the reader's everyday life, but are part of it. As I have explained, it is for this reason – the need to acknowledge that stories (the imaginary) are not separate from experience – that I have chosen to read the Internet through theories of fantasy. Debates in feminist literary theory have for some time attempted to deconstruct the notion of an oppositional relationship between theory and experience, between 'reading' and 'the real world'. If ethnography involves close engagement with the subject, then feminist literary criticism entails just such an engagement with a text (but, crucially, does not imply, as 'virtual ethnography' does, that such an engagement can be conflated with a proximity to the other, that is, the author of the text).

Theories of reading thus enable us to get closer to the ways in which particular sites produce a sense of community, rather than starting out from the assumption that community is simply 'out there' waiting to be studied. By reading websites as texts, it is possible to track the precise means by which a 'sense of community' is constructed: through intonation, through explicit or implicit addresses to an 'ideal' reader, through intertextual references and hypertextual links, to name but a few. As Lynn Pearce has argued, texts do produce affective responses in the reader; so, for example, she writes of her own 'jealousy' on realising that the feminist texts she thought she had 'discovered' were also speaking to other women (1994: 90–1). What is more, she argues, such affective readings work to produce a sense of belonging, often for several different groups of readers at a time, and it is the interplay between feelings of inclusion and exclusion that accounts for the pleasures of reading:

> While I, the reader, exist in dialogic relationship with the text ... I am nevertheless positioned by it, and the challenge and excitement of the reading process depends upon my not knowing, in advance, if it will embrace me or reject me: position me as an ally or as an antagonist (1994: 92).

Crucially, Pearce suggests that a real relationship exists between reader and text: one which is profoundly rooted in and shaped by the reader's lived experience (and is also, one could therefore add, an embodied relationship). By reading websites as texts, following Pearce, it should be possible to track the ways in which they like other texts work to produce a sense of community (or indeed of exclusion). It is also necessary to be aware of the ways in which the Web text works to position the reader, challenging assumptions about authorial intentionality which result from the assumption of proximity to the author. Instead, my account engages with poststructuralist literary theory, in which the liberal humanist notion of intentionality is displaced, as Pearce summarises, by a focus on the impact of texts on the construction and interpolation of the subject (Pearce 1994: 94 n3). Hence, I would suggest that an understanding of online community might be reached through proximity to the text, and not simply through some assumed computer-mediated proximity to the other. In methodological terms, this translates into an emphasis on close reading as a means of approaching online texts. In the section that follows, I will explain what I mean by close reading, before going on to outline how I have used this method in the following chapters.

If the Internet text is by its nature fluid, always in construction, this is in some sense true of all texts. Moreover, the changing nature of the Internet text tends to foreground issues of theoretical judgement, whilst the intimate connections between text and author constantly call into question the relationship between researcher and subject. The great difficulty in carrying out a textual analysis of community on the Internet lies in the need to negotiate the space between text and textual production, to retain the possibility of making judgements whilst avoiding violence. So, for example, the early experiences detailed in the personal account above, resulted in my producing some very negative and critical readings of online communities in the early stages of my research. This approach has been tempered as my own newbie status has transformed into a more participative role (albeit one in which I am constantly aware of a critical distance, since even when using the Internet in my leisure time I am constantly aware of the desire to find possible objects for my research). As the term 'close reading' implies, my method of textual analysis depends on getting close to the text, and the increasing integration of the Internet into everyday life, at least within Western academic cultures, can hence be seen as productive. However, the assumption of proximity implied by the term needs further elaboration.

As Sara Ahmed argues, close readings carry the possibility of judgement: yet in order to be reflexive, it is necessary to suspend the desire to make generalised judgements. However, she argues:

> Close readings may suspend general judgement. However, the possibility of judgement is not negated by closer readings: indeed, getting closer to the text also involves a form of distanciation without which closeness would constitute the violence of merger. Moving from proximity to distance, a closer reading of ... texts make judgements through engagement. This approach to closer readings is hence bound up with ethics, with the meta-discursive question of what makes some readings more just than others (Ahmed 1998: 9).

As we shall see, the ethical concerns outlined by Ahmed are of crucial importance in dealing with self-published texts such as home pages. It is in engaging with theories of fantasy and virtuality that I have experienced most keenly the problem of assuming a position of authority, of assuming my right to make 'just' readings. This issue is of particular importance in carrying out a textual analysis of the Internet. For example, I have argued that my approach to textual analysis avoids making assumptions about authorial intention. In this, it draws on the work of feminist literary critics who have long argued that the relationship between reader and text should be seen as dialogic. Such an account allows for an acknowledgement that readings are situated, that different readers will approach a text in different ways (Pearce 1994). The need to avoid fantasies 'knowing' the author's intention through an 'authentic' textual encounter, therefore, becomes a political imperative. My account takes this further to suggest that, in studying virtual culture, it is crucial to be aware of the dangers of making assumptions about the author as well as about the reader. This is perhaps best illustrated by an example.

In Chapter 5 of this book, I deal with pro-ana websites: that is, sites that celebrate eating disorders. In order to understand how these sites work to produce a sense of community, I argue, it is absolutely essential to avoid assuming that they bring one into proximity with 'real' anorexic subjects, that they somehow let the reader get inside the author's mind. Websites, since they lack the authority of other textual forms (as I argue in my reading of personal homepages) are particularly vulnerable to such a reading which would, however, precisely cross over into 'the violence of merger'. Therefore I would reiterate that close reading implies a closeness to the text, that is, a careful reading that pays attention to the ways in which texts use fantasy to produce particular effects: it does not, cannot, imply a proximity to the other's body). My work on pro-ana does make judgements: but those judgements are directed at readings of pro-ana in the mass media that precisely assume that by reading pro-ana texts, it is possible to get close to the author, to acquire 'knowledge' about the bodies, and the lives, of others: and that this knowledge then gives the reader the authority to impose the violence of censorship. Such an approach to reading is indicative of what Stanley and Wise have termed the 'uncharitable academic three-step' (1990: 46). In *Feminist Praxis*, Stanley and Wise argue that feminist research must question the ways in which knowledge claims are made. Traditionally, they argue that sociologists have tended 'simply to judge "other" against "self" and find it wanting simply because it is "other"': instead, they argue that feminist researchers should 'assess what is being said in its own terms', paying attention to its own definitions of what constitutes 'knowledge' and 'truth' (1990: 47). This is what a close reading grounded in feminism attempts to do. Indeed, Stanley and Wise state that in order to produce reflexive research which avoids judging the other, one must be aware that '[any] piece of writing can have different readings made of it' and that '[m]ore and less generous readings are always readings made in relation to ... those of other positions and arguments and account' (1990: 47). Therefore, by reading texts closely as texts, rather than as a means of getting close to the other, it becomes possible to assess how those texts define 'community' and 'belonging' in their own terms, and how they seek to invoke an affective response, whilst staying aware of the danger of positioning the other as object. Such issues are foregrounded in dealing with texts precisely because of the feminist researcher's engagement with feminist epistemology, with its emphasis on the importance of understanding the power relationships that can arise in the meeting of researcher and subject. Perhaps by reframing the encounter between researcher and subject as one of interest, it is possible to call into question the ways in which we are continually reading and making judgements, in 'real life' as well as online. If reading implies a positive attachment, and movement-towards an object, then this has the potential to reframe our assumptions about inherent power relationships between researcher and subject. The 'additional skin' that encloses body-and-book also potentially encloses the body-being-read, involving reader and author in a relation of intensity in which new forms of engagement are possible.

CHAPTER 2

(Un)deleted Subjects: Mourning, Violence and Community

What is at stake in the notion of 'new' media, and how do desires and fears about 'newness' shape our lived experience of being online? These questions have informed media discourse on digital culture from the outset. In July 2000,[1] the *Guardian* newspaper published an article which set the tone for public discourses and debates about online subjectivity, establishing a script from which subsequent popular discussion of cyberculture have barely deviated. The piece takes the form of a discussion between 'cybercafé pioneer' Eva Pascoe and the social scientist John Locke, on the subject 'can a sense of community flourish in cyberspace?' The debate was commissioned in the light of a contemporary survey – the first of many – which, the introduction to the article claimed, revealed 'how little people are involved in their local communities'. For example, it found that one in three British people had never met their next-door neighbours.[2]

1 The timing of this debate is of course significant, occurring as it does shortly after the so-called 'millennium bug' failed to deliver the promised apocalypse expected on 1 January 2000. The importance of 'the bug' cannot be overestimated in providing a context for both utopian and dystopian accounts of digital culture: for an entertainingly bathetic account of the ways in which the stockpiling of food, ammunition and so on resulted in nothing more apocalyptic than 'gentle mocking', see Gere 2002. Gere, however, notes that whilst the apocalypse failed to materialise, 'it was an apocalypse in another sense, an *apo-kalypteiin* – an uncovering or disclosing of what had previously been hidden' – in this case the 'almost total transformation of the world by digital technology' (2002: 9).

2 In fact, it becomes clear from reading the article that the actual question asked of the research subjects was whether they had spent a whole evening in the company of their next-door neighbours, which suggests a rather narrow model of 'the social'.

However, the debate (which took the form of an exchange of letters) focussed not on whether a sense of community could exist in cyberspace (both accepted that it could), but on whether virtual communities were in danger of replacing 'real' communities.

For Locke, virtual community is problematic because it involves what he calls 'de-voicing'. Human communication, he says, is essentially embodied: 'we think of it as a process of the mind, but it's done by bodies: faces move, voices intone, bodies sway, hands gesture'. On the Internet, where 'the mind is present but the body is gone', the speaker is reduced to a 'person-typist' whose mood and personality can never really be known. Summarising the argument of his book, *The De-Voicing of Society*, he goes on to claim that spoken language 'works' precisely because of this embodiment. By language 'working', he means that it helps convey the truth about the speaker's intentions: 'Speakers, especially those wishing to deceive, would gladly eliminate glances and tones of voice that reveal nefarious intentions, but listeners need these to avoid being duped'.

For Pascoe, it is precisely this undecideability of the virtual subject's identity that makes online communication superior to speech. In this sense it is both a continuation of and an improvement upon the partial anonymity of the telephone. Virtual technologies allow the possibility of new, utopian models of community because they erase social markers. In face-to-face conversation, Pascoe is aware of her positioning as Other, 'a foreigner and a woman active in the IT industry'; as such, she says, her experience of online communication has been liberating: 'on numerous occasions I've benefited from being able to hide behind the label e.pascoe while commenting on technology issues'.[3] Virtual communities, then, allow the individual 'to be heard on merit'. They are a potentially liberating space in which everyone is equal:

3 As owner of the cybercafé chain Cyberia, Pascoe presumably feels no further need to court anonymity in this way; nevertheless, the café's name, suggesting dissidence and exile, strikes a playful note of defiance against the male-dominated culture of e-commerce.

Dear John,

I take your points. But the human voice carries not only the mood and temperament of the speaker – it also betrays gender and social position through accent and vocabulary, along with other variables that can be used to the speaker's disadvantage. The telephone has perpetuated the misfortunes of the ethnic minorities and 'less equal' members of the community by delivering the cues on which the society judges the importance and weight of the comments made. For the first time, the Internet allows us to cut out such irrelevancies as gender or social grouping and lets the merits of the communication shine through without distractions ... The human mind is simply too limited to dissociate the merit of the argument from the socially constructed weighting of whose words matter and whose can be ignored. The Internet has provided the first truly equal communications platform – and it's finally moving us beyond the biases or prejudices that have infected our minds since Neanderthal times (Locke and Pascoe 2000).

This, then, is Pascoe's manifesto for a cyber-utopia in which everyone is equal. Her ideal appears to be one of an online culture based upon conversation, in which everything is permitted except the discussion of difference. Her use of the term 'betrayal' suggests that differences of gender, race, and class are shameful secrets that naturally exclude individuals from 'the society'. In this view, difference is naturalised as the property of some bodies; such bodies are always in the process of being judged by, and hence excluded from, the larger body of 'the' society. The insertion of the definite article here ('the' society rather than the more usual 'society') is significant: it serves both a functional purpose (that of obscuring a central flaw in the argument, the notion that one can be outside society itself rather than simply being excluded from certain sections of society) and an emotive one (with its connotation of secret societies). There seems to be a contradiction here between the evocation of a classically liberal, neutral subject, and an apprehension of 'the' society as biased and hostile. One must become neutral, putting aside the 'irrelevancies' of difference in order to enter society: nevertheless, that society, constructed here as a harsh, judgmental and perpetually watchful presence, is far from neutral. However, Pascoe does not follow through with this line of argument; in the next sentence she suggests that it is not 'the society' that is prejudiced; rather, prejudice is a disease, one which 'infects' the human mind. Significantly, she says that it has 'infected our minds'; hence, the notion of disease is linked to the 'we' of community, or to put it another way, the human race is naturally prone to prejudice, and as a result has failed to build the ideal community to which Pascoe would have it aspire.

All that is about to change, though, with the advent of virtual technologies, to which Pascoe attributes both medicinal and Messianic powers of transformation which will enable users to transcend the limitations, not only of the flesh, but of the voice and hence of identity itself. Crucially, the cure for prejudice is not for 'other' subjects to pass as white middle-class men (although that is certainly implicit in Pascoe's argument), nor is it concerned with making white, middle-class male identity visible. Instead, she longs for a world in which all subjects are neutral and unmarked. This, together with her refusal to view her position as 'a woman and a foreigner' in political terms, constructs passing as an unproblematic, neutral act. Pascoe's own apparent confusion here leads her into absurdities, notably her claim that 'the telephone has perpetuated the misfortunes of ethnic minorities'. 'The Society' must not be blamed for its endemic racism, sexism and class bias (for nobody would choose to become infected with a disease, and disease itself has no agency); therefore it must be the other's own body that betrays her, or failing that, her voice. In contrast with feminist accounts of difference, which have focussed on the need to listen to the voices of women and the need to find a voice, this account requires that all voices be silenced for ever; for Pascoe, that silencing would be no great loss. Passing, in this view, is simply a pragmatic strategy through which to deal with those whose minds have become infected with prejudice. For Pascoe, then, passing in cyberspace is not so much a case of black skin, white masks (Fanon 1970), as of blank and featureless masks for all; but this cannot alter the fact, implicit in her argument, that the face behind the mask is always assumed to be white, and that the free and equal conversation of cyberspace must be closely regulated if those masked others are to avoid 'betraying' their secret.

Partly, the debate here is about the function of language: the speakers negotiate the debatable territory between the notion of, as Denise Riley has it, 'How to Do Things with Words' – the title of Austin's germinal work of linguistic theory – and 'How Words Do Things with Us' (Riley 2002: 3). Each speaker inhabits, in his or her own way, the tension between seeing language as relational, a process of becoming – what she calls 'language as speaking us', and 'our status as freely choosing users of language' where language is 'that outward unconscious which hovers between people' versus language as an authentic mode of self-expression which '[swims] upward from the privacy of each heart' (2002: 4–5). On the one hand, both Pascoe and Locke share an acknowledgement of the intersubjectivity of language: for Locke, in the form of speech as performative and reproductive of community, and for Pascoe in the way that language works to embed subjects in existing power relations. However, each displays a belief precisely in language as coming from the heart, although interestingly this is more evident in Pascoe's passionately argued case 'for' the virtual, than in Locke's more conservative account. For Pascoe, the self is not produced through power relations but is merely fettered by them. In this rather confused position it is by 'getting beyond' lived experience that the virtual self, in all its potential, is capable of emerging. This resonates with Brian Massumi's notion of the virtual as potential, to be sure: but this notion of 'potential' is one wholly aligned with late capitalism's reduction of potential to competencies for material success. If the idea of 'potential' has an affective dimension, it is a tendency to produce 'confidence': a highly problematic virtue which Massumi memorably sums up as 'the emotional translation of affect as capturable life potential' (2002: 41). This plea for self-expression in and through the virtual hence ends by ironically reproducing a neo-liberal ideal of subjectivity which precisely privileges individualism at the expense of the self.

Partly, the problem with this position is a practical one: since anything impinging on race, national identity, gender – any one of a proliferation of identity labels – is forbidden, one wonders exactly what Pascoe's ideal liberal subjects would find to talk about. This is not a frivolous question: it is not necessary to take a feminist, or any other, position to see that it would be nigh on impossible to have any kind of meaningful discussion spontaneously whilst simultaneously avoiding all such cues. Perhaps they would be discussing theory, if one can imagine such an activity taking place without bodies. This question of 'what to talk about' was central to early debates on virtual identity, and as such I will examine it more closely below.[4] Here, I want to turn to Locke's response in order to illustrate how both participants are apparently blind to the wider implications of Pascoe's statement. His response does not address the underlying assumptions of power in Pascoe's model of cyberspace; instead, he merely comments rather cryptically:

> Years ago, a TV commercial advised Americans that 'It's not nice to fool Mother Nature!' The reference was to dairy companies that wanted viewers to buy margarine instead of butter, but the same can be said of humans who would have us believe they are someone else. We mess with human biology at our peril, and those who conceal their unique identities do exactly that, however understandable their motives (Locke and Pascoe 2000).

The problem with this simile is that whereas Pascoe is looking forward to her vision of a utopian online community, Locke, along with the 'neo-Luddites' who claim that virtual community is destroying an implicitly superior geophysical community (Doheny-Farina 1996, Talbott 1995), presupposes there to have been a previous, golden age in which everyone ate butter, all the time. Whilst the use of this image neatly interrupts Pascoe's rhapsodic vision of community, Locke fails to engage with the problems inherent in her argument precisely because he is invested in the same notions of authenticity and 'truth'. Hence, a dualistic relation is firmly established between online and real-life communication. This debate exists purely as a performance of the struggle to turn dualism into hierarchy, with each participant claiming to be on the side of authenticity.

I have quoted from this article at length since I think it illustrates the problematic nature of the debate around virtual communities. By

4 Indeed, this question is central to the problem many early commentators had with homepages and blogs, namely that 'just' reading individual's life stories would be too boring and hence unsustainable: this in spite of the simultaneous proliferation of biographical and confessional genres in television, publishing, and art. For a fuller discussion of this early prejudice towards biographical forms of online media, see Chapter 3.

comparing these two statements, we can see that the debate has become polarised. Both sides assume that the Internet is leading people to create new communities that are in some sense taking over from 'real' neighbourhoods, and participation in these communities involves the erasure of characteristics that are assumed to be visible attributes of the body, such as gender and race. They differ only in that Pascoe argues that this potential for the members of virtual communities to become unmarked subjects is inherently desirable, and that it might lead to the development of more and more utopian online communities. Locke, on the other hand, whilst he sees these developments as inevitable, believes the disembodied community of cyberspace to be undesirable, dystopian: although he does not quite articulate his concerns, preferring to mutter darkly about the dangers of 'interfering with nature', a strategy which typically characterises most objections to technological advancement.

However, despite the suggestion of heated debate inherent in the article's structure, I have argued that these arguments represent two sides of the same coin; by becoming fixed along dualistic lines (utopia vs. dystopia), discussions of virtual community have reached a stalemate in which both sides implicitly share the same assumptions, and each seems oblivious of the ways in which those assumptions are structured through discourses of power. For cyber-utopians like Pascoe, online belonging entails a sense of responsibility to the 'we' of the online community. The community space is constructed through the performance of a lack (of difference): the liberating, communal space of virtual community comes into being through each participant's performance of an identity unmarked by gender, race, class, national identity, and sexual identity. As Vicki Bell has noted, the citational nature of identity is central to a feminist understanding of what it means to belong, in the sense that 'the performativity of belonging "cites" the norms that constitute or make present the "community" of the group as such' (1999: 3), and this is certainly true of online belongings. However, in Pascoe's model of virtual community, the community comes into being not through a 'stylised repetition of [public] acts' (Bell 1999: 3), but rather through the repetition of private acts of erasure. The individual is thus burdened with the work of erasure: with one finger always on the delete key, they must remove all reference to those identity positions which may be seen as disruptive, in order for the utopian virtual community to come into being. The article cited above (and many others like it) represents one vision of online community: one which, however, is by no means universal. In practice, discussions of experience, difference and embodiment are by no means taboo in cyberspace; indeed, the proliferation of websites, bulletin boards and newsgroups devoted to the discussion of every topic from racism to childbirth suggests that vast sections of the online population would dissent from this view of the benefits associated with online belongings. Nevertheless, the mass media continues to focus heavily on the pleasures and dangers of anonymity, and of passing, in its discussions of online community. The obsession with these themes stems, I think, precisely from the innate conservatism by which the notion of online passing displaces responsibility for social problems like racism and sexism from 'the society', onto the individual. As long as technology exists which allows 'foreigners and women' to get on, to fight the 'disease' of prejudice, society itself cannot be held responsible if some members of those groups are unable or unwilling to take the advantages it offers. Failure to participate is hence re-positioned as indicative of a kind of self-defeating passivity.

Nevertheless, I do not think we should be too quick to dismiss Pascoe's position. This fantasy – of perfect disembodied beings (silicon life forms?) exchanging ideas of pure, crystalline reason – is a very powerful one, and one need only consider her palpable weariness at having to speak 'as a woman and a foreigner' to see why. Indeed, my own tentative forays into 'computer cross-dressing' resonate with the sense of sheer relief at (albeit temporarily) becoming not so much unmarked as unreadable.[5] It is possible, however, to acknowledge the power of this fantasy without accepting it as therefore an ideal state of affairs. To be sure, the work of being (readable as) Other is, as Pascoe suggests, onerous. But it does not follow that one must therefore hope for a future in which all difference is erased.

5 For a discussion of the origins and implications of the term 'computer cross-dressing', see Ferreday and Lock 2007.

What is highly problematic about the liberal notion of online identity that Pascoe takes up, is its implicit presentation of erasure not as a weary response to the labour of embodying otherness, but as active, progressive, and positive. This 'claiming' of erasure is presented as hopeful, but this upbeat account conceals its own hopelessness, its frustrated acceptance of prejudice as an unshakeable fact. In this sense, it only serves to reproduce an unbridgeable gulf between those who are continually engaged in deletion, and those subjects (white, male, heterosexual, English-speaking), who have nothing to delete.[6] The form of online belonging suggested by these narratives, then, involves a fantasy of taking on white male privilege by achieving a form of agency that is assumed to be unavailable in 'real life'. But this performance of online identity as unmarked identity is not limited to the 'we' of virtual communities. There is always a larger 'we' at stake, that is the notion of the Internet as a whole, and this larger 'we' is deeply entwined with discourses of global community. Below, I examine the notion of unmarked belonging, paying close attention to the slippage between different performances of unmarked online identity and their implications for questions of online belonging.

6 Pascoe's argument hinges on this idea that it is possible to have nothing to delete. However, this is in itself a problematic claim, given that popular anxieties surrounding the Internet have focussed on the figure of a white, male stalker who disguises his identity in order to make contact with vulnerable subjects. It is precisely the focus on subtraction that allows Pascoe to ignore the ways in which an erasure of identity might be problematic. The cyber-stalker's disguise, in contrast, is usually imagined as additive: the stalker *takes on* the characteristics of other groups, for example by pretending to be a child.

'He opened these doors of utterance': from Cyber-utopia to Communities of Hate

Early accounts of web community are haunted by a deep longing for the frontier. Rheingold's book is of course subtitled *Homesteading on the Virtual Frontier*, but there are multiple other examples. It has been widely argued that the use of the frontier metaphor produced limited readings of the Internet community (Ulmer 1994, Milne 2000). What is more, despite a general shift away from the technocentrism that dominated cyberculture studies in the 1990s, debates about what it means to see cyberspace as a frontier continue to proliferate in current popular discourse, as well as cultural theory (Wood and Smith 2005). Clearly, in the textually mediated environment of the Internet, a great deal is at stake in the repetition of particular stories, particular images. As Esther Milne noted in 2000, the 'mobile army of metaphors' associated with online communities might be read as alienating by readers who are not white, male and middle class. Further, she points out that the repetition of these metaphors has the side effect of making feminist critique seem marginal, irrelevant. As Milne argues, it should be noted that the preoccupation with particular metaphors dominates our 'current understanding of new writing technologies' (2000: 105). These metaphors reveal much about the fantasies, and especially the fantasies of belonging and exclusion that are at stake in our understanding of virtual communities. For Milne, fantasies that continually reiterate the notion of the Internet as a new frontier suggest that the online environment arouses the desire for conquest, for mastery. This desire, she claims, is always conceptualised as inherently masculine, but is also classed and situated firmly within the culture of an imagined, idealised United States. For example, she cites John Seabrook's rewriting of the frontier fantasy, in which he identifies with both Francis Parkman and Henry David Thoreau (hence mastering both

West and East).[7] However, she goes on to say that elsewhere Seabrook is 'a little too Ivy League' for some readers. She cites, for example, an almost comically overblown passage in which he compares browsing through the Well's archives with 'walking through the Princeton boathouse in the dim light after crew practice, with those big lacquered wooden rowing shells bulking out at you in the gleaming dimness' (Seabrook cited in Milne 2000: 105).

Milne's work typifies a sense of unease that characterised rather more cautious feminist accounts of the period which were concerned with avoiding some of the perceived excesses of 'cyberfeminism'. Certainly, her call for metaphors to be taken seriously is a necessary corrective to some of the more breathless accounts of the time. A more troubling aspect of her argument, though, is a tendency to regard metaphor itself as somewhat suspect which manifests as a generalised rejection of 'hip' language: as though imagination itself were somehow decadent. For example, as a feminist, she says, she is unable to share 'the irony and share the hip sensibility' that characterises much of the cyber-writing of this period; and it is through this discourse of 'unhipness' that feminist politics comes to be seen as archaic, as obsolete in the new, virtual age. As she puts it, 'I am, no doubt, still labouring under the assumptions, misconceptions and limitations of the analogue paradigm' (2000: 105).

The metaphor of the frontier is inextricably linked to the notion of utopia: the vision of cyberspace as a new found land invokes ideas of religious freedom, as well as colonial privilege. As David F. Noble argues in *The Religion of Technology*, the development of technology in the West has throughout history been influenced by and intertwined with religion, particularly with millenarian strands of Christian belief. This relationship between religion and technology was, at its apex, inseparably from the project of colonising the American West: its 'true centre', he writes, was 'the promised land of the New World' (1997: 88):

7 See also Healy 1997: 58–60 for a detailed deconstruction of the connections between *Walden* and early political narratives of the 'information superhighway'.

> Perhaps nowhere is [the] intimate connection between religion and technology more manifest than in the United States, where an unrivalled popular enchantment with technological advance is matched by an equally earnest popular expectation of Jesus Christ's return. What has typically been ignored by most observers ... is that these two obsessions are often held by the same people, many of these being technologists themselves ... Artificial Intelligence advocates wax eloquent about the possibilities of machine-based immortality and resurrection, and their disciples, the architects of virtual reality and cyberspace, exult in their expectation of God-like omnipresence and disembodied perfection (Noble 1997: 5).

It is not difficult to find religious rhetoric in the field of cyberstudies. When R.W.B. Lewis, in his study of nineteenth-century American literature, wrote of the 'individual emancipated from history [and] easily identified with Adam before the Fall' (cited in Noble 1997: 89), he might easily have been describing the ideal virtual subject. That phrase 'emancipated from history', in particular, seems to epitomise certain paradoxes which are always implied in discourses of online belonging. On the one hand, cyberculture is rooted in postmodern culture. Although it was originally a by-product of the defence industry, its first viable use was as Arpanet, a communications network for academics which was quickly claimed as a sort of object lesson in postmodern subjectivity, a 'test object', to take Sherry Turkle's useful phrase somewhat out of context (1995: 27). This entailed, on the one hand, an acceptance of Baudrillard's view of postmodernity as the collapse of linear time and the advent of 'catastrophic' time, a shift which according to Franklin et al. 'brings with it a collapse of the distinction between originals and copies and the redistribution of authorship' (Franklin et al. 2000: 53). However, the fantasy of the Internet as virgin territory has proved particularly compelling to some commentators, with the result that the project of online communities has been not so much about the collapse of linear time, as the end of one chapter in history and the commencement of a transformative new world order. As we have seen, the project of building this brave new world often requires that some subjects erase those aspects of their subjectivity that might be seen as problematic. Online religious groups have seized upon this notion of erasure and have tended to value the Internet as a site for community-building precisely because of its ability to bring together those subjects who imagine themselves to be 'superior', whilst excluding others.

For many right-wing religious groups, the project of community building has centred on the 'issue' of sexuality. Unlike some other forms of difference such as race and gender, which are more likely to be imagined as visible, immutable qualities of particular bodies, these groups see sexual difference as invisible or behavioural, and hence capable of being erased. Homophobia – though the term hardly does justice to the sheer strenuous *labour* that goes into their constant reproduction of a sense of outraged loathing – is central to these groups' identity. The hatred of the sexual Other is reinforced by the notion that the homosexual is invisible and is hence the enemy within, the stranger among us who must be cast out in order to ensure the purity of the community. In other words, the homosexual subject is asked to take on a new identity, to allow other members of the community to assume that she is heterosexual. It should be apparent, then, that there is a connection to be made here with the Internet community's attitude to difference. Indeed, one of the advantages of online communication, according to Mark Poster, is that it becomes impossible to tell the difference; one of the virtues of online communities is that textual interactions tends to render all forms of difference 'invisible'. For Poster, this is an unambiguously desirable side-effect of virtual disembodiment:

> In bulletin boards like the Well, people connect with strangers without much of the social baggage that divides and alienates. Without visual clues about gender, age, ethnicity and social status, conversations open up in directions that otherwise might be avoided. Participants in these virtual communities often express themselves with little inhibition and dialogues flourish and develop quickly (Poster 1995: 70).

This argument is echoed in the work of William Mitchell (1999), who claims that cyberspace is the ultimate democratic space because it allows individuals to express their opinions in a way that transcends what he calls 'the geocode', that is to say the spatial factors such as postal codes that serve as markers of social status. Even Margaret Wertheim, in an otherwise perceptive analysis of utopian visions of cyberspace, praises the Internet for its ability to erase class difference. She notes that 'for the first time ... Americans graduating from high school and college are finding they are unlikely to have a higher standard of living than their parents', and goes on to quote one of Turkle's subjects who said that 'MUD got me back into the middle class' as evidence that cyberspace allows those who find themselves in reduced circumstances to become 'energetic and productive cyber citizens' (Wertheim 1999: 287).

Read alongside early fantasies of online utopia, the widespread fascination with the theme of erasing otherness calls into question any optimistic vision of cyber-utopia as an inclusive site of belonging. The most famous of these is perhaps Howard Rheingold's seminal book *The Virtual Community*. Rheingold, following J.C. Licklider, sees cyber-communities as founded on shared interests:

> Life will be happier for the online individual because the people with whom one interacts most strongly will be selected more by commonality of interests and goals than by accidents of proximity ... my friends and I ... are part of the future that Licklider dreamed about, and we often can attest to the truth of his prediction (cited in Moser 1996: 121).

I want to focus here on the particular view of belonging that is being constructed in the examples cited above. For Rheingold (1993) and Poster (1995), belonging comes into being when individuals with shared interests choose to come together, creating an online community. That community is then fantasised as perfect; because the 'interest' pre-exists online belonging, the argument goes, there is no potential for serious disagreement. However, this fantasy is flawed since it does not account for the fact that a community may deem some interests to be divisive, and hence unacceptable. A decade after it was first written, then, the optimistic view of virtual culture outlined in *The Virtual Community* seems rather more problematic. Whilst the Well, and other communities based on the same model, have continued to thrive, the very idea of 'shared interests' suggests that their appeal may lie, not in erasure of 'real-life' attributes, but precisely in their ability to facilitate discussion of 'real life' experience. Web users are as likely to be united by gender, nationality, profession and so on, as by their erasure. What is more, the recent exposure of BNP membership in the UK shows that 'shared interests' can mean many things, not all of them benign. One need not share Locke's pessimism about cyberculture to feel unease about an unbridled celebration of the Internet as a site of belonging, and indeed critical theory in the late 1990s highlighted the problematic nature of a tendency to celebrate a generalised notion of 'difference' whilst promoting a model of virtual community that tends to erase real difference in favour of a homogenous, Americanised identity. For example, Jon Stratton writes that the stories that get told about digital culture tend to be rooted in narratives of American citizenship:

> [T]he Internet as a community represents a nostalgic dream for a mythical early modern community which reasserts the dominance of the white, middle-class male and his cultural assumptions. Far from the present day attempts to construct heterogeneous nation-states founded in on an acceptance of difference, the image of the small town community is located in the melting pot politics of homogenisation into a new, unitary American national identity (Stratton 1997: 271).

Similarly, Wilbur points out that the metaphors of the frontier are 'steeped in traditions of imperialism, rough justice and the sometimes violent opposition of any number of others:' nevertheless, he notes with concern they have been taken up with enthusiasm by liberal computer users who might be expected to be more wary (2000: 46–7). He suggests that it is politically imperative to pay attention to the uneasy connection between the frontier, which he describes as 'near-primitive' (2000: 47) and the supposedly idyllic online community described by Rheingold. Indeed, one could argue that the frontier is an appropriate metaphor for the reality of an Internet dominated by United States-based commercial interests and dogged by problems of access. As Stephen Talbott has argued, one implication of the frontier narrative is that there cannot be enough land for everyone, and that this might lead to further hierarchies developing between those marginalised groups who are able to establish an online presence, and those who are not (1995: 48–9).

The debates over frontier metaphors highlight the tension which has always existed between academic optimism, and actual inequality. As David Gauntlett points out, this tension can also be seen in academic discourse concerning the 'public sphere'. In the early 1990s, he argues, it was assumed that 'when even more people had access, the net would bring about a healthy public sphere' (2000: 16), with every member of society contributing to a vast, democratic public discussion of current political issues. In practice, however, he argues that this vision was unlikely ever to materialise: firstly because only interested people participate in online discussions, but also due to the fact that access to the web is still highly limited, and in any case such a huge discussion between millions of people would be unworkable.

By reading early metaphors of cyberspace alongside later debates concerning access, then, it should be clear that the textual formations through which online communities are imagined, have real consequences for members of the community (as well as for those who do not have access). This is not to claim that it is necessary to adopt a wholly pessimistic view of virtual community: however, it is important to acknowledge that inequalities which exist in geophysical communities, might be reproduced online, and that it is precisely through those metaphors that are intended to portray cyberculture as liberating that inequalities tend to be reproduced. As James Porter notes, '[I]n a society or community with inherently unequal participants, or with a long history of inequality, the appeal to the liberal enlightenment view may have the effect of maintaining the status quo' (1999: 242): and this, I would suggest, is the function served by the notion of virtual homesteading. The fantasy of heading for the frontier, of making a fresh start, therefore carries the traces of that which is not fully present in the text: the problems, differences and inequalities that are being concealed. For all its optimism, then, the story of the frontier implicitly stands in for anxieties about the possible failure of the utopian project. Some accounts of virtual community have tended to normalise particular interests and identity positions, presenting them as authentic, with the result that other identifications are reduced to the level of mere 'baggage'. That is, they are presented as superfluous material attachments that burden the subject and that can be put down in order to facilitate the flight to the frontier: however, such a flight is always threatened with failure, with the suggestion that utopia might simply fail to materialise, or that it might collapse into dystopia. I have argued that the liberal notion of utopia might mask real political effects that are conservative in character. Here, I want to look more closely at the ways in which the notion of 'utopia' draws on religious narratives.

Here, the term 'baggage' is significant, since it the notion of giving up physical 'belongings' in order to belong is again suggestive of religious discourse. Just as one is asked to put aside worldly riches in order to enter the kingdom of heaven, those differences, which might be seen as (potentially) constructing the richness of human experiences and relationships, must be put aside if one is to experience fully a sense of online belonging. Hence, this view of community differs from that of 'real-life' communities, which is more likely to privilege materiality and shared experience, as Anne-Marie Fortier points out, 'Belongings refers to both "possessions" and *appartenance*. That is, practices of group identity are about manufacturing cultural and historical belongings which mark out terrains of commonality that delineate the politics and social dynamics of "fitting in"' (1999: 42).

This is not to claim that 'belongings' are unimportant in fantasies of online community like that outlined by Pascoe. Rather, what is at stake is the surrendering of one set of 'imaginary possessions' in exchange for another. The 'imaginary possessions that ... a people cobble together from the past and the present' (Probyn 1996: 68) (that is, any pre-existing identifications outside the Internet community) are what is surrendered here. The Internet community is 'cobbled together from the past and the present' only in the sense that one is encouraged to see one's own history as merged with, and subordinate to, the history of the Internet itself. A hierarchy of experience is constructed, in which diversity is acceptable only insofar as it does not disrupt the Internet community itself; whilst the community may be read as transgressive in itself, its integrity must not be threatened.

Pascoe's vision of cyber-utopia, then, far from encouraging communication on a level which transcends gendered, racial, sexual, and class difference, is open to becoming dystopian/totalitarian precisely because it permits members of different groups to communicate but without discussing those differences. Again, what is at stake here (as in discourses of religious homophobia) is the question of telling the difference (Garber 1992). In order to belong fully to the online community, a participant is expected to perform the role of unmarked subject. According to Poster

(1995), this subject's age, social status, gender and race are to remain undetermined in order that the conversation may flow as freely as possible. However, this is not to say that the subject has no such characteristics, rather that he or she should conceal those attributes that are deemed to be especially disruptive; that is, those associated with 'difference'. As Lisa Nakamura has noted, in live role-playing games, 'Players who elect to describe themselves in racial terms, as Asian, African American, Latino ... are often seen as engaging in a form of hostile performance, since they introduce what many consider a real life "divisive issue" into the phantasmic world of cybernetic textual interaction' (1995: 183). The utopian view of cyber-community outlined above, then, is not one of justice for all, nor is it imagined as a forum in which issues of difference may be openly discussed. Rather, the virtual community is imagined as one in which the white, middle-class heterosexual subject need not be threatened by the visible presence of the other, and where 'others' can experience, albeit briefly, the pleasure of passing as 'unmarked'.

This focus on becoming unmarked is not only problematic for virtual communities themselves. Although the impact of online violence should not be underestimated, these assumptions become more dangerous when we consider the ways in which the virtual community is imagined as mapping onto the 'real world'. If an ideal community is one in which difference is erased, this allegedly new, transformative, cutting-edge model of utopia also comes to be more acceptable as a means of imagining a real-world utopia constructed along similar lines. The fantasy of virtual communities, here, lies in the notion of the virtual space as a forum in which new social forms might be developed that will then be used to benefit the whole world through the benign global networks outlined above. All this typically means that the discourse of virtual community pays little attention to the ways in which virtual communities often re-present the social mores of the real world, or at least the world of the information-rich. As Mark Nunes suggests, this assumption of the essential newness of virtual communities obscures the ways in which these 'ideal' societies represent what he calls a 'banal ideal', one that merely 're-creates the world as we find it, rather than challenging it' (1997: 171). I would go further, suggesting that the idealism we invest in virtual communities assumes a challenge to 'the world as we find it' even when no such challenge is present. However, the outcome is the same: Nunes notes that '[while] some may dream of "societies more decent and free than those mapped onto dirt and concrete and capital", most online culture has more to do with an endless repetition and circulation of the same personal, social and political strategies that have served as the dominant expressions of (real) modern space' (1997: 171).[8]

God Hates Fags is perhaps one of the best-known Christian fundamentalist sites on the web. It is a non-interactive website, set up and maintained by Benjamin Phelps, pastor of Westboro Baptist Church in Topeka, Kansas in association with his grandfather Fred Phelps, who originally founded the church in 1964. Phelps first achieved notoriety in 1991 when he organised a picket of the San Francisco Pride parade, to 'warn this evil city that they're going the way of Sodom'. In 1997, the church's members were ordered by the Supreme Court to limit their picketing activities after targeting a local Episcopalian church that they claimed had promoted gay rights. Since the ruling, church members have continued their campaign of homophobic picketing. However, it is as an online promoter of homophobic and other forms of hatred that Phelps has achieved notoriety on an international scale. On paper, Westboro Baptist Church's website seems like the perfect example of the Web's utility as a means of giving voice to small, marginalised community groups, and of bringing together people who share 'a commonality of interests and goals'. This, like other homophobic fundamentalist sites, appropriates discourses of cyberspace as essentially liberating and utopian. However, the fantasy of utopia at stake here, is, in line with the fundamentalist sentiments of the site's authors, not metaphorical but literal. The sites claim the notion of

8 In any case, the web itself is in a sense 'mapped onto capital', since most pages are funded by banner advertising. Often, this has unintentionally bathetic consequences. For example, at the time of writing, on the homepage of the hate site Surfing the Apocalypse (www.surfingtheapocalypse.com), the portentous tone (featuring animations of electrical storms against a black background, red lettering in the *Exorcist* film typescript) is somewhat spoiled by a banner advertising British Gas Plumbing and Pipes Insurance for £4.00 a month.

'shared interests' as a means of justifying their activities, but the interests that members share happen to include insisting that creationist dogma be taught in schools, picketing the funerals of those who die of Aids or as a result of homophobic attacks, and promoting the harassment of gay men and lesbians, and any other subject whose sexuality is felt to place them beyond the pale.

The website is hence rooted in the Church's real-life existence as a pressure group. However, Westboro Baptist Church's website seeks to transcend the limitations of the local community, claiming to represent a much wider imagined community of obsessively homophobic religious fundamentalists. This community was an early adopter of web technologies, despite its dated look, and has as its focal point a website with no explicitly interactive features (such as live chat, bulletin boards, or even a guestbook where the visitor could post responses to the site's content). The banner for the site is an illustration reminiscent of the clipart images more often seen on homemade flyers, showing a small red-haired white boy, carrying a sign bearing a stylised image of two stick figures engaging in what appears to be anal sex (although this only becomes clear from the context), with the words 'FAG SIN'. The accompanying text is a quote from Leviticus saying only '… and therefore I abhorred them' (ellipsis in original): this slender remnant of scripture represents the only concrete biblical evidence that God in fact, as advertised, 'hates fags'.[9]

Since its inception in the early 1990s, the church's website has expanded to include scripture content, press room, coverage of 'other issues' including anti-Catholic content, videos, FAQs in English and Spanish, and a (to this reader at least) largely incoherent blog consisting of answers to questions supposedly posed by the general public. The replies combine playground abuse of the questioners with often lengthy quotations from scripture in a sprawling overview of the church's message. A response to one question, asking how the church can hope to preach worldwide, as it claims, begins, 'Dear Crybaby Kay! You silly loser', and continues:

9 www.godhatesfags.com, accessed 28 November 2008.

> Our job is to PUBLISH!! We do that in many, many ways. It includes, but is not limited to: Standing on the streets; sending out News Releases (they include good words of reproof and instruction AND information); talking to people on the phones (dozens, daily); answering emails (even from brutes); web pages (including with words, audio of sermons and songs and videos with words, songs, photos, MANY PHOTOS and images and articles to connect the dots for you haters and rebels); other internet – when the unclean birds take the words, etc. and post, post, post, share, fuss, snarl, etc.; Media – they publish the words and show the words, they show the images, they help you haters to sift through this little flock of slaughter so you KNOW our manner of life and you KNOW that we walk before you honestly with the TRUTH of God … [t]hat is how our God rolls! He opened those doors of utterance unto us …[10]

What is interesting here is the rather dual image of virtual space as, on the one hand, an extension of the fantasy pairing of America/Sodom that underpins much of the site's content, but also as a pure, god-given space. The Internet is taken to be an answer to Paul's prayer, in the epistle to the Colossians, 'that God would open unto us a door of utterance, to speak the mystery of Christ'. The key fantasy here is one of one's prayers being answered, of a presiding intelligence making sense of the chaos of 'words … post, post, post', the dangerously unregulated heteroglossia of the unsaved: indeed just as Bakhtin's heteroglossia represents a pulling away by multiple voices from the move to a standardised language (Bakhtin 1981), the 'post, post, post' of the Web is here imagined as a pulling away from god. In using the Web, the believer is imagined as self-consciously taking up god's work. In contrast, 'media', by reporting on Westboro's activities, are portrayed as also doing god's work, but unknowingly; although these mainstream reports may be critical, their role is simply 'to show'; they 'publish the words … show the images' (and in this sense, no publicity is bad publicity). The distinction here is between passive 'showing', and the internet as the site of an active engagement between 'good' and 'evil'; as the site, perhaps, of a virtual Armageddon.

10 www.godhatesfags.com/written/sermons/outlines/Sermon_20080615.pdf, accessed 28 November 2008.

Whilst God Hates Fags and other sites like it primarily express the fantasy of a post-apocalyptic New Jerusalem, they do so by referring to fantasies of the nation (as a space which must be purified in order for this apocalyptic transformation to take place); through a kind of pose of dumb insolence which refuses to acknowledge that anything offensive is being expressed (the word 'colourful' makes this point particularly impressively); and most of all through a knowing appropriation of the language of virtual community (here re-imagined in distorted form as a community of haters). This is rooted in the local community producing the site, who, from being a small, marginal force, are re-presented as a community of knowers attempting to promote 'the truth' about life in the United States. Whilst all four of these communities are imagined in the same style through a fantasy of imminent apocalypse and the redemption of the elect, they are not simply analogous to one another, and indeed are often in conflict. Further, the church's activities are not limited to the online sphere: the affective community being constructed by these sites is inseparable from its connection to offline bodies and lives.

Whilst all communities are to some extent unaware of their own violence, their own blind spots, Westboro Baptist Church's claims of peacefulness often stretch credulity to a greater than usual extent. Here is the site's description of church member's 'peaceful' protests:

> WBC engages in daily peaceful sidewalk demonstrations opposing the homosexual lifestyle of soul-damning, nation-destroying filth. We display large, colourful signs containing Bible words and sentiments, including: GOD HATES FAGS, FAGS HATE GOD, AIDS CURES FAGS, THANK GOD FOR AIDS, FAGS BURN IN HELL, GOD IS NOT MOCKED, FAGS ARE NATURE FREAKS [sic] ... FAGS DOOM NATIONS, etc.[11]

The site's authors are able to claim such sentiments as 'non-violent' precisely because of the way that violence is imagined purely in terms of physical act: that is, as embodied. Discursive violence, the violence

11 www.godhatesfags.com/written/wbcinfo/aboutwbc.html, accessed 28 November 2008.

of the text, is not recognised as such. Reading the passages above, I am reminded of Esther Milne's frustration at her inability to share the ironic 'hip sensibility' to be found in some accounts of cyberculture: the process of reading *moves* me, challenging (though not ultimately displacing) my views about freedom of expression. My reading of the site is not, cannot be, dispassionate. I find it difficult to maintain any sense of critical distance at the notion of picketing a funeral, and then going online to publicise the activity and exhort others to do the same. The site is not unaware of its ability to stir up deep emotions, although it refuses to acknowledge that the reader's negative affective reaction is anything other than the whining of a 'cry baby' who cannot handle the truth. Indeed, the site is frustrating precisely in that it consistently assumes the reader's sympathy. For the site's authors, a community of 'fag haters' already exists within the wider, corrupt national community of the United States; the site merely serves to unite this community and to provide it with resources. Nevertheless, the statement is itself part of the process by which the site attempts to construct a community through a process of rehabilitation, which aims to re-position hatred of homosexuals both as a political position, and as an identity position. The site assumes that the experience of hatred, like that of other extreme emotions, has been wrongly constructed as essentially private, even impossible to articulate. The Westboro Baptist Church's writings assure us that it can and must be articulated, that 'our' hatred (and the reader is always assumed to be on side; the site is never defensive in tone, and never attempts to address its critics) is shared by others. The community exists 'inside' individuals; by making hatred public and visible, the community can surface, becoming visible in the public domain.

This site, and others like it, provide a chilling new perspective on the notion of 'shared interests' as a basis for community. I am not claiming that the notion of community is therefore somehow invalid: only that we need to pay attention to the ease with which narratives of community can be appropriated by advocates of hatred. But it is useful, as well, to read sites like God Hates Fags, for the insight they give us into the ways in which inequalities might not only be carried over from offline into online communities but actually be heightened, not least by the liberal rhetoric of free speech in which the intended victims of such assaults are urged simply to ignore them, even as they are imposed upon an ever-increasing number of victims (Porter 1999: 234–5). In order to justify their attacks on outsiders, hate sites reproduce discourses of virtual community alongside fundamentalist dogma. So, for example, Westboro Baptist Church claims that it is necessary to draw together a community based on a shared homophobic response in order to protect the larger community of the nation from destruction. In order to construct the virtual community, then, it is necessary to mobilise fantasies of the nation as it might be in an ideal world; the community does not simply represent the wider community of the United States; that is, it is not a 'virtual America'. Rather, it draws upon a fantasy of the nation as perfectible, and this fantasy assumes a desire to purify the nation by destroying or expelling the hated Other.

The central structuring fantasy of the site is the displacement of the violence of erasure onto the figure of 'God', such that expulsion of the Other is imagined as the direct work of god. God, not the Phelps family and their cohorts, is presented as the ultimate author of the site; hate speech therefore becomes not just the expression of a political position which is being defended as 'more enlightened' or as 'saying what others are afraid to say' – although both are important themes – but a means of using the possibilities afforded by the Internet to speak for god. God is presented as a marginalised subject who finds, in the Internet, a means of self-publishing. The figure of god is a means of re-invoking a unitary, masculine authority against the frightening heteroglossia of cyberspace, but is also democratised: god is 'just like us', just a regular guy, in that he publishes his views online, complete with cheap clip-art images; god thinks like us, feels like us, hates like us. As Michael Cobb's brilliant exposition of religious homophobia reminds us, fundamentalist accounts of the Bible must refuse the truth that 'the Bible is a massive and textually unstable document, which must be translated, implied [sic], refined, interpreted and applied in very ingenious ways all the time'; this 'rhetorical complexity' is ignored in favour of a trumpeting of god's word as 'simple and true', a process he says is exemplified by Westboro's use of scripture (2006: 23–4). But this simplification is not confined to the selective quoting of scripture. It is rooted in the construction of god as a simple individual with simple tastes. This version of 'god' has personal tastes: he enjoys a colourful sign, and doesn't like being mocked. He has emotions which are an amplified version of his disciples. He likes a joke, has a crude sense of humour, and can be coarsely sentimental and simple-minded (not for nothing does the site speak of Bible 'sentiments', not ideas or concepts). Yet at the same time he is the god of the Old Testament, capable of unleashing a plague through his sheer rage: this god is pure affect, pure hatred: indeed, the notion of a god who 'hates' may be a deliberate inversion of mainstream Christianity's assertion that 'god is love'. Indeed, a section on the site is entitled 'God Loves Everyone: the greatest lie ever told',[12] and purports to prove 'God's hate and wrath for most of mankind' through the citation of 701 scriptural passages. To be consumed by hatred – and the Phelps family consists of generations of a single family, all of whose lives are given over to the promotion of hate speech – is truly to have accepted god into one's heart.

Importantly, this notion of 'God as hatred' requires a critical reappraisal of 'hate' itself. Feminist and postcolonial critics have paid considerable attention to 'hate'. In these important accounts, 'hate' is considered in two connected ways: firstly as hate speech, and secondly through a focus on intimate bodily practices of disgust (hooks 1992, Lorde 1984, Ahmed 2004). These accounts have tended to focus on the other's body as an object of hate, as in Sara Ahmed's close reading of Lorde, which takes Lorde's phrase 'the hate' as the starting point for an insightful consideration of what it means to live 'as' an object of hate and to experience an affective encounter in which one is positioned as an object of disgust (2004: 53–4). In order to consider the meaning of the word 'hate' in the term 'god hates fags', I think we need to re-frame this notion of hate as both grounded in, and productive of, an affective encounter between dominant and marginal bodies. Through the appropriation of online space, 'hate' comes to signify something different, to do different work. Ahmed's account focuses on the intimacy of hatred, and this trope is

12 http://www.godhatesfags.com/written/reports/20060331_god-loves-everyone-lie.pdf, accessed 8 December 2008.

certainly repeated in much of the material on the GHF website. The notion of 'preaching' itself, of having the 'doors of utterance' opened, itself implies an Other who is being preached to; in this sense, the online is imagined as giving access to the sinful Other in order that he may yet mend his ways. In other words, the site, like all spaces used for proselytising is imagined as an interactive space, orientated to a dual audience (the faithful who form the community, and the other who must be preached to in order to be incorporated). But there is another, parallel narrative at work that constantly undoes this work of interactivity. In order to explain what I mean by this, it is instructive to return to the story of Sodom and Gomorrah, the founding myth that underpins the site's fantasy narrative concerning the origin of the Aids 'epidemic'.

The story of the cities of the plain provides the site with a founding myth. In the biblical story, found in Genesis Chapter 19, the cities of Sodom and Gomorrah were supposedly destroyed by god after several of the menfolk demanded of righteous Lot that his male guests be sent out to them 'that we may know them'.[13] In the story, the righteous are allowed to flee Sodom, but Lot's wife looks back, and as punishment is turned into a pillar of salt. Lot's wife is an important figure for fundamentalist Christianity: for example, one FAQ site addresses in serious and scholarly terms the question, 'why haven't we found Lot's wife?' concluding that:

> The place that Lots [sic] wife killed [sic] was never meant to be a memorial – she perished as the result of God's judgment. Her body was reduced to ash and salt – That whole area is now salt – its [sic] not just one tiny pillar somewhere so we wouldn't expect to find one human shaped mound or anything. The bible warned that they would 'be consumed' Genesis 19:17.[14]

13 For consistency, biblical references are taken from the King James version of the bible, specifically the online version which is available along with several other translations at: http://biblecc.com. This appears to be the version preferred by the Westboro Baptist Church, although some scriptural quotations appear to be in colloquial language and are hence presumably taken from more recent translations.

14 Taken from the site 'Jesus, Dinosaurs and More!', a creationist website: see http://www.angelfire.com/mi/dinosaurs/lotswife.html. The dinosaurs apparently make, albeit coded, appearances throughout the Old Testament, thus proving evolution

Sodom of course gave its name to the practice crudely represented in the site's masthead by the two stick figures. In the image, one figure appears to be bent at the knees, while the other approaches him from behind while holding on to the place where a human's waist or hips would be. These two images – that of Lot's wife transformed into a pillar that is 'not a memorial', and the reduction of 'fags' to a stick-figure representation of 'sodomy', are central the work that 'hate' does on this site. Crucially, 'hate' is tied up with reductiveness and with the work of erasure.

It should be clear that the God Hates Fags site equates Aids, which it sees as an epidemic sent directly by god, with the conflagration that engulfed the cities of the plain. Specific groups and communities are repeatedly identified with Sodom: sometimes 'gay' areas such as San Francisco, sometimes the 'gay community', sometimes the United States itself. In this account, the affective moment of disgust is denied: one does not have to acknowledge homophobic disgust in oneself, since god is always already engaged in 'hating fags' and acting on that hatred: he is doing his best to destroy the hated object. 'Fags' are thus doubly erased from the text. Despite the overt performance of preaching, the implied object is always already damned. 'Hatred' thus refers not to the affective encounter of disgust, but to the work of erasure itself, of making (the other) absent. Hate is thus not 'felt' as a passionate repudiation of a loathed other, which is to say it is not an affect in Tomkins' sense. 'Hate' is an absence of emotion, a closing off of the other and an absolute denial of the other's capacity for feeling. In doubly reducing 'fags' – first to a discrete sexual practice, and then to a simple visual signification of that practice – the site becomes a denial of the other's subjectivity. The texture of everyday life – the loves, friendships, fears, sufferings, anxieties, and anger of the other – are edited out. Further, it is a denial of intersubjectivity, a refusal to be moved but also a kind of ritual performance of speaking 'to' the other which is simultaneously a speaking into the void. To be moved is to look back (and hence to be consumed). In order to look forward,

---

to be a myth (and hence rather pleasingly demonstrating, if nothing else, that even fundamentalist readings of texts require a certain amount of interpretation for their true meanings to become clear).

the convert must gaze into a future in which all emotions have passed through the prism of God's hatred to be subsumed into the single emotion of hate. Desire is still the primary affect, as in Tomkins' model, but desire leads inexorably to the void that is god-as-hate. In this overwhelmingly negative worldview, preaching to a body in a coffin suddenly makes perfect sense: the other, being already damned (or living in the hell of god's wrath) was never really there to begin with. In other words, god-as-hate is Žižek's notion of interpassivity taken to the extreme.

According to Žižek, interpassivity is the inescapable shadow of interactivity, its 'shadowy and much more uncanny supplement/double'. He identifies how theories of cyberculture make much of the notion that 'the passive consumption of a text or a work of art is over', such that we now interact with the screen rather than simply staring at it: all liberal and utopian claims for the possibilities of cyberspace rely on this fantasy of interactivity. This masks the fact that what one is interacting with, often, is not a single, identifiable other individual, but the Big Other; imagining oneself to be engaging in new encounters with unknown others, the observer becomes doubly passive. This is not to say that interpassivity is not experienced as an encounter, nor that it is not affective: the example he uses is that of an academic who 'authentically' suffers through accounts of rape and murder in Bosnia 'while calmly pursuing his academic career'. Ironically, for Žižek, the ultimate example of interpassivity is the suffering Christ who 'redeemed us all not by acting for us, but by assuming the burden of the ultimate passive experience' (2008).

God Hates Fags takes this a step further. Here, any encounter with the Other carries the risk of being consumed into the void represented by the signifier God. In order that the believer not be consumed, the Other must be made to suffer. However, this involves the believer in a double bind, since it is precisely recognition of the Other's suffering which carries this risk of annihilation. The Other must thus be positioned as always already in hell, already obliterated. In this temporality of hate, to be 'a fag' is to be already dead. 'Hate' thus refers not to the heat of the affective encounter, but to a completed act of erasure. To say that 'god hates fags' is not to claim that God sits around brooding over the disgustingness of 'sodomy'; rather it is to claim that the hated other does not really exist, indeed never really existed. 'Hate', in this account, is inseparable from a fantasy of the utter annihilation of the hated Other. It assumes a completed act of annihilation.

Despite the dystopian violence of Phelps' vision, then, I do not think it is enough to argue (as a reading of Margaret Wertheim's work might suggest) that such manifestations are simply an example of a medium with great potential for spiritual growth, falling into the wrong hands. Wertheim seems to predict the use of the Internet to promote hatred when she writes that '[T]here is every potential, if we are not careful, for cyberspace to be less like Heaven, and more like Hell' (1999: 298). This reading of virtual culture tends to normalise the idea of a utopian internet community, from which deviations occur only as the result of insufficient vigilance. In GHF, the desired object – what we might call 'heaven' – is hell, if hell is imagined as being inside the void of god's hatred; as an empty universe where there are no Others. What is more, the invocation of a group of right-thinking cybercitizens – the 'we' who must be 'careful' – reproduces the very liberal rhetoric which, as I have argued, tends to perpetuate, or at least obscure, power structures within online communities. Indeed, the notion of 'the online community' invoked here seems, ironically, to reproduce the notion of a single unlimited community which, if it is not conterminous with all mankind exactly, is certainly conterminous with all (responsible) users of the internet. As I have shown, it is by appropriating the notions of universality and redemption that underpin utopian theories of cyberculture that Phelps and his family are able to present their site as a site of community. I would suggest, then, that the notion of a community that has the potential to be good, but is constantly under threat from deviant outsiders, is inadequate. Rather, it is necessary to pay attention to the ways in which utopian rhetoric might be appropriated and itself become a means of reproducing online and offline violence.

Mending Communities: The Virtual Aids Quilt

> The weaving of complex designs demands far more than one pair of hands, and textiles production tends to be communal, sociable work allowing plenty of occasion for gossip and chat. Weaving was already multimedia: singing, chanting, telling stories, dancing, and playing games as they work, spinsters, weavers, and needle-workers were literally networkers as well (Plant 1997: 67).

For the fundamentalist websites cited above, the imagining of the online community is inseparable from fantasies of the nation state and Christian eschatology. I now to turn from the excesses of those sites, and to examine a different category of affective community on the web. As I have argued, the communities above construct a fantasy that assumes that the values of the online community will eventually be carried forward into the real world. The sites construct a virtual world that is constantly in the process of expelling hated others. Indeed, the expulsion of those others constitutes a performance of the desire to eliminate those others altogether. Similarly, communities of mourning aim to bring together and make visible a community that is perceived as already existing in the material world.

The Virtual Aids Quilt began life as a website that was set up on behalf of the NAMES foundation to provide an archive of the original Aids quilt, and to provide wider access to the quilt. The quilt itself, which was begun by activists in San Francisco in 1987, consists of 44,000 panels measuring three feet by six, each commemorating the life of a person who died of Aids. Lovers and family members were encouraged to make panels as an act of community building. The website reminds the reader that there is a historical connection between the act of quilting, and notions of community and shared memory:

> Quilt making has always been a unique way of creating a sense of community. When family members and friends gather to sew quilts, they also weave a tapestry of stories and memories, as colourful and beautiful as the quilts themselves. Over

> the years, the AIDS Memorial Quilt has created its own community of family and friends who have lost someone to AIDS.[15]

In this account, the quilt is presented as a means of making visible a 'virtual' community that already exists, consisting of those who share the common experience of having 'lost someone to Aids'. The quilt is envisaged as a celebration of diversity, specificity and difference whilst also giving a sense of empowerment through belonging to a large and influential community. Whilst it has always been known as the 'virtual quilt', the original version of the site was not 'truly' virtual; rather it used the then new technologies of the Internet as a means of displaying a physical artefact, and providing a communal space. The online 'quilt squares' were hence reproductions of real-life fabric squares, and it is this version of the quilt I want to examine first.

When the Aids quilt project began in the 1990s, its status as a community-building project was criticised by some writers and activists for not being as all-inclusive as the account above might suggest. The project was criticised for presenting a sanitised and unthreatening view of the disease (and, by extension, of the 'gay community'), and for the ease with which the quilt has become assimilated as a commodity within mainstream consumer culture (Harris 1985). Others rejected the quilt as too sentimental. Most famously, the late, then HIV-positive director Derek Jarman described the project as 'horrible, quasi-religious, false', and went on to say, 'I shall haunt anyone who ever makes a panel for me' (Jarman 1995). Whilst ACT-UP activists have been critical of what they see as a failure to address less comfortable issues such as sexuality and sexual practise. The feminist cultural theorist Marita Sturken claims that the quilt is problematic precisely because it appropriates the imagery of quilting. By failing to engage with the history of quilting as a feminine activity, she argues that it excludes women, and in doing so presents the experience of Aids as a 'highly eroticised male-only zone' in which only a few women's experiences are represented (1997: 202). Whilst these criticisms are contradictory, they both arise from a feeling that the quilt fails in its

15 www.aidsquilt.org/community.htm, accessed 28 November 2008.

promise to create a sense of community. Although the image of a quilt suggests an essential homeliness and a sense of comfort, these accounts raise the uncomfortable suggestion that some subjects might feel more 'at home' in this community than others.

The virtual quilt website attempts to address some of these criticisms, and to present a more diverse and complex view of community. The main section of the site consists of a database, which is still in the process of being updated to include all 44,000 panels. The database contains photographic images of the panels, which the user can browse at random, or search for specific panels by name or number, using the built-in search engine. The archive is currently being expanded to include further documentary information about the subject of each panel, including photographs, letters and memoirs. As I have stated, the act of contributing to the quilt is imagined as one of healing, which gives survivors a sense of consolation through the awareness of larger community based on a shared sense of mourning. However, the website also lists more explicitly political aims. Through giving wider access to the quilt, its goal is 'to use the Aids memorial quilt to bring an end to Aids' by illustrating the size of the epidemic, raising awareness, assisting in public education projects, and raising funds for 'community-based Aids service organisations'.[16] In an interview quoted on the site of the virtual quilt's corporate sponsor, the software company Infolink, the NAMES Project Foundation's director Anthony Turney reiterates the importance of a sense of community in achieving these goals:

> The Memorial Quilt web site is a perfect example of how technology can impact the community in a very humane way ... We are thankful for the expertise and support all these companies have given us, and with them, hope to bring awareness to communities around the world about those who suffer from AIDS.[17]

16 www.einet.net/directory/165567/NAMES_Project___AIDS_Memorial_Quilt.htm, accessed 8 December 2008.

17 ww5.aegis.org/news/bw/1997/BW971114.html, accessed 28 November 2008.

Here, the term 'community' is being used in a variety of different ways. In the first sentence of this quotation, 'the' community is positioned as a group of people 'out there', who need to be educated, whose lives the quilt could impact in a positive way. In the next sentence, however, this view immediately shifts in meaning, becoming more complex. Now it is the more diverse 'communities' who are being addressed, although these communities are still positioned as needing education. The website itself adds yet more different forms of community. The site is described as 'a "virtual" community where you can share memories and thoughts, chat with other friends of the Quilt, and find information and resources about HIV/AIDS'. On its main menu there is a section entitled 'community', which is split into three sections headed 'HIV/Aids info', 'Memory Book', and 'Chat'. Each section uses a different kind of interactive technology to produce different 'communal' experiences, some of which feel more communal than others. Of the three sections, the 'info' section feels least interactive. It simply leads to two pages of US and international statistics on HIV and Aids, and to a links page listing the websites of other research and charitable organisations. This section is arguably the most likely to be useful to people who are, or think they might be HIV positive, since it gives details of advocacy and healthcare services, for example. Yet, curiously, the feeling this gives is one of being hurried to some other site; this is hardly a communal experience. The site itself includes no information on living with Aids, suggesting that the community referred to in the site menu, whoever it might include, excludes people who are currently living with the disease. In a sense, this is only to be expected; after all, this is a memorial site whose very existence is rooted in the shared experience of having 'lost someone'. However, the site fails, for example, to address the concerns of those survivors who are themselves HIV positive. Rather, it draws on a sense of tragedy and loss as a means of giving the 'wider community' – people, by implication heterosexuals, who might be unaware of the seriousness and scale of the problem – access to a more enlightened community of mourners.

The next item on the Community menu is the Memory Book. This section is presented as a resource for the community of mourners, where survivors can 'share memories and stories about a loved one lost to Aids'.

Whilst the site's authors imply that the resource can be used by other friends of the quilt as well, this is not actively encouraged. The site states that 'it is also a space where people can write about their feelings, thoughts and ideas about AIDS, about the Quilt, or about the experience of making a Quilt panel'. The memory book consists of an online bulletin board. Users can type a message into an email form, which is then permanently displayed on the site. The bulletin board format also means that other users can respond to these messages, carrying on a public conversation which is permanently accessible to other readers. The Chat section is a live chat facility. It is not a private space, since any visitor to the site can either participate or simply read other users' conversations. Such a discussion is by definition anonymous and ephemeral; the site's owners keep no record of these conversations and it is not possible for users to record them.

These three sections of the site's 'community' suggest that there are in fact three separate communities. The first is the community at large, which is comprised of people who have not been diagnosed HIV positive (though it does not necessarily exclude those who are simply worried that they might be). This is the community that is in need of education and consciousness-raising. The second, larger space is given over to a community of mourners and people with Aids, and is rooted in a sense of shared mourning and memories of shared experiences. The third more ambiguous space, the chat room, may include people from any or none of these groups, although it is pitched at what we might call 'friends of the quilt'. This section, being comprised simply of an online chat window, leaves no record (interestingly, since the site is primarily concerned with memory and with the work of creating a permanent archive). Whilst this space might be read as opening up the possibility for more creative forms of communication between members of the community, I think there is also a hierarchical structure at work here. The Memory Book is used mainly for making unofficial additions to the quilt by posting entries in memory of the dead and for asking practical questions about, for example, how to make a quilt square or how to include the iconography of the quilt in funeral rites. Indeed, the name Memory Book itself suggests that this space is open to those who have memories of people with Aids.

However, the wording (suggesting that one might use the space to share 'thoughts, feelings and ideas' about Aids, but not personal experience of having Aids) makes it clear that the site is a community for mourners, not a forum for discussing the disease itself. The community is hence founded on the lived experience of certain bodies, yet a sense of belonging is contingent precisely upon the death of those bodies, a death which allows mourning, and hence entry into the community, to commence. The chat room, in contrast, is open to all. This includes, by implication, those who do not have memories (that is, people who have no personal experience of living with Aids) or who do not wish to 'share' such memories on the site's terms. The presumption that the website can only function as an extension of the quilt's memorial function, that is as a community which is also a permanent memorial, works to conceal the ways in which the subject with Aids is implicitly excluded from that community.

The quilt itself is equated with the act of community building, yet the quilt database occupies a separate section of the site. However, the section entitled 'community' is separate from the quilt itself. Whilst the quilt is the reason for the site's existence, the foundation of the model of virtual community on offer here, its squares are buried deeply within the structure of the website. Since the database is constantly being updated, the database is often closed for maintenance. What is more, the built-in search engine often proves unable to cope with the sheer volume of site traffic. Both these factors mean that the quilt database is often offline and inaccessible. Yet this seems appropriate since the site is not concerned simply with presenting the quilt itself as spectacle. Instead, the website is emblematic of the process by which the web, nominally a much more visual, and less interactive, space than other forms of online community, works to create a sense of belonging. Although the site's original purpose was simply to make the quilt visible to anyone who wishes to see it, what emerges is a picture of a community defined by a central absence that has its origin in the death of an entire generation. The website, then, answers the need to make good the loss in some sense by bringing survivors and sympathisers together, to make visible the community of mourners. The sense of community it invokes is hence based on a longing to make this loss visible. This making-visible is crucial to the work of the web community and could not, I think, be carried out as successfully in any other medium since it is through the accessibility of the web that the site becomes a community as opposed to simply a memorial. By setting up the Aids memorial as a text which is constantly being modified and added to, the quilt community performs a constant engagement with the loss of an imagined future for those who have died. As such, it stands as a powerful rejoinder to homophobic sites, which aim to create a sense of community precisely through the denial and mockery of that loss.

The current version of the virtual quilt has moved on, however, to be more fully 'virtual', in that it now consists of a distributed network of sites, and, crucially, in that it is possible to create a memorial square that exists only as an online image, and not as a 'real' fabric square. Separate action groups, organisations and geographic areas have their own 'sections'. The Aids Action Committee of Massachusetts is typical in that it allows users to create individual web pages in memory of their loved ones. These can include visual material resembling a quilt square, but they can also be purely textual and can include a blog-like guestbook, allowing other mourners to add their words. What is more, the site is no longer limited to those who have died, but can be used to 'honour' others affected by the disease, as the organisation's homepage describes it:

> The Virtual AIDS Quilt is AIDS Action Committee's online program that allows you to design a personalized web page in honour of a loved one who has been affected by HIV/AIDS. This is your chance to convey the experience of this disease and fully capture the life of your friend in a safe and easily accessible space.
>
> Alternately, you may want to honour someone still living with the disease; a friend who has done much for the HIV/AIDS community; or your own experience as an HIV/AIDS volunteer, educator, advocate, or ally.[18]

In the original quilt website, a perhaps unconscious correlation is made between Internet and patchwork. The internet itself can, after all, only be experienced as a series of colourful squares, however sophisticated the content. What is more, in making this connection, a sense of

18 www.aac.org/quilt, accessed 28 November 2008.

continuity is created between past and present, old and new media, which speaks powerfully to the need to carry the dead with us into the new world. In online terms, sewing and weaving are metaphors for the work of community, not least in Sadie Plant's still-visionary writing from the 1990s (Plant 1997). The contemporary virtual quilt has up this metaphor, pushing it further and further, so that patchwork becomes more than just a metaphor for diversity, but is itself performative. Consider the connections being made her: between radically different media; different forms of 'new' media; different voices within the pages themselves; building to give a sense of a vast network within the wider community. The contemporary Aids quilt is thus a working out of a potential, a virtuality, inherent in the original quilt. I am using potential here in Massumi's sense; the virtual is, for Massumi, a 'pressing crowd of incipiencies and tendencies' and is hence 'a realm of potential' (2002: 30). This is particularly helpful in understanding the ways in which the virtual quilt works in terms of temporality. The virtual quilt mobilises the asynchronous format of online communication to disrupt the linear temporality of mourning that sees the dead as 'in the past' and needing to be 'got over'; although, simultaneously, it 'contains' such narratives to the extent that they are helpful for members of the community (so, for example, individual squares may represent a longing for closure, as well as a passionate desire to remember). In Massumi's terms, this reworking of oppositional categories of past and present, real and unreal, is precisely what characterises the virtual. Potential, he says, is the site where

> [Futurity] combines, unmediated, with pastness, where outsides are enfolded and sadness is happy (happy because the press to action and expression is life). The virtual is a lived paradox where what are normally opposites coexist, coalesce, and connect … (2002: 30).

The contemporary, more networked quilt should hence not be seen only as a fragmentation as an original, coherent site. Rather such a fragmentation is always already inherent in the quilt itself, since it is through this very fragmentation that the community of those affected by Aids emerges, not as a single cause but as a patchwork of difference. The 'press to action' emerges through fragmentation. Above, I have used 'deletion' as a way of thinking self-writing as performative, as a way of enacting regimes of power upon the self. To have one's finger on the delete key is to write with caution, with an apprehension of the proximity of potential violence. Writing/deleting is the inverse of the writing-as-liberation, that is sometimes assumed to reach its apotheosis through new technologies, through the harnessing of the hardware and software of late capitalism for subversive purposes. For hate sites like God Hates Fags, Aids itself is imagined as little more than a form of textual deletion: with chilling detachment, other bodies, other lives, are figured as nothing more than a kind of regrettable mistake now mercifully corrected with a stroke of the editor's pencil. It is not so much that the online environment makes this possible: more that (as ever) the online is a space in which offline realities become visible and are reproduced. The computer screen becomes both a symbol of the repeated daily 'screening' out of the experiences, realities, dreams and emotions of other lives. Hatred is a violent repudiation of proximity, a refusal to be touched by the hated other; the online refusal of hatred mirrors this, but it is also simultaneously a refusal of depth. The screen is imaged as just that: a flat screen, which does not open onto other worlds, other lives. Communities of hate are hence constructed precisely through the refusal of any but a partial experience of virtual spaces. We are 'going the way of Sodom'. A fictional city, destroyed in a fictional act of erasure by a god imagined as some kind of colossal editor sharing the writer's own views. For the authors of God Hates Fags, the virtual becomes an extension of the holy book in fundamentalist Christianity: it is at once a text that describes and defines reality, but simultaneously it is reality. In the text of Genesis, the cities of the plain are destroyed: through the writing of their destruction, that destruction becomes pre-determined and inevitable. Aids is imagined, similarly, as a textual intervention that stands in for divine endorsement of the author's desires.

If the human reality of living with Aids can be reduced to a mere act of deletion, one of the things the virtual Aids quilt does is to 'patch up' the ragged holes left by death, by absence. A quilt is made from patches, each one complete in itself and yet part of a whole. To patch something up is not to make it good as new: the presence of the patch at once reveals the fabric to be torn, and gestures to a desire to repair the tear while realising that nothing can ever be made good as new. In this sense it has a powerful resonance as a metaphor for mourning. What is more, patches are made from scraps, from the remnants of that which is used, that has been worn to death; it speaks to an imaginary past in which nothing was wasted, nothing thrown away; traditionally, for this reason, patchwork quilts have always symbolised memory, nostalgia, a sense of attachment to that which is (almost but never quite) lost.

Again, the question of whether a subject can be lost is central to the experience of using the internet. The virtual quilt uses a search engine to allow users to 'find' the squares representing individuals. Through search, there is a sense that individuals cannot be lost; nobody is ever more than a Google search away: old friends, lovers, classmates can be found in an instant, a process that might once have taken weeks or months of dogged inquiry. The residue of this fantasy of traceability is the haunting sense of those who cannot be Googled: to be not-Google-able is to join the anti-community of runaways, escaped criminals, refugees, fleeing witnesses, the socially marginal: and, of course, the far vaster community of the dead. The internet is like a vast patchwork, but it is one from which many are missing. By creating a virtual quilt square, one stakes out a tiny corner of this vast territory in the name, perhaps, of one who died too soon to stake his or her own claim: this one page figuratively patches over the rent where there might have been a blog, a homepage, a MySpace page, all the threads that make up the warp and weft of an online presence. A patch at once stands in for and refuses absence: it is a visual record of absence. Above all it stands for a defiant refusal of the notion that some bodies, some lives, can simply be cropped out of existence (and if 'deletion' is a way of thinking about the editing of life-texts, then perhaps by extension we also need to think in terms of 'cropping', given that online content is visual as well as textual). The work of (virtual) sewing is a labour of love through which the lost are 'patched in', stitched back into the emerging and developing community. Unlike Lot's wife, who is destroyed by her single doomed act of attachment to her lost homeland (and this turning back towards the burning city is a perfect dramatisation of what Tomkins means by attachment as a movement towards the desired object), the virtual quilt represents a desire for a fixed monument in this most shifting and transient of spaces: a refusal to be erased, to be reduced to metaphorical salt and ashes.

I began this chapter by presenting a close reading that asked whether a sense of community could flourish in cyberspace. In fact, as the two websites I examine above demonstrate, the notion of 'community' is central to the appeal of virtual experiences. I have presented these two sites alongside one another because they deal with the questions of visibility raised by Locke and Pascoe (2000) in very different ways. Whilst the newspaper debate suggested that some loss of visibility is a worthwhile price to pay for the construction of a utopian community, homophobic websites illustrate the dangers that arise when one group decides that it is precisely the visibility of a certain category of subject that is preventing such a community from coming into existence. Whilst sites like God Hates Fags continue to lobby for the erasure of gay subjects, the Aids quilt website provides a site of resistance precisely because it harnesses the visual elements of the web in order to make visible a loss. In this, it refuses the work of erasure, since it insists that the virtual community is important precisely because of its ability to take aspects of lived experience that might otherwise remain hidden, and make them not only visible, but the very basis of a sense of belonging. It is very different from the visions of Eva Pascoe and Howard Rheingold, both of whom assume the construction of virtual communities to be a utopian project that involves the casting off of old allegiances along with 'irrelevancies' such as gender and social grouping. In practice, the highly visual and commercialised culture of the web is just as likely to provide a sense of community as more obscure sites of virtual belonging such as chat rooms and UseNet groups, and this sense of community is perhaps less likely to require the erasure of specificity and difference. Instead, it is based on a sense of shared experience and, importantly, shared emotion.

As I have demonstrated, such a community has its problematic elements, not least that the site's design and structure are likely to appeal to some subjects more than others. One of the recurring themes of this chapter has been the assumptions that are built into web communities about the kinds of readers who are being addressed. So, for example, it is fair to say that the majority of readers would not feel at home in the imagined community constructed by the homophobic websites, yet the site constructs that community precisely by addressing the reader as an accomplice. The cropping-out of all non-conforming viewpoints, the fantasy that 'everyone must share our desires, and he who does not share them is no true subject' is never allowed to slip for a moment, and it is this, paradoxically, that produces such an uncanny sense of alienation in the reader.

As we shall see in the next two chapters, it is common practice for websites to invite readers to make themselves at home (or make themselves comfortable). However, the appropriation of this practice by hate sites raises the question of who feels and home and why, and as such touches on key questions about the ways in which websites interpellate some readers into the virtual community and exclude others, and about the work that the reader is expected to do if she wishes to achieve a sense of being at home in a given online community. In order to engage with these questions, the next chapter returns to the question of visibility and to ask what happens when subjects choose to accept, or reject, the task of self-erasure.

CHAPTER 3

At-home in Cyberspace: Home, Belonging and Subjectivity

What does it mean to have a home, to be at home, on the web? In the previous chapter, I showed that in utopian readings of online community, a 'sense of belonging' arises from a fantasy of becoming unmarked: good cyber-citizens are those who are willing to engage in acts of self-erasure, taking care to avoid all reference to such 'irrelevancies'. Indeed, according to this fantasy, the work of self-erasure speaks to their most cherished desire, since it allows them to feel that they are helping to build the community. I went on to ask, what can these unmarked citizens talk about? Here, I want to recast this question, if one refuses the imperative to become unmarked, can one ever really be at home on the Web? In other words, how does one construct a self that can be lived as at-home on the web?

In this chapter, I examine how homepages, personal webcams and blogs expand existing myths about home, by analysing some of the ways in which questions of home and subjectivity are intertwined. 'Home' has been imagined as a fixed space to which one returns, or from which one originates: as a private space, or as the site of belonging to a larger cultural or family group. Whilst fantasies of homing on the Web draw on all these visions of home, the way in which the site itself is imagined as home is less important than the relationship between home and subject. In cyberspace one does not create a home, and then simply 'move in'. In this context, the term 'home' (as in personal homepages, for example) refers not primarily to a space, but to a state of mind; being at-home implies that the subject feels at home, not that home itself is a fixed space. To be at-home in cyberspace, then, one must construct a self that can feel at-home. One way to do this, as we have seen. is through a process of erasure, of becoming 'unmarked', which allows one to experience a virtual holiday away from the pain of maintaining a bodily identity that is imagined to be marked as Other. For offline as well as online communities, the notion of being-at-home always raises questions about subjectivity and identity: whilst these sites of 'home' are very different in form, they are both real and fantastic. In this chapter, however, I look at the ways in which specific sites of online belonging negotiate the relationship between the real and the imaginary through fantasies of being-at-home. In order to do so, I examine how two different categories of website, the personal homepage and the personality-testing site, present themselves as spaces in which one can come to feel at-home, and provide different strategies for achieving this. The former does so by refusing the possibilities offered by the anonymity of cyberspace to present a more traditional notion of home, and the latter by presenting a toolkit which one is encouraged to use in order to construct a self which is marked by other, less contentious identity positions than those of race, class, gender and sexuality.

All the pages I look at here do present 'home' as space, especially by attempting to evoke a sense of homecoming. Home is positioned as that which awaits us at the end of a long and tiring journey, the place where one can finally shed the weight of 'irrelevant' identity positions (and the positioning gaze of others) and be oneself. This fantasy of homecoming might draw upon a sense of finally being able to speak out about one's day-to-day experience, as in the case of personal homepages (the online home as an extension of the real home); or it might involve an escape from the constraints of the 'real-life' home (online home as refuge). Crucially, though, this view of home as a remote space, a space at which one arrives, conceals the work that goes into constructing the self that feels at-home. I want to start, then, by looking at personal homepages as a space on the Web that precisely negotiates the different ways in which 'home' is imagined as a fixed space. I look at the ways in which these pages work to destabilise the boundaries between public and private, and simultaneously to construct (and police) other types of boundaries.

A Home on the Web: Personal Homepages

In early writing about cybercultures, the notion of what it meant to be at-home in cyberspace was addressed through questions of authenticity. The question of what makes an authentic online subject, or how one engages with cyberspace in the most authentic way, has given rise to a proliferation of proposed solutions. These range from the writings of Allucquére Roseanne Stone (1995), who writes evocatively of the queer possibilities for gender subversion offered by virtual technologies, to the cyberpunk fantasies of Rudy Rucker who, in the earliest days of the Internet proposed the web as a site of postmodern identity fragmentation: 'don't come together: come apart' (1992: 210). Others have suggested participation in text-based MUD games as the answer, particularly when this experience included cyber-sex between two or more fantasy identities: indeed, for Julian Dibbell, whose cyber-autobiography *My Tiny Life* (1998) and essay A Rape in Cyberspace (1993) have been hugely influential in shaping popular understandings of online experience, it is only through 'surrendering' to the experience of cybersex that one can truly come to understand the true nature of virtual reality (1993: 40). What all these accounts shares, apart from a debt to the cyberpunk novels of William Gibson, was a conviction that an authentic sense of being-at-home in cyberspace derives precisely from the sexy and slippery possibilities offered by its destabilising of traditional notions of authority which depend upon a fixed sense of identity.

In this sense, the emergence of what might be termed personal sites, or sites tied to a specific offline identity, might be seen as yet more evidence that the Internet has fallen prey to the commercial and the literal, that it has failed hopelessly to fulfil its early promise. These personal sites, with their emphasis on the author's real-life experience, day-to-day experience, and everyday relationships, mobilise the notion of 'home' as site of fixity. It is reassuring, safe, to Google an absent friend, old roommate, or ex, or to make contact through Facebook with an acquaintance briefly encountered at a conference: beyond the comforts of Schadenfreude (the so-called 'friends-reunited' effect) there is a deeper comfort of feeling that everything is in its place, that we are all present and correct (although this fantasy is subject to violent moments of rupture when the other is not, or no longer, present). However, whilst not denying the importance of this fantasy I want to suggest that in order to understand the powerful appeal of personal Internet sites we need to read beyond a rather narrow view of the homepage as narcissistic and conservative, and to think about how homepages work to construct a subjectivity that is at once virtual, and rooted in the everyday.

This is not to claim that the homepage is necessarily a site of resistance. Indeed, homepages are constructed through a process that involves leaving out some details whilst including others; and what is left out may well be an awareness of difference. However, throughout their history, homepages have been the subject of often baffling hostility in media discourses of cyberspace, a hostility that is all the more interesting when we consider that media panics around the Internet have otherwise centred around anonymity (Ferreday 2008). Because they continually remind readers of the importance of lived experience in creating a sense of being-at-home, these pages have come to be seen at best as refusing the process of erasure outlined in the previous chapter; and at worst as the naïve and pointless outpourings of those who are too limited to grasp the possibilities offered by digital technology. However, such a criticism rests on the false assumption that these pages simply represent a series of facts about an individual's everyday life. Rather, I would suggest that homepages allow the author to bring together details from everyday life, with aspects of their fantasy life that would otherwise be invisible.[1]

For their critics, homepages are characterised by a lack which stems precisely from an absence of authority on the one hand, and of desire on

1 This became very clear in the course of my own research, with Simon Lock, on cross-dressing. For men blogging about their experiences of transvestism, *both* 'drag' and 'drab' self-presentation were widely felt to be incomplete as identity performances. The homepage or blog was valued in that it allowed 'transvestite identity' to become visible as a complex and often contradictory set of identity positions: it was this very contradictoriness, and not the mere act of wearing feminine clothes, that constituted 'transvestite identity' on the web (Ferreday and Lock 2007).

the other; or, where desire is acknowledged as a factor in their production, it is constructed as immature or neurotic (as 'attention-seeking', for example). Whilst the anonymity of MUD games or chat rooms offers the ability to explore, discover and gratify new desires, 'home' implies fixity. Such a notion of home calls to mind Nalina Persram's characterisation of home as a place where there is 'being without longing' (1997: 213). As Sara Ahmed has argued, this privileged state of comfort precludes the potential challenges of thinking, as well as the restlessness of desire; it is a place 'too comfortable to question the limits and borders of her or his experience, indeed, where the subject is so at ease that she does not think', and where the subject 'does not over-reach itself through the desire for something other' (2000: 87). This suggests that that home (as opposed to say 'property') is imagined as inseparable from the subject. Home is an extension of one's subjectivity and also performative: it is through being at home that the subject comes into being.

It is precisely an investment in this powerful notion of 'home' as not-thinking and not-desiring (and hence as a place which one leaves in order to attain experience and maturity) which gives homepages and other personal sites their prosaic image. The personal homepage, then, is always presented in opposition to other more uncertain spaces, and this opposition is imagined as centring on the presence or absence of desire. Clearly, such a reading (which simply 'carries over' existing notions of home as a private space and then attempts to apply them to virtual homes), is limited, not least in its failure to account for a crucial and unique quality of personal homepages, that is their location on the boundary between public and private. Personal homepages are attacked since they are identified with a highly conservative notion of home; yet their very location in cyberspace and in particular their accessibility makes any such identification impossible. For example, the act of constructing a homepage speaks precisely to feminist critiques of home as a space where one does not need to think, since this is a home one must build oneself, from scratch. Indeed, since a virtual home is not physically necessary in the same sense as a 'real' home. Virtual homelessness cannot be equated with the real thing, no matter how strong our insistence that fantasy is part of the real. I would argue that it is less likely to be experienced as taken-for-granted, as neutral. The process of creating a homepage (and, by extension, of constructing an identity in cyberspace, albeit one which may be unfixed and temporary), then, involves conscious thought as well as desire. The processes of learning simple programming techniques, writing copy, and assembling images represent a process of materialising the fantasy self and making it visible in the real world. In blogging, this self is given a temporal dimension which, being written in diary form but often read asynchronously, disrupts the dominant Western notion of 'the self' as something on which we work, the project with an endlessly deferred endpoint implied by fantasies of perfectibility.

Despite all this, the homepage has often been positioned in opposition to more 'authentic' forms of online belonging. An article by Edward Rothstein, published in the *New York Times*, set the tone for a kind of high-handed dismissal of homepages which came to popularise a view of homepages (and their authors) as mediocre, trivial and attention-seeking. After its publication in 1995 this article was widely circulated via online bulletin boards. As a result, it has had a considerable impact on the ways in which these sites are perceived. The authors of the first major survey of personal homepages, carried out by the Personal Home Page Institute in 1996, state in their introduction that their work is intended as direct response to Rothstein, which they say 'sums up our prevailing distaste' for these pages (although they do concur with him that homepages are 'useless' (1996: 1)). Although the authors do not define who they mean by 'we', the invocation of an inclusive pronoun positions the authors of homepages as Other, as the object of a disapproving collective gaze. Whilst the authors do state that they intend to put an end to such discrimination, this statement implies that at the time of writing, the authors of homepages are excluded from the 'we' of online community.

Returning to the original article after all these years (and eight years is a long time in the life of the Web, which is generally understood to have originated in 1993), I am struck by the elitism of Rothstein's argument. The article begins with a quotation from a personal homepage the author claims to have 'tripped over' recently:

> 'Hello, I am Stuart Roberts ... I have big feet.'
>
> This proclamation raised some expectations that somewhere under the photo of Roberts would be an explanation of this fact, some elucidation of its importance or implication. But that was all: a Web page devoted to podiatric disclosure ... [T]here are resumes, photos of significant others clothed and unclothed, and endless lists ... (Rothstein 1995).

Whilst this account captures the experience of sifting through hundreds of personal homepages with scathing accuracy, it is deeply problematic (not least in its ethically questionable treatment of the, possibly fictional, Roberts). Most problematic of all is the assertion, firstly that homepages are inane and useless because they are concerned with the minutiae of everyday experience, and secondly that this lack of quality, this embarrassing outpouring of trivia, is the product of a culture that allows too many people access to the Web. It is simply untrue to suggest that there is 'too much' access to cyberspace whilst huge sections of the world's population have no access at all, due either to poverty, cultural exclusion, or language barriers. Hence, this assertion suggests a highly westernised, classed and gendered notion of 'the community'.

Nevertheless, Rothstein insists the means of production in cyberspace has become too open, and that this openness leads to a vision of dystopia in which CompuServe's homepage service attracted 10,000 users a day at its inception in November 1994, 10,000 people 'all proclaiming their own versions of Roberts' big feet' (Rothstein 1995). His horror is such that I wonder, almost with sympathy, what he would say about the subsequent explosion of blogging culture and social networking sites whose purpose is often to capture the minutiae of everyday life. His distaste seems to stem from a desire to establish the boundaries of what is considered publishable material. Homepages, like autobiography, threaten the distinction between public and private, between those narratives that are considered fit for public consumption and those that are private, domestic, and unspeakable. Hence, Rothstein's position of privilege as technology columnist of the *New York Times* could be read as under threat from the sheer proliferation of voices online (as, for example, the authority of a book reviewer might be threatened by the proliferation of online book groups and reader reviews on sites like Amazon.com). What this article does, then, is mobilise this privilege to police the boundary between publishable and unpublishable, between the authoritative voice of the professional journalist, and the inane outpourings of the amateur. In order to do this, it is extremely selective in its use of examples as well as in its assumption that the examples given above are in fact as inane as the author insists. It presents material out of context; we do not know, for example, whether Robert's thoughts on the size of his feet are in fact simply vacuous outpourings or, perhaps, part of a larger piece of comic writing. Finally, the article contains a number of untested assumptions, not least that the 'endless lists' that are a feature of many homepages are entirely arbitrary, consisting merely of pointless trivia.

Yet studies of personal homepages have suggested that the listing of 'what I think is cool' (Miller 1995) is an essential factor in constructing online identities. Lists of favourite books, music, comics and so on, together with lists of links to other websites, work to construct a sense of community through an appeal to shared tastes or experiences; as such, they may represent complex social and cultural histories. What is more, these lists are only one example of the ways in which personal homepages use material borrowed from the public domain in order to construct a sense of self, and as such they demonstrate how these pages blur the boundaries between public and private, not just by making the personal public, but also by making the public personal (Chandler 1998). Whilst Chandler argues that this process works through the appropriation of images and brands from consumer culture, Thomas Erickson suggests that the Web precisely offers a site of resistance to consumer culture; it is a site where 'individuals can construct portrayals of themselves using information rather than consumer goods as their palette' (Erickson 1996). Following from Erickson's argument, I would suggest that homepages involve a fantasy of becoming visible, of establishing an individual voice within the Internet community. However concerned with real life, homepages are fantastic in that they are motivated by a longing to be heard and to be recognised as one's 'real self'. However, this version of the 'real self' does not transcend categories of race, class, gender and sexuality. Instead, it may be partly defined by them. The fantasy of visibility inherent in personal homepages, then, is one that understands 'individuality' as situated, since a unique self is constructed by a combination of traditional identity categories, and through engagement with popular culture. This fantasy is not simply individualistic, since its value lies in making one's self visible to the rest of the online community.

Rothstein (and whilst the article is old in Internet terms, his argument is anything but obsolete) also detects an element of fantasy in personal homepages, but he sees this element of fantasy in a negative light. His analysis is underpinned by assumptions that are rooted in psychoanalytic theory, especially when he appears to suggest that the motivation for producing a homepage is simply infantile and neurotic, motivated by sheer (unmerited) attention-seeking. The pages are 'advertisements for the self', and 'everyone wants attention'. He ends by dismissing homepages as 'sophomoric' (Rothstein 1995). This attention seeking is imagined as fundamentally egotistical; the authors are presented as compelled simply to put facts about their lives 'out there', with little concern for the reader. However, it is debatable whether blogs represent an attempt at publication in the rather narrow and privileged form in which it is read here. I prefer to read homepages as a form of amplified selfhood: a means of making the self intelligible to others (rather than simply reproducing the offline self), in ways that can often become surprising. If we see blogs and homepages as sites of intersubjectivity, any judgement based on their merit in comparison to print media (or which condemns them, as Rothstein does, as simply a widely available form of vanity publishing) is simply irrelevant. Furthermore, since most homepages provide some means of contacting the author, either through a comments box, links to MySpace and Facebook profiles, or the inclusion of email addresses, they are constantly in dialogue with the reader, allowing the online self to make contact with others. Or, as Hugh Miller puts it, 'the personal homepage ... provides an opportunity for people to describe their selves and personalities to the world' (1999). It is precisely this act of 'presentation' which makes homepages unique.

As I have argued, the self that is presented to the world through these pages consists of a combination of real-life information about the subject's job, home, and family, together with more fantastic elements.

The element of fantasy need not involve a description of the author's fantasies: it may be built into the design of the site itself. In any case, not all homepages follow such a conventional structure. For some authors, homepages and blogs are used to construct explicitly fantastic identities. As such, they illustrate my point that all homepages involve to some extent the creation of a fantasy self, a claim that has implications of this for the broader notion of being-at-home I introduced in my opening remarks. In the following sections, I look at two types of sites which both attempt to construct themselves as sites of being-at-home, but in very different ways; and this difference centres on their negotiation of the relationship between the fantastic and the real.

Virtual Vampires: Home, Subjectivity and the Fantasy Self

While homepages are generally grounded in offline life, this is not to say that offline identities are simply reproduced online. A case in point are subcultural homepages. Here, I am interested in one such subculture: online vampires. Perhaps because of its traditionally middle-class roots as well as its high profile in the work of William Gibson, the Gothic subculture was an early adopter of digital technologies, and has generated various spin-offs, including a thriving group of bloggers who identify as 'real-life vampires'. The cyber-vampire is an ambiguous figure, not least because at first glance, the idea of being-at-home as a vampire seems like a contradiction in terms. The figure of the vampire, in fantastic fiction, is precisely that of the outsider, the monstrous Other. In traditional vampire fictions the vampire cannot be at-home because, as Other, it is not understood as having subjectivity; instead, it exists precisely in order to define the boundaries of home; the vampire lurks in the shadows, emerging after dark to haunt the world outside the lighted windows. Indeed, one could argue it is 'home' itself in the traditional sense which brings forth vampires. As Rosemary Jackson notes, in Victorian vampire fiction 'a bourgeois family structure ... gives rise to its own undead, suggesting that the law contains, through repression, its "other"' (1981: 120). Later feminist accounts have focussed on the transgressive potential offered by this outsider status, focussing in particular on the ways in which contemporary vampire fictions re-work conservative models of gender and sexuality (Auerbach 1995, Wisker 1998, Dyer 1988). Gina Wisker's account is typical of this approach. In an account which contrasts vampire stories with romantic fiction, whose privileging of the heterosexual couple relationship, she says, 'leads to binary oppositions of black/white, right/wrong, male/female, social insider/outsider and all the destructive rigid duties this ... encourages', she argues that the vampire exists to disrupt these oppositions:

> Vampire fictions and the figure of the vampire are a direct assault on such conformity, but while conventional vampire fictions openly trouble and terrify, they eventually restore order: the weak and the victim are sacrificed, normality continues. Not so in contemporary women's vampire fictions which refuse the romantic and conventional vampire formulae, providing genuine alternatives. Crossing the boundaries of these binaries is one of all vampire fiction's great transgressive strengths. Vampire fictions reverse and undermine value systems exposing their limitations. They seize and build on that which is feared and abjected (Wisker 1998: 52–3).

In cyberculture studies, the vampire has been taken up as a symbol of the possibilities offered by new technologies. In an article entitled 'What Vampires Know', Allucquére Roseanne Stone uses the character of Lestat from Anne Rice's *Interview with the Vampire* books (texts which provide much of the inspiration for online 'vampires', as my reading of vampire homepages shows) as a figure who embodies the notion of identity as performative. Stone imagines that the vampire's immortality allows him to observe how generations of humans are confined to act out the same subject positions, whilst his own location on the boundaries between human and monster gives him a unique insight into the flexibility of those positions, especially in virtual communities:

> He sees people trapped, stuck in their particular gender positions, in their particular subjectivities, not able to make the jump to seeing subject position as a boat that's momentarily at anchor, but that can actually move through a sea of possible subject positions. The vampire would like to be able to make that more visible. He talks about it in terms of the Dark Gift that turns one into a vampire. He would like to see more people being vampires, but he hasn't figured out how to bring that about yet (Stone 1993).

The virtual vampire is a liminal figure, who occupies the debatable lands between life and death. Hence virtual vampires call into question oppositional categories: fantastic/real, online/offline, self and other. We can extend this metaphor of the cyber-vampire in order to discover more about what it means to be at-home in cyberspace, and the ways in which this being-at-home is tied up with the notion of identity, of constructing a 'real' self (which may include some elements of the RL self and leave out others). In doing so, I do not entirely concur with Wisker's view that vampire fictions are always subversive, or that they always allow categories of gender and sexuality to be questioned. As Allucquére Roseanne Stone has pointed out, subject positions may be open to change, but such change can only occur within the cultural constraints that surround the subject; and these constraints do not simply disappear when one enters cyberspace (Stone 1995). Moreover, a site that sets out to disrupt one set of boundaries may inadvertently reinforce another. For example, many of the vampire websites I looked at were created by women, who clearly understand their appropriation of imagery and characters from vampire fiction to be empowering. This sense of empowerment also applies, sometimes, to their identities as lesbian or bisexual women. Nevertheless, the sites are often problematic and even conservative in tone, not least because of the normalisation of whiteness that is such an integral part of vampire/gothic subcultures. I want, therefore, to think through the notion of 'subversiveness' in a slightly different way. Rather than claiming that vampire identities themselves are subversive, I would suggest that the sites are animated by a fantasy of subversion. The desire to be subversive, whether it is by claiming to be a vampire and sharing blood-drinking tips, or simply by allowing strangers access to a 'private' diary or webcam footage is, I think, a factor both in vampire websites, and in more general attempts to build an online home. Whilst homepages cannot be subversive in themselves, fantasies of subversion *may* open up the possibility for real acts of resistance, not least through the refusal of injunctions to become unmarked.

Vampires are most useful, in that they embody some of the contradictions of online homing. One of the ways in which the homepages address these contradictions is through attempting to make the world of vampirism – traditionally an abject and menacing place – feel welcoming, so that the visitor as well as the vampire author herself feels at home. Despite their use of explicitly fantastic themes, many of the vampire sites I looked at in the course of my research draw upon various, often highly domestic, images of home. Whilst the home in question is as likely to be a cave, coffin or castle as the suburban family home identified as a common image by other researchers (Miller 1995, Arnold and Miller 1999, 2000), names like Ravinn's Boudoir, Cinnabar's Playhouse and Mileena's Chateau all invoke private, delimited spaces: each can be read as representing a homestead, to use Rheingold's term.[2] This notion of a vampire homestead is used in two ways. Firstly, these images address other 'vampires' in order to construct these Web pages as a place of refuge, relaxation, comfort, or safety. On the other hand, they may simultaneously address the reader as one who has strayed or been drawn into the vampire's lair; while one is invited to enter as a guest, this invitation is often presented as slightly mocking or threatening. I want to focus, here, on one example, Mileena's Chateau, which is the personal web page of one 'vampire' woman.[3] I have chosen to look at this site in detail because it is typical, in design and content, of vampire homepages, and because it deals directly with questions of hospitality and being-at-home.

On first loading the page, a dialogue box appears prompting the user to enter 'your name (or anybody's name)'. A message then appears into which the text is inserted, to form what looks like a personal greeting. But

2 www.geocities.com/Area51/Chamber/4140/Naward.html; http://www.geocities.com/SouthBeach/Docks/6409/; www.geocities.com/Area51/Chamber/4140/, accessed 8 December 2008.

3 www.geocities.com/Area51/Chamber/4140/.

this greeting is ambiguous in tone. Although the user is urged to make herself at home, it is assumed that she is uncomfortable to begin with. The text begins, 'Take a wrong turn? How delightful!', establishing the fiction that the user has arrived at Mileena's 'home' by mistake. The text continues with an invitation to 'sit down [and] make yourself at home', before going on to introduce Mileena with the statement, 'I am a vampire'. The greeting continues in this ambiguous tone, assuring the reader that she is quite safe and asking her to look around and feel at her ease, whilst using emoticons (such as ::grin::) and warnings to 'behave yourself' to suggest that all is not quite as safe and comfortable as it seems.[4]

This site is significant, I think, since it addresses the question I raised in my introduction concerning the relation between the personal and the public in quite a sophisticated way. As Hugh Miller has pointed out, images of home are often mobilised to create a sense of hospitality, despite the fact that the conventions of building a personal homepage make it impossible to limit or restrict access (although, I would add, it is possible to structure access, as in the 'members only' areas of the Sanguinarius site discussed above). According to Miller, the granting of selective access is 'part of the essence of welcoming (real) visitors to your (real) home'. As he argues, this welcoming is structured so that, for example, one might choose not to allow casual acquaintances into certain sections of the house, whilst others never make it further than the front door. In personal homepages, it is not possible to do this; nevertheless, the 'fiction of permission, of a particular gift of access, is still valuable' (Miller 1995: 2). Mileena's homepage adds another dimension to this interaction between author and user, since her granting of access is presented as conditional. Although the user is urged to make herself at home, this welcome contains the hint of a threat, creating the illusion firstly that it is possible to 'misbehave' when visiting a personal homepage, and secondly that the author (who is always implicitly at-home in this space) has the authority to respond to any such misbehaviour. In fact, the site's interactivity is

4 www.geocities.com/Area51/Chamber/4140/index2.html, accessed 28 November 2008.

restricted to the personalised greeting mentioned above, and a guestbook in which readers can post their comments on the site. On the most obvious level, the reference to 'misbehaviour' could be a coded reference to the author's practice of deleting any abusive or critical comments posted in this forum, but it also works to construct a sense of the author's being-at-home which, rather than simply giving the illusion of selective access, actively works to maintain the boundaries between author and reader. The greeting page is not only a 'fiction' constructed to mirror or recreate the experience of being invited into a real home, although it is partly that. It also works to construct a sense of the author as at-home and as present in the virtual space. The author is present to the reader as a subject speaking with authority, that is, speaking from a sense of being-at-home. This speaking from home involves a direct refusal of the injunction to be an unmarked subject. The statement 'My name is Mileena. I am a vampire' is simultaneously a statement of belonging (to the group of people who call themselves vampires), and of specificity (I am this vampire, not just any old generic vampire): Mileena is hence both connected to, and separate from, a wider community of vampires.

As I have noted, the reader's position is less fixed. Whilst the author's authoritative tone suggests that the reader is being addressed as a non-vampire (a position which, I think, is implicit in the suggestion that the reader is in danger), the boundaries constructed by this reading are not fixed. The very ambiguity of the reader's position calls into question the boundaries of the fantasy vampire community to which Mileena belongs. Whilst the hint of danger in Mileena's welcome could be read as Othering, as constructing a dichotomy between inside and outside, and between vampire and non-vampire, other aspects of the site seem to embody Donna Haraway's assertion that 'boundaries shift from within; boundaries are very tricky' (1991: 201). Indeed, the walls of the 'castle' itself are not fixed: the reader is asked to visit again in the future: 'For I am always changing the design of my chateau'. What is more, the slightly remote and chilly tone gives way, once inside, to a more intimate feel characteristic of 'normal' homepages. The site includes a journal, poetry, and photos of Mileena and her friends. This demonstrates two important characteristic of online homes; firstly, that they allow the user to negotiate different levels of access (giving an impression of gradually becoming accepted into the author's home), and secondly that they are unfixed and subject to change. A reading of this site thus opens up the possibility that relations to home, the boundaries between who is and is not at-home in a given (online) space, may also be open to change. The reader is constantly offered opportunities to contact Mileena via ICQ (live chat) or email, or by posting comments to the guestbook. In this way, it is hinted, it might be possible to learn how to build one's own home in the online vampire community, a possibility which is imagined through the vampire's ability to create new vampires.

The creation of new vampires is also an important theme for Sanguinarius, another female vampire whose homepage has grown to become Sanguinarius.org, a web portal that also hosts its own web ring, and hence represents a resource by which individual homepages can be organised into an active community.[5] The web ring works to organise a community of blogs and websites, organised into a central 'ring' of links which allow the user to move from site to site, or to access a central site (called a hub), which lists the individual member sites, and permits authors to apply to add their own homepages to the ring. Sanguinarius is one such ring, whose eponymously titled hub site is subtitled 'support for vampires' and is aimed at those who would identify themselves as real vampires. Its directory listing on Webring.com describes it as a an interactive site 'dedicated to building and serving the vampiric community by providing info, support & various resources for real vampires, blood drinkers, psychic/energy vampires, blood fetishists, & Vampyre lifestylers, as well as those who are curious'. Lists such as this are commonplace in the publicity material for web rings, as well as on personal homepages themselves; a proliferation of identity positions: even outsiders are positioned as 'the curious'. The site itself is a vast resource containing information and FAQ pages, details of forthcoming RL and online events, support pages, chat rooms and even a vampire dating service. These resources include a FAQ (frequently asked questions) section which addresses 'the curious',

5 www.sanguinarius.org/, accessed 8 December 2008.

providing explanations of the vampire lifestyle and the reasons why some users consider themselves to be vampires.[6]

Like Lestat in the article by Allucquére Roseanne Stone quoted above, the site is preoccupied with the Dark Gift, or what it calls 'awakening' or 'turning' (mortals into vampires). The process of 'awakening' is clearly an important component of the fantasy of revealing (and constructing) a 'real' self; by describing how she converts humans into vampires, Sanguinarius is able to re-assert her fantasy identity, taking on the power and authority of the vampire. But I think that 'turning' can also be seen as an initiation into the community and, by extension, into a sense of being-at-home on the Web. By entering Sanguinarius' home, the reader may begin the journey to being converted and hence coming to share Sanguinarius' sense of belonging; that is, the user moves from the passive status of reader, to a state of being at-home. This impression is reinforced by her insistence on a sense of responsibility for the so-called 'donor' who wishes to take this step. Under the heading, 'how do I become a vampire', the site outlines the ways in which members of the community are responsible for new members. The most important aspect of this, the site suggests, involves the development of a sense of belonging, as the following extract suggests:

> Another good thing would be to introduce them to the community, as well as to instil in them a sense of when and how to (and not to) 'come out of the coffin' to another or others; how to safely conceal themselves and their practices and activities from those who would in some way prove detrimental to their personal safety, security or peace of mind; how to defend themselves in various situations, be it confrontational, physical, verbal, or what have you; how to proceed in contacting authorities, and present themselves and their situation / case to the authorities in such a way that they will not be dismissed out-of-hand as a crackpot and ignored.[7]

In other words, being-at-home, in this community, is imagined as involving both visibility (on the Web), and invisibility (the ability not to 'come out of the coffin'). Whilst 'vampire lifestylers' might be visible

6 www.sanguinarius.org/faqs/index.php, accessed 28 November 2008.
7 www.sanguinarius.org/terminology.shtml, accessed 28 November 2008.

in the RL community, vampire websites further aim to make the visible legible; that is, they insist that what might look to the outsider like a 'vampire lifestyler' or a member of a gothic subculture, is in fact a 'real' vampire who needs to drink blood in order to stay alive. The 'real', in this sense, refers to sense of self that includes fantastic as well as RL elements. The sites suggest that it is only by making this 'real' self visible and accessible to others, that one can really be at-home; indeed, these homepages exist primarily in order to facilitate the display of the 'real' self. This self, far from being unmarked, is highly marked: it is specifically concerned with reproducing a marked identity position, that is based on having a fantasy in common.

A crucial aspect of these sites is that they allow others to be invited into the community. This welcoming of outsiders takes many forms, and is always partial. Whilst visitors might be invited to 'make themselves at home' at a particular homepage, this at-homeness is temporary, and this is emphasised by the mocking, slightly threatening tone adopted by site administrators like Mileena. Nevertheless, this is not to suggest that homepages ultimately work to reinforce a notion of home as fixed, or that they ultimately position the reader as other. Like the vampire itself, these homepages always suggest the possibility of a transformation in which those who are not at-home come to be included in the community. By inviting the user to make her own page, or to link to an existing page, they offer the possibility that the boundaries of 'home' itself might be open to change. This is not confined to openly fantastic sites: indeed, all homepages contain elements of fantasy, as well as references to lived experience. In this way, homepages disrupt dualistic models of online belonging which position the virtual in opposition to the real. My reading problematises this view, suggesting instead an approach which pays attention to the ways in which a homepages invoke notions of the 'real' and the RL to produce a sense of being-at-home on the Web. Such a reading calls attention to a crucial difference between virtual homing, and traditional Western notions of being-at-home: that is, that online homes are not already constituted as spaces of comfort and safety, but are created through fantasy.

I have argued that vampire homepages suggest that the real self is produced through fantasy. That is, they are concerned with appropriating elements of fantasy fiction to construct an identity that feels more authentic than one's lived experience in the material world. Such an appropriation consists of explicitly fantastic claims, such as claiming to be immortal, to be sensitive to sunlight, and to have a biological need for blood. The 'real' self combines these elements with aspects of RL, since vampire homepages may include photographs of the author, photographs of their house or city in RL, and descriptions of embodied practices that fall outside the 'vampire' character (such as favourite foods). The homepages in this section, in contrast, privilege the element of RL over that of fantasy. Nevertheless, a close reading of these sites reveals that they, too, combine representations of RL with elements of desire, especially the desire for visibility. Whilst their content, with its domestic imagery and 'family-friendly' language that makes repeated appeals to notions of 'the ordinary' and 'the everyday', constitutes anything but an 'assault on conformity' in Stone's phrase (Stone 1993), the very location of that content on the Web allows the familiar narratives of suburban family life to be repeated with a difference. Moreover, by disrupting the boundaries between the private and the public and by depicting lived experience in an unedited (though not unstructured) form, these sites continually question the injunction to become unmarked, creating new forms of being-at-home which are open to the acknowledgement of desire and of difference. Before I go on to analyse how this potential is exploited by specific sites, I want to outline the history of webcams, and explain a little about how they work.

Living on the Web

In keeping with the homely image cultivated by the sites below, webcam technology originated in the domestic. The first simple webcam was developed by a programmer at Cambridge University, who positioned a small camera beside the coffee machine in the staff common room and wired it up to the building's computer network. A frame-grabber posted updated individual frames of film to the network every few minutes, allowing researchers to check whether coffee was available before going downstairs. Since the expansion of the Web in the early 1990s, webcam technology has become cheap and widely available; there are now thousands of cameras broadcasting on the Web from both public and private locations, some using the original 'frame-grabber' format (where a new frame appears at regular intervals), and, more recently, using streaming video footage. The simplest of these that are used on personal homepages are 'deskcams', which sit on top of a personal computer and monitor, and transmit pictures of the user sitting at his or her desk. Whilst this practice adds an element of RL or face-to-face communication to the homepage, it is I think simply an extension of the usual practice of posting photographs and representations of oneself. The difference is that some homepages are entirely based around webcams, so that the webcam itself becomes the point of the site; and it is with these sites that I am concerned here.

One such site is 'Debbie and Stephen', the homepage of a heterosexual couple in their early thirties who live in Eastbourne, England, and who have two children. Their site has two streaming webcams, broadcasting live footage from their living room, and from on top of their computer, which appears to be in the dining room (though archive shots show that it was previously kept in the bedroom). The site also contains the other, more typical features of a personal homepage, which include CVs, photo galleries (including holiday and wedding photos), details of their favourite music, recordings by Stephen's band, and a blog.[8]

At first, the site (like all webcam sites) feels oddly disorientating. This is partly because it has no FAQ section and (in contrast to the vampire sites with their endless desire to explain, educate and justify) offers no explanation for the two protagonists' decision to post footage of their everyday life on the Internet. This lack of information makes sharply visible the extent to which Web users rely on conventions like the FAQ page for orientation, for guidance as to how one is supposed to read a particular text. Most disorientating, though, are the webcam pictures themselves, with their strange silent pictures of a family going about their daily lives,

8 www.debbieandstephen.com/index.php, accessed 28 November 2008.

however illusory this impression may be, and however mediated by the presence of the camera. Although the authors are aware of the users presence (since the website displays how many 'guests' are online and alerts the owners of their presence), the effect is one of haunting, of being present in another's life whilst remaining unseen oneself. This feeling is heightened by the absence of invitations to 'make yourself at home', which are frequently a feature of personal homepages but which, my research suggests, are less likely to appear on webcam pages. This omission, I think, stems from an awareness that one makes oneself vulnerable by allowing strangers access to one's 'real' home; there is a desire to re-establish boundaries between the visitor and those who appear on the site, even as those boundaries are laid open. Whilst webcams necessarily call into question the boundaries between public and private simply by allowing at least partial access to private lives, then, the boundary between who is and is not at-home remains fixed. This differs from the shifting relations embodied in conventional homepages (for which the vampire, with her ability to 'turn' mere mortals to her own uncertain condition, is a useful metaphorical figure). Continual references to 'our home', together with the lack of sound and the webcam users' tendency to ignore their visitors (except on websites where the visitor's presence is an integral part of the experience, such as sex sites) reiterate and reinforce the authors' at-homeness, and the reader's exclusion. Watching Debbie play with her two small children whilst working intermittently on her home computer, I am struck not by a sense of being invited into the home, but of being an uninvited guest: because I know so little about these people, the spectacle of their lives, displayed on my computer screen, only heightens my feeling of not being at-home.

However, the effect of this is to emphasise the fact that the protagonists themselves are very much at-home, both in their offline homes, and in their related space on the Web. The inclusion of a guestbook and chat spaces suggests a longing to reach beyond the boundaries of that home, and the desire to 'make new friends' provides a rationale for the site's existence, which further invokes a desire to transcend the boundaries of the domestic notion of 'home' suggested by the nuclear family unit. The silent images on the screen contradict any sense of transgression on the user's part by reminding the user that the site's owners are always, in a sense, unknowable, in spite of their visibility. This model of being-at-home, then, is less dependent on the notion of permeability, of inviting others to make themselves at-home, than that used by the fantasy homepages above. Rather, it suggests that being-at-home implies the construction of a space in which one has authority. Whilst the decision to install a webcam could be read as a refusal of authority (and after all, such a high level of visibility might expose the subjects to danger), the site itself constantly displaces 'home', constructing it as a geophysically located space to which only the subjects themselves have access. Yet the premise of the site rests precisely on the assumption that by simply looking at the website, negotiating its archive pages to find out more about the family, the viewer can come to share their sense of being-at-home. The result is a homepage that raises questions about what it means to be at-home, whilst refusing easy answers.

Whilst sites like Debbie and Stephen's could be read simply as inviting voyeurism, such a reading only partially accounts for the process by which the viewer is invited to make herself at-home precisely by taking up a position which threatens to become voyeuristic. Yet this being-at-home is always partial, and its terms are decided by the author of the site, who decides where to position the camera as well as when to turn it off. These sites involve a performance of an idealised 'real life', and the extent to which such a performance is itself transformed by the presence of the camera. What is visible on the screen is never simply 'real life', but rather a performance which attempts to represent the 'real' self in a way which, while it is more centrally concerned with the subject's actual geographic location, nevertheless draws upon a fantasy of controlling the ways in which one's life is seen by others.

Above, I have problematised the hierarchical model in which homepages are positioned as amateur, inferior and, crucially, concerned only with the mundane facts of the subject's real life. Rather the term 'real' itself can be read and understood in a number of ways. When Sanguinarius, the vampire website, describes itself as a resource for 'real vampires', it is mobilising the notion of 'realness' in a very different way from a webcam which shows the user's real bedroom. In the former example, 'real' refers to an authentic fantasy self. Whilst the authors and readers of vampire websites might be indistinguishable from ordinary teenagers as far as their family, classmates and teachers are concerned, the language used by the site suggests that it is their hidden fantasies and desires that constitute the true self; hence, one is a vampire if one really, truly desires to be. In webcam sites, in contrast, 'the real' means the subject's life in the material world, as opposed to the virtual. Since it would be extremely difficult to stage the conditions required for a webcam-based homepage without the technical and financial resources of a TV series like *Big Brother*, it is safe to assume that these sites do indeed provide some level of access to the subject's everyday life, and that they show real people in their real-life homes. My account, then, centres on an analysis of the shifting and contingent ways in which 'the real' and RL are mobilised in personal homepages. This approach shows that there is a need for a more complex understanding of what it means to be at home in cyberspace and the means by which 'real' and RL selves might make themselves at home in different and sometimes contradictory ways.

In this section, I have argued that both types of personal homepage examined above represent a site of resistance to the unmarked identities demanded by other types of online space. I want now to look at online quiz sites which, I argue, take the opposite approach, engaging with the challenge of constructing an unmarked identity in the visually-orientated space of the Web. The development of a personal homepage is a means of establishing a sense of being at-home on the Web that refuses to construct an unmarked subject, and hence does not require the subject to erase what might be felt as crucial aspects of her identity such as gender, race and sexuality. I think that the criticisms of these sites cited above are motivated precisely by an awareness that they have the potential to refuse the project of 'becoming unmarked', a project which, as I noted in the previous chapter, is central to popular notions of the ways in which human relations might be transformed in the age of the Internet. This notion of cyberspace as a site of transformation and liberation depends upon the 'dream ... that through new computerised technologies we can leave behind the hierarchies and "unfreedoms" of gendered and racially marked identities' (Seidler 1998: 20). I would suggest that the appeal of such a 'dream', for its supporters, lies not simply in moving away from 'unfreedoms', or irrelevancies; equally important is the fantasy of having the freedom to rediscover and share one's 'true' self, the self which is constructed, in liberal thought, as lying 'beneath the skin'. Whilst it is not true to claim that all personal homepages necessarily resist this view of the self, they are at least more open to resistance and to allowing subjects to reach their own definition of what constitutes a 'real' self. Becoming unmarked is, I think, not simply a matter of erasure; rather, it also involves an attempt to uncover what lies beneath what it terms 'skin-deep' identity positions. In the next section, I look at the ways in which personal development quizzes aim to answer this question, and to offer new identity positions to fill the vacuum left when one omits references to more traditional sources of identification.

Interactive Self-discovery

> Emode is the fastest growing site on the Internet today because we provide truly interactive, viral content about the thing people should care most about ... themselves (James Currier, founder of emode.com).[9]

All the versions of home I have listed so far evoke, to some extent, notions of comfort, relaxation, and freedom. Homepages are only one way of thinking through the question of home, though: I am also concerned, here, with the question of what it means to feel at-home in cyberspace (and specifically on the Web). So far, I have shown that the literature on homepages often presents 'comfort' itself as a necessary precursor to liberation; from the position of comfort afforded by being at-home, the breathing space that comes from emerging as one's true, unencumbered self, one can set out to participate in, and hence construct, an ideal community. Nevertheless, the work of erasure involved in obscuring one's race

9 http://web.tickle.com/, accessed 28 November 2008.

or class seems to suggest a different affective response that entails discomfort, stress, and an overriding sense of constraint. Ironically, it could be argued that the subject is likely to be most self-conscious when engaged in the work of erasing these identity markers (and hence constantly aware of the possibility of slips), since one of the dangers of passing is that it always involves the risk of being caught out (Ahmed 1999).

The producers of interactive media, such as 'personal development' quizzes, have been quick to present their software as the ideal means of 'uncovering' this 'true' self. This process of discovery is, they suggest, the only real way to feel at-home in cyberspace. As I have noted, the notion of being-at-home in cyberspace is always intertwined with questions of identity, and in this case, the two come together in the concept of self-discovery. In these interactive sites, the romantic idea of homecoming is strongly identified with this concept; 'finding oneself' is imagined as identical to 'the journey home'. The 'true' self, however, consists not of the RL self (which is constricted by 'unfreedoms') nor some self-created fantasy construction, let alone any combination of the two. Instead, the user is dependent upon 'expert' opinion. The sites ask multiple-choice, forced-answer questions about seemingly random preferences and behaviours. The user's answers to these questions are interpreted, and the site then tells the user who she 'really' is. These answers, it is suggested, can then be used to create a sense of self with which one can feel more at-home in cyberspace.

Interactivity has long been associated with self-discovery and self-revelation. For example, there are a number of chain emails in circulation which ask the recipient to complete a questionnaire containing a series of personal questions (favourite colour, food and so on) and send them on to friends, often with the incentive of having a wish granted or avoiding bad luck. Similarly, 'geek codes' included in the signature file at the bottom of an email communicated trivial personal information about the writer, albeit in cryptic, coded form (Star 1995: 1–28). The current proliferation of online self-test sites originated partly from these codes, and partly from the electronic distribution of 'purity tests', checklists of questions which were originally used by American schoolchildren to rate their levels of sexual experience. According to Armory.com, a website that collects some of the most popular interactive purity tests, these questionnaires were first converted to interactive data files in 1989 by a programmer named Eric Lechner. In 1994 they were converted to HTML, allowing them to be accessed on the world wide web. However, as I shall go on to argue, the design and content of contemporary quizzes owes as much to women's magazines as to developments in programming.

There is a proliferation of sites offering interactive tests that claim to reveal hidden aspects of one's 'true', 'inner' self. These sites are immensely popular; one of the best-known is Emode (renamed Tickle since the time of writing) which won the 2002 Webby Rising Star award, an annual award which is presented by the Academy of Digital Arts and Sciences to the fastest growing website of the year. The site provides a range of personality tests ranging from the pseudo-scientific (such as the Ultimate IQ Test, and a personality test loosely based on Myers-Briggs personality typing) to the frivolous (What Breed of Dog Are You, What's Your Flavour, and so on).[10] In a press release, the site's founder, James Currier, pointed out that the site has 14 million registered members who have completed some 85 million tests between them. Although this service is largely funded by advertising, the site has recently begun to make a profit since it began to offer users 'the ability to continue their self-discovery experience' by purchasing longer and more detailed reports. Indeed, profit is central to the site's self-image; when asked by the organisers of the Webby awards to contribute a five-word acceptance speech (a practice which is supposed to result in 'creative and humorous' responses), Currier came up with '50,000 new members daily – profitable', according to the Webby Awards website.[11]

Nevertheless, the site may owe some of its success to the skill with which it disguises this hard commercial imperative, presenting instead a space in which users can feel at-home. The help page, a resource for users wanting more information rather than advertisers or competitors, presents a very different view of the site's purpose or 'vision':

10 For a full list of tests, see web.tickle.com/, accessed 8 December 2008.

11 http://www.webbyawards.com/webbys/current.php, accessed 28 November 2008.

> We've built Emode to be fun, simple, and – dare we say it – meaningful. After all, life is a journey. We want to help you explore it. With a service that moves, inspires and connects you, Emode is your refuge from the daily grind …
>
> Emode is a group of designers, writers, artists, Ph.D.s, and engineers with a common vision: to substantially improve the way people discover and connect with the important ingredients of their lives – entertainment, information, experiences, and each other.[12]

These themes of discovery and connection are symbolised by the site's logo, which uses Flash animation to morph the 'o' in 'Emode' from a view of the earth from space, into an open sunflower. The blue planet represents a vision of potentially limitless, global community (Franklin, Lury and Stacey 2000), whilst the flower symbolises self-discovery, the blossoming and opening-up of previously undiscovered aspects of the self. This message is continued (and tied to a strong corporate image) in the text, which reads 'the #1 destination for self-discovery'. As we can see, the site draws on some of the notions of home I examined above in that it presents itself both as a private, personal space ('your refuge from the daily grind'), and as a point of homecoming, and a communal space ('your #1 destination'). Yet the boundary between private and public is unstable: one is encouraged to take tests in order to find out hidden truths about the self, but then to share them with others (both the Emode community as a whole, and one's own real-life and/or online friends and acquaintances). 'The private' is not a space where one is alone; rather the distinction is between intimate others (friends), and strangers. Hence, a refuge from the daily grind does not necessarily mean retreat from real-life communities. Instead, the site offers a new form of communication that transcends the daily grind. It suggests that one might be able to connect with existing acquaintances in a new way, one which owes more to the idealised community embodied in the blue planet, than to the exigencies of day-to-day life. So the site presents itself as a refuge and also a place of homecoming: but crucially, one from which the user is encouraged to reach out, through the image of travel, to other members of the community.

12 www.sagastevin.com/TestYourself/Emode.html, accessed 28 November 2008.

Users are encouraged to buy into this sense of being at-home by becoming members. Whilst many of the site's tests are open to non-members, joining the Emode community entitles the user to certain extras, which in theory enable her greater access to the interactive elements of the site. Members' quiz results are stored, and used to produce a monthly email newsletter whose contents are modified to match the interests of the individual user; they are also stored in a personal section of the site where they can be reviewed, or shared with other users. Finally, members can set up an address book which, like an email address book, stores the details of their friends so that they in turn can be 'invited' to join. If these friends do go on to join, the user can then view their test results as well as her own. Like a homepage, then, this personalised space might be read as simply a fixed point in cyberspace, a home into which one invites others so that they can participate in one's personal life. Indeed, it is a more explicitly privatised space than a conventional homepage, since the user has much more control over who has access to the information contained in her account; it is not simply open to the public (and indeed, it is possible to provide even more structured access by, for example, forbidding some friends to see the results of particular tests). What makes this site unique, though, is its vision of home and subject as mutually constitutive. That is, the member's personal space is not simply a space in which to discover and express her true self; rather, it is a fantasy space which allows users to live the dream of becoming unmarked by constructing and performing a new form of identity. For example, the more tests a user takes, the more accurately Emode is able to customise the email newsletter to appeal to her 'personality type'. Hence, contrary to the explicit claims made by the site to be a tool for 'self-discovery', we can see that users are, in fact, constantly engaged in the work of producing a coherent and individualised self, but one which belongs to a coherent and recognisable 'type'. Self-discovery is hence not simply a private pursuit: instead, it is the basis for a performance of identity. This performance serves to distract others' attention away from what has been left out. By performing an identity in which 'the individual' is constructed through categories such as colour, flavour, favourite song and so on, it is implied, one can forestall curiosity about one's gender, race, or class.

In order to understand what kind of self users are encouraged to construct, we might look at the content of some of the more popular tests. At first sight, it is clear that whilst Emode's may be precisely drawing on the desire to put aside such 'unfreedoms', the site itself reproduces a number of assumptions concerning the gender, race, nationality and sexuality of its users. The site makes clear distinctions between those elements of the user's identity that are considered speakable, and those that are not. So, for example, users are asked to give details of their gender and age when they join, but the site carefully avoids asking for information on racial and ethnic background, unlike other sites such as Queendom, which asks for this information for 'market research' purposes. When the site does ask for personal information, it is for what it presents as purely practical reasons. For example, it needs to know the user's gender for the purpose of quizzes such as 'what's your style', so that it can recommend different clothes for men and women. Sexuality is treated in a similarly practical manner. When users first take one of the many tests that are contender with sex or 'dating', they are asked to 'tell us whether you like men or women'. They then select one of two check boxes, and the information is stored and used in conjunction with later tests. The effect of this is to undermine Emode's unwritten policy of inclusiveness, since such a choice allows for no ambiguity, and no changes in preference. In going along with a perceived need for the user to become unmarked in order to participate in the wider Web community, it denies itself the simpler option of asking users how they identify at the current time, and thus allowing them to position themselves as transgender or bisexual, among other possibilities. The whole point of such sites is, after all, to give the Internet user something to talk about other than where she situates herself within these categories.

What the site puts in place of these troubling identifications is a proliferation of more or less trivial identifications, all based loosely on the notion of discovering one's 'true' personality. The user can take tests to find out their 'humour style', 'work style', and 'personal [clothing] style', as well as which type of food and breed of cat or dog they most resemble, what colours they should wear in summer, and which celebrity is their 'ideal match', among others. Each test takes the form of an interactive multiple-choice questionnaire, with the questions frequently relating to preferences in consumer goods, media and celebrity culture. For example, the quiz entitled 'What are You Looking for in a Relationship?' asks the user to choose which movie they would most like to 'act out' from a list comprising *When Harry Met Sally*, *Nine and a Half Weeks*, *Parenthood*, and *Love Story*.[13] Another question in the same quiz asks which product, if any, they would most like to buy from the homewares department at Macy's department store. In other words, all the quizzes assume the user to be middle-class and to be at least familiar with aspects of American popular culture, which perhaps explains why it asks no questions about background, nationality or income. The effect when one has never heard of a particular product or celebrity is jarring: it disrupts the carefully contrived sense of being-at-home, of refuge, referred to above.

The identities constructed through this site, then, are not unmarked. Rather, they are marked in a way that is less likely to be seen as disruptive than that produced by the homepages presented above. Indeed, as I argued in the previous chapter, the unmarked itself becomes the mark of privilege, and is hence marked. Crucially, being-at-home in the Emode community involves familiarity with consumer culture. Indeed, it involves positioning oneself entirely through such a culture. Tests like 'What's Your Flavour?' take this process further, encouraging the reader to present herself as the object of consumption. Similarly, 'Who's Your Movie Star Double' suggests that celebrity culture is archetypal, so that any user can be understood by comparing herself to a particular movie or television actor. It is simply a matter of finding the right flavour, the right actor. The site, then, works to produce identity on two levels. Firstly, it assumes that the reader wants the answer to a particular set of questions that are themselves marked. The reader's concerns are assumed to be identical with those of women's magazines and advertising, chiefly relationships, sex, food and clothes. Secondly, it allows the user to align herself with particular products and stylised identities. For example, when a female user takes the 'Who's Your Movie Star Double' test mentioned above, the site

13 web.tickle.com/quizzes/show/1143, accessed 28 November 2008.

might return the result, 'Cate Blanchett' (despite constant implications of unmarkedness, the result is always matched to the gender of the user: having ticked the box marked 'female', one cannot be matched to Russell Crowe or John Cusack). It does not matter that the person taking the test does not in the least resemble Cate Blanchett, as the site's rationale for this result suggests:

> An intellectual like you needs to be played by someone who understands how to be deep without being boring, someone who can grasp complicated subjects and make them seem clear cut, someone like Cate Blanchett ... Cate has shown the world that being smart can be sexy ... Cate's a natural to star as you because she, like you, has a good head on her shoulders. And she isn't afraid to use it.[14]

In other words, the quiz is based on sorting users into a number of stereotypes – intellectual, ingénue, sex symbol and so on – and then assigning a celebrity archetype to each one. Cate Blanchett is simply the actor whose on-screen image is considered to be 'intellectual' in comparison with other movie actors.

Yet it is significant that the test does refer to movie stars rather than other high-profile women. It does so because it assumes that whatever other qualities she may possess, the user needs constant reassurance that she is sexually attractive according to the standards of mainstream heterosexual culture. In this case, the user is assured that although she may identify as 'smart', she is also 'sexy' and possesses 'glamour' and good looks (despite the fact that the test itself does not ask any questions about the user's looks).

By taking a number of these tests, the user is encouraged to build up a kind of composite character profile, which can then be used to make herself legible to others. For this reason, it can be seen that the sense of community relies on members of the community sharing a common culture. In order to understand what another member's profile is telling you, it is necessary to know what Cate Blanchett or Angelina Jolie represents rather than simply assuming that the user resembles these actors

14 web.tickle.com/quizzes/show/1144, accessed 28 November 2008.

physically, or is a fan of theirs. Similarly, the user needs to know what kind of person tastes of chocolate, and why they are different from someone who tastes of lemon or vanilla. Membership of the Emode community is hence far from unmarked, although the site claims otherwise. Moreover, membership depends upon being able to read others' profiles correctly as well as making a profile of one's own. Here, being-at-home is not simply a matter of interacting with technology. Rather, the user's sense of being-at-home is related to their ability to 'fit in'. In order to do so she must have some knowledge of popular culture and an interest in a very narrow, highly feminine and consumerist set of interests. Here, we can see a direct contrast with personal homepages, which have been described as spaces where users 'can construct portrayals of themselves using information rather than consumer goods as their palette' (Erickson 1996). Instead, quiz sites draw 'acceptable' differences from consumer culture as a means of excluding other, more 'problematic' kinds of difference. The result is that users not only come to construct 'portrayals of themselves' entirely from references to consumer goods, but that these portrayals come to stand in for the self. Hence, whilst quiz sites are explicitly concerned with the differences between subjects, they conceal the extent to which some forms of difference are constantly being excluded.

Another test site, Queendom, offers its users a different way to address the problem of not fitting in. In contrast to the 'fun' approach taken by Emode, Queendom, which calls itself 'the world's largest testing centre', presents its tests as scientific tools. These tests are offered to employers as a means of testing potential employees' aptitude for certain jobs, as well as to individuals seeking opportunities for 'personal development'.[15]

Originally, the site worked along the same lines as Emode, offering a combination of free, short tests, and longer more 'serious' tools including personality typing and IQ testing. So far, then, Queendom is the same as the sites above in that it offers a fantasy of the authentic self, which becomes present to itself and which transcends inferior identities constructed through raced, gendered and classed experience, and which

15 www.queendom.com, accessed 8 December 2008.

can hence feel at-home in both online and RL settings. More recently, Queendom has changed the focus of its flagship Type A Personality Test in a way that has a significant impact on the relations of being-at-home and fitting-in outlined above:

> Type A Personality Test – Revised
>
> Want to know if your personality is bad for your health? Go to the new completely revamped Type A Personality Test and find out! Type A characteristics have been linked to an increased risk for coronary heart disease and cancer ... Complete results include ten sub-scores, such as competitiveness and negativity, and a practical no-nonsense advice section which includes tips on living a healthier, more balanced lifestyle.[16]

The test divides users into three personality types labelled A, B and C. Type A is described as over-stressed and likely to suffer from the diseases detailed in the quotation above. Type C is under-stressed, and likely to suffer from depressive illnesses, whilst only type B is described as normal. Since there are only three categories, users stand a much higher chance of finding themselves in one of the abnormal categories, than in category B. This test, then, asks questions about the user's ability to fit in, that is to cope with life in the online and RL communities, then relates this information to the idea of fitness. Some personalities are too competitive, too aggressive or too 'negative': they do not fit in, and hence risk becoming literally unfit.

However, unlike Emode, Queendom does not simply offer ways of fitting into the online community. Instead, it assumes that users are motivated to take its quizzes as a result of the desire for a healthy body as well as the desire to find themselves. Indeed, the site seems to draw on a sense of anxiety, suggesting that Web users are unable to function in the 'real' world. This is most evident from a reading of the advertisement above, which contains a link to Queendom's sponsor. Although the site does not overtly advertise the fact, Queendom.com and its corporate

16 http://www.queendom.com/tests/access_page/index.htm?idRegTest=1126, accessed 28 November 2008.

partner Psychtests, which supplies aptitude tests to employers, receive corporate sponsorship from the multinational pharmaceutical company Glaxo SmithKline. The link given in the email above does not say this; it simply displays the invitation, 'visit our sponsor', which turns out to be a link to a website advertising the antidepressant drug Paxil entitled 'Paxil – Your Life is Waiting!'[17] The implication is that users who 'fail' the Type A Personality test might like to try medication as a means of fitting in, of feeling more at-home in the body as well as in the online community. At the moment when the user clicks on the Paxil link, the purpose of the original quiz changes. Rather than simply being a means of understanding one's own personality, it becomes positioned as a diagnostic tool. The implication is that it is only a short step from being able to determine one's personality type, to feeling qualified to diagnose one's own health problems. Rather than offering ways to build a self that is at-home, then, this site encourages users who do not feel at-home to identify as pathological. The site contains further quizzes, which allow the user to test herself for depressive and personality disorders. It then provides information on how to obtain the drug, including guidelines for conducting telephone interviews with prospective doctors and psychiatrists in such a way as to determine whether they are likely to prescribe antidepressants, and how to describe 'symptoms' in such a way that the doctor is convinced that such a prescription would be appropriate.

The site also provides resources including a checklist that the user can print out, and refer to during these 'interviews', including a list of criteria such as professional experience, means of payment and, crucially, 'I want a therapist who has access to antidepressant medications like Paxil'. The rest of the site constitutes little more than an advertisement for the drug, which is graphically represented as an iconic image of brightly coloured capsules. The production values of this image are similar to those of the chocolate sites that I discuss in Chapter 4: every effort is taken to enhance the appearance of the capsules, so that they appear as an object of desire. They are digitally enhanced to appear bright and shiny, and are displayed

17 http://www.paxilcr.com/index.html?a=paxil, accessed 8 December 2008.

floating in front of an ethereal, light-blue background.[18] As such, they are removed from their context as medicine in order to be presented as just another commodity. As a commodity, Paxil comes to stand in for the reader's own anxiety and sense of not being at-home. The drug can, therefore, be presented as the answer to the problem of not being at-home.

Crucially, this website uses its connection with a well-known personality testing site to market a potentially dangerous drug as a means of fitting in, of constructing a self that is able to feel at-home in all social situations and not merely online. For example, the diagnostic test for 'social anxiety disorder' asks the reader to rate her response to 17 questions including, 'parties and social events scare me', 'I am bothered by blushing in front of people', and 'I avoid activities in which I am the centre of attention'. None of these statements seem particularly indicative of pathology, yet simply answering 'a little bit' to all the questions prompts the site to return a diagnosis of social anxiety disorder. Indeed, it is almost impossible to be pronounced healthy by the test. Even a score of zero produces the following response:

> Your score is not typical of a person suffering from social anxiety disorder. However, if your participation in this self test is due to concerns you may have about your overall well-being, we strongly encourage you to make an appointment with a qualified healthcare professional to discuss your feelings ... We encourage you to make an appointment with a qualified healthcare professional to discuss your symptoms.[19]

Simply taking the test is enough to mark the user as a potential case for medication. The repetition of an almost identical sentence within the

18 The image of commodities floating in mid-air is often used as a means of emphasising their fantastic desirability: in the next chapter I provide a reading of a commercial for Royal Mail, which also shows commodities floating (although in this case they are out of reach).

19 www.paxilcr.com/. The diagnostic tests have been removed from the site since the time of writing, but the same questions are displayed at the top of the page relating to each psychological disorder as a guide to self-assessment, accessed 28 November 2008.

same paragraph is particularly significant here, since it contains a slippage in which 'feelings' become 'symptoms'. Despite the fact that a desire to feel at-home may have motivated the user to try online test sites in the first place, the alliance of Queendom and Paxil uses hypertext to lead her to the conclusion that the only way to address this desire is through medication. The medicated subject, it is implied, feels at home everywhere and is liberated from even the mildest social anxieties. I would suggest that what is happening here is that the desire to feel at-home is conflated with the desire to conform, a fitting-in that is equated with physical fitness. Fitness is defined as fitting-in; the message is that by taking a drug to avoid feeling uncomfortable and anxious, one can not only feel at home but also avoid serious illnesses such as cancer and heart disease later in life. Fitting in is hence imagined not only as a duty (and the Paxil site is emphatic that 'family and friends' will also benefit from the subject's taking the drug) but also as a matter of life and death. The message is clear: fit in or die. To be depressed, to be affectively disordered, as the medical terminology goes, is to be threatened by oneself: the potentially violent (and hence divided) self must be made whole in order to be integrated back into society.

In other words, sites like this one involve a shift from a paradigm in which the community comes into being as a result of the user's fantasy of being visible or being understood, to one in which the commercial interests determine what the user's desires ought to be. Unlike homepages, these and other commercial sites work with the perceived desire for self-erasure to produce the notion that being-at-home is dependent on the acceptance of certain norms, as well as consumption of a particular product. This is very different from the situated fantasies produced by the vampire homepages above, and from the webcam sites in which the fantasy at stake is precisely that the viewers take the subjects as they find them, requiring an acceptance of 'real' selves (and real homes). Instead, the personality tests create a self that is lived as at-home through engagement with ready-made products and fantasies; and it is through shared experience of these that a community comes into being. For all their interactivity, then, these websites produce communities of passive subjects.

Conclusion

I have examined how 'home' is used to articulate two different approaches to the problem of becoming unmarked. Further, both personal homepages and quiz sites construct the idea of being at-home through an appeal to the notion of difference. Being at-home is presented as involving the ability to be oneself, although the sites imagine the self in very different ways. On the surface, homepages appear to allow their authors to resist the desire to become unmarked, whilst quiz sites attempt to work with this desire, allowing users to construct a self that is still marked, but in a highly individualised way that does not include differences of race or class and also excludes gender and sexuality to a certain extent.

However, such an oppositional reading is partial, in that it conceals the extent to which both types of site might both conceal and reveal various forms of difference. So, for example, vampire homepages insist that their authors are 'different' from 'mere mortals', and in doing so they construct the 'real' self as composed of both material reality, and fantasy (Mileena's Chateau, Sanguinarius). These sites are hence valuable in that they allow psychic reality to become visible, and in doing so they problematise the distinction between the fantastic and 'the real'. However, by focussing on one particular site of difference whilst extending hospitality to the reader, vampire sites refuse to examine the possibility that some subjects may be less able to feel welcomed into the online home than others. For example, the sites do not question the implicit whiteness of the ideal vampire, and their readings of vampire fiction does not pay attention to the fetishising of whiteness that is inherent in many of these fantasy texts, despite the fact that vampires like Sanguinarius may digitally enhance their photographs so that their skin appears to be literally white.

The quiz sites again appeal to notions of difference, suggesting that it is possible to imagine a model of inclusivity in which all subjects are able to reach a state of feeling at-home by using interactive technology to create and perform a coherent self. However, the effect of these sites is that they bring in some differences in order to facilitate the erasure of others. What is more, the 'unmarked' or unproblematically marked subject they construct is in fact marked through identification with Western consumer culture. In order to create the self that is at-home, paradoxically, one must already be at-home with certain forms of cultural knowledge and practice.

One thread running through this chapter has been that of comfort; the self that is at-home is that which is comfortable in certain spaces. In the next chapter, I relate this notion of comfort specifically to online consumer culture, asking how themes of belonging and community are used to create a sense of comfort in the role of consumer. Once those old unfreedoms are removed, the self – chocolate-flavoured, Blanchett-like, introverted, untidy and reminiscent of a pug – is much more comfortable: and the notion of comfort – of being a subject that is at once comfortable with oneself, and longs to be comforted – is central to the structuring narrative of life in late capitalist digital culture: that of the self as consumer.

CHAPTER 4

Cyberconsumption: Pleasure, Fantasy and Online Shopping

'The commercial' is generally reviled in cyberculture theory. For a while, at the time of the dot-com bubble, it seemed as though there might indeed be something essentially anti-commercial about the Web, that claims for counter-cultural authenticity made on its behalf might turn out to be justified. At the time of writing, online shopping is the only area of consumer culture that continues to grow, despite a global recession. In the last decade, online shopping has become embedded in everyday life: for many in the West, the virtual subject is primarily a virtual consumer. Yet the implications of consumption as a site of community and identity practice remain under-explored in cultural theory. Here, I want to examine the ways in which consumer culture appropriates discourses of community, disembodiment and networking to produce a new fantasy figure: the cyber-consumer.

Online shopping has always adopted and adapted the language practices of virtual community, an approach pioneered by sites like Amazon, founded in 1994, whose cultural visibility, based on its customer review system, far exceeds its commercial success: the site struggled to make a profit even as the failure of its anonymity settings, and the resulting exposure of literary egos, became the subject of urban myth. Studies of e-commerce have largely reproduced this discourse of community, arguing that one crucial component of commercial success online is 'the creation of virtual communities among the consumers of a company's product' (Blanchard and Markus 2002: 1): this, it is claimed, creates 'feelings of belonging' that lead to 'satisfaction and commitment' (2002: 2). Here, I am interested in the ways in which online shopping mobilises ideas about public and private, embodiment, desire, and emotion, and how these relate to wider cultural theories of consumption. For example, Anne Cronin brings together themes of belonging, identity and consumption in the context of offline shopping. In *Advertising and Consumer Citizenship* (2000), Cronin examines the relationship between the consumer culture, and notions of 'belonging' within Western culture. For Cronin, advertising plays a key role in constructing discourses of belonging, and hence in shaping the ways in which consumers identify with a specific cultural group. Similarly, historical accounts by Rachel Bowlby (1997, 2000) and Mica Nava (1992) that focus on gendered experiences of shopping, as well as on the ways in which shopping has been presented as empowering. Cronin's account focuses on the ways in which advertising works to construct the consumer as a gendered subject; and this analysis has also been extended to studies of online shopping. For example, Angela Medhurst (1998) has examined the ways in which online supermarkets construct the cyber-shopper as female, whilst Nina Wakeford (2000) has written on the marketing of shopping sites to women via offers such as free email accounts. Cyberconsumption is deeply gendered and classed: online shopping itself is a defining practice of middle-class identity, at least in the West; and the figure of the cyberconsumer, a narcissistic subject drifting in a space of fantasy, dreamily clicking on the objects of her many and shifting desires, is an implicitly feminine figure.[1]

If the cyber-consumer is a feminine subject, she is also one whose femininity is imagined as constrained by the demands of life under late

1 At the time of writing, the *Sunday Times* is running extracts from a book by the doyenne of lifestyle publishing, India Knight, whose previous book *The Shops* was a guide to better living through consumption, and paid considerable attention to the new possibilities for shopping afforded by the Web. In her current book, *The Thrift Book*, Knight advises readers to shop locally and online in order to avoid excessive consumption, and hence avoid being seen to indulge in overconsumption in a time of recession. This makes me wonder whether part of the appeal of online shopping may be precisely that it allows shopping to become a private activity: not that it allows us to spend less, but that we are not *seen* to be spending. In this it differs from the fantasy of shopping locally, where one is seen to be consuming but in a way that is imagined as inherently virtuous ('The Thrift Revolution', *Sunday Times Style*, 1 November 2008, pp. 10–15).

capitalism: online shopping is presented both as a manifestation of that famously feminine skill-set, 'multi-tasking', and as its antidote. Increasingly, consumer culture seems to take for granted the notion that the consuming subject is overworked, teetering constantly on the edge of burnout. It is as though life is a disease which needs constant treatment in the forms of escapism, self-indulgence and fantasy. This is demonstrated by the two fantasy tropes that dominate online consumer culture: comfort and safety. In the previous chapter, I proposed that these terms are central to ideas about being-at-home. Whilst online homes like the vampire Web pages I examined in that chapter often attempt to think through the differences between online and RL homes (and the implications of this for the comfort and safety of their inhabitants), online shopping makes no such distinction. Instead, I propose in this chapter that online shopping sites construct home as a privileged space from which to shop, a space in which one is already comfortable and safe. According to this fantasy, it is when one leaves this space that one encounters discomfort and danger, hence the desirability of online shopping as a means of avoiding both. Therefore, my argument is structured around two imperatives which are often used to evoke the unique experience of online shopping: 'shop from the comfort of your own home', and 'shop from the safety of your own home'. Yet it could be argued that the constant, mantra-like evocation of these terms suggests anxiety; the online shopper, perhaps, seeks comfort precisely because she feels uncomfortable.

To use the term 'consumption' interchangeably with 'shopping', as capitalist interests would have us do, is itself a strategy which seeks to depoliticise acts of consumption by masking the connection of each individualised purchase to a wider consumer culture which is materially exploitative. Hence, my argument is not concerned simply with dot.com shopping sites; rather it is animated by an awareness of the wider implications of consumer culture, especially in relation to constructions of difference. Drawing on bell hook's essay 'Eating the Other' (1992), I expand Patricia Wise's view of virtual reality to suggest that in Western consumer culture, 'other' cultures and bodies, like women in Wise's work, are imagined as 'always already virtual' (Wise 1997). That is to say, existing practices of othering and stereotyping become more visible in cyberspace, where the removal of perceived physical danger/involvement results, I argue, in an unrestricted (though not unambivalent) celebration of unbridled consumption.

Internet consumption (imagined as having 'the world at your fingertips', but from within the safety of one's own home) implicates the consumer in a fantasy of 'safe' encounters with the other. Hence, the point-and-click culture of online shopping becomes embedded in a broader fantasy of virtual travel in which virtual shopping is imagined as an opportunity to experience and to consume the Other in a way that does not trouble one's sense of comfort and safety. With the removal of physical constraints ('comfort') comes a heightening of these fantasy themes and an attendant sense of deferred responsibility. First however, I want to turn to two examples that illustrate how online shopping has been imagined and presented to the public as a means of negotiating desire.

'Only Virtual': Online Shopping and Desire

From the very beginning, the idea of virtuality has been embedded in popular narratives of online shopping. The Christmas 1999 television advertising campaign for Royal Mail, starring Elton John, emphasises this point.[2] The first ad seems to address the popular belief that online communication is in danger of replacing 'snail mail', although this is implicit. Instead, the commercial focuses on the continuing necessity of the postal service in the digital age. In the opening shot, John is shown at a desk, dressed in a black sequin-encrusted jacket reminiscent of that usually worn by Liza Minnelli. Gazing at a computer screen on which is displayed the image of a high-heeled satin shoe, which glides out of the screen to rotate, transparent and just out of reach, above the singer's head.

2 Bates Worldwide (1999) 'Royal Mail Consumer Services' available at http://www.visit4info.com/advert/Royal-Mail-Royal-Mail-Consumer-Services/3698, accessed 8 December 2008.

As he is bombarded with a proliferation of virtual packages, including an extravagantly camp French poodle, a voiceover points out, virtual shopping involves a measure of frustration, since 'when you buy things online, that's all they are – virtual'. The voiceover goes on to reassure the viewer that, thanks to Royal Mail, these commodities can be delivered before we know it.

A subsequent ad, this time for Royal Mail's business service, opens with a blank hot-pink screen and a voiceover asking 'what network can you rely on to reach your customers ... in a way that makes them happy?' As the strains of the Elton John power ballad 'I Want Love' swell to a crescendo, the pink screen breaks apart to reveal Elton rising from his desk with a joyous cry of 'mail!' as a crowd of stereotypical celebrity flunkeys – smartly dressed and preppily groomed – enter, each carrying a vast pile of brown paper packages, including the aforementioned poodle. Grabbing one pile, he flings it in the air; the ad ends with the star buried under a pile of boxes: grinning, he turns to camera and utters the single word, 'magic'.[3]

The date of this ad is significant, as is the choice of Elton John as a spokesperson to represent the figure of the ideal cyberconsumer. We can see 1999 as perhaps the peak of the Blair era, after the death of Diana and Tony Blair's historic speech, but before the disaster of the Millennium Dome, widely seen as emblematic of the shabby and meretricious aspects of the New Labour project (let alone the massive disenchantment that was to follow). 'Sir Elton', as the press referred to him, came to represent this joyous, reckless period of unprecedented consumer confidence, a time when personal identity in the West became finally and irrevocably bound up with consumer goods. Sir Elton, with his legendary parties, is an enabling and a Dionysian figure: perhaps the analogy is more exact if one thinks of the camp reincarnation of the god in Scrooge, Brian Desmond Hurst's iconic 1951 film of *A Christmas Carol*. Elton, camp as Christmas grinning hugely in the face of timid fears about the safety

3 Bates Worldwide (1999) 'Royal Mail Consumer Services' archived at http://www.visit4info.com/advert/Royal-Mail-Royal-Mail-Consumer-Services/3698, accessed 8 December 2008.

of online shopping, is the anti-Scrooge, a symbol of liberalism in every sense of the word, of abundance and excess. In his lawsuit against a former accountant the following year, it emerged that he had spent thirty million pounds in two years: newspaper accounts of the trial note that the court was particularly perplexed by a bill of almost £300,000 for flowers: to which he responded simply, 'yes, I like flowers'.[4] As a highly visible gay man, yet one who embodies a reassuringly camp stereotype, Elton-as-cyberconsumer works to inspire and comfort the audience, who may feel less secure about the risks of online shopping.

In its invocation of anxiety about packages that are 'only virtual' until they arrive as highly material brown paper packages carried by an army of uniformed postal workers, this ad identifies a tension that is implicit in virtual reality; that is, 'virtual' experience is not necessarily linked to any improvement in one's material circumstances. Rather, virtual shopping privileges the element of fantasy which is present in all acts of consumption to the extent that the commodity, the thing itself (although this term is problematic since the thing itself is also constructed partly through the fantasies of the consumer) becomes less important than the desire for the commodity. In fact the Royal Mail commercial misses the point: it is precisely the deferral of the fulfilment of desire – albeit a deferral that can be enjoyed because it is known in advance to be limited – that provides much of the pleasure of online shopping. To be sure, shopping site exists to 'produce' desire in the way that advertising does: but it does so by appealing to the sense of newness, of a promised land waiting to be discovered. The internet is imagined rather as the strange room in one's house that one discovers in dreams: completely new and surprising, yet somehow always having been there. Yet instead of a room it is a parade of marvellous shops, right here, on my own desk. Through the discovery of this cabinet of wonders, it is implied, I can finally acknowledge consumer desires which were previously destined to be denied, thwarted.

4 C. Gordon, J. Aston and J. Colley (2000) 'Elton John Spent £40m in 20 Months', *Independent*, 15 November, http://www.independent.co.uk/news/uk/home-news/elton-john-spent-pound40m-in-20-months-622287.html, accessed 8 December 2008.

The apotheosis of this trend is the high fashion site Net-A-Porter. Its founder, Natalie Massenet, has become something of a business icon: a woman who succeeded where so many others failed. The site launched in 2000, in the middle of the very period at which the dot.com bubble is generally perceived to have 'burst'. According to one newspaper account, Massenet's success was due to her ability to anticipate potential customers' desires. Massenet, it says, 'a freelance fashion editor working the glamorous but usual … wished she could "click" on fashion pages and buy what she saw as soon as the desire hit' (Davies 2004), and it is this intuitive connection between 'clicking' and the sudden 'rush' of desire that sums up Massenet's understanding of the Internet's potential to transform clothes shopping. Davies goes on to cite Massenet's claim that 'ninety percent of what we buy is the result of an "oh my God!" moment': the language parodically evokes the moment of orgasm, suggesting that at the moment of 'clicking', reason is overthrown by a charge of insurmountable desire which is simultaneously a consummation of that desire. Despite the language of desire, however, touch is seen as unimportant: 'many people say that everyone wants the possibility of touching and feeling when purchasing clothes, but I believe that's no longer true necessarily,' Massenet says:

> Touching is considered to be part of the buying process just because that's how it has been done until now. But you don't have to touch a Mercedes to work out that you want to own it, and you don't need to touch a pair of Jimmy Choos to know you want to wear them (Davies 2004).

The Net-A-Porter web page is laid out to resemble that medium which is, for Western feminist thought, emblematic of the manufacturing under late capitalism of impossible desire: a fashion magazine. The first page one encounters resembles the pages of a glossy magazine; the style a hybrid of cover and editorial fashion page (incidentally, in 'real-life' fashion magazines, these high-concept editorial pages are known as the Well: ironic, then, that this ultimate space of virtual capitalist desire shares a name with Rheingold's ultimate space of decommercialised collectivism). The art direction mirrors that of the magazine format, so for example the HTML links are visible only when one hovers the mouse pointer over the page: clicking anywhere on the cover will take the reader to the relevant editorial; by clicking again, it is possible to buy the clothes featured on the models. Setting up an account means that this happens instantly, with minimal interaction from the shopper. The clothes then arrive, lavishly wrapped, the next day or, in London and New York, within four hours. The style is very much high fashion, reproducing the language and imagery that came to dominate high fashion from the late 1990s onwards, a mood of conspicuous consumption best summed up by the frequently repeated word *luxe*: the prevailing tone is one of fevered self-indulgence, of shameless bling and unfettered commodity fetishism: of It-bags, 'precious' fabrics, exotic skins, 'bling', 'ghetto fabulous' fashion and 'statement' jewellery. Through the site is concerned with the jargon of the fashion industry, not with the quasi-therapeutic language associated with the mid-market glossies and reality television. One is hence invited to engage with the magazine text and, through that text, to enter into the world of the fashion 'insider'. This is hence a fantasy of speaking back not through critique, but through participation. Although it might be argued that participation comes at a price, this is not quite true: the effect of seeing these rarefied goods laid out for inspection is to suggest accessibility. If the user lacks the funds to buy the goods, she can at least buy into the fantasy of being 'a fashionista', au fait with the language of the fashion industry (and this is a strategy that has since been taken up by print media and television, through the weekly style magazine *Grazia* as well as through numerous TV makeover shows).

As we have seen, touch is de-centred as a means of engaging with clothes: and this is tied to a more general sense of disembodiment: one shops as pure point of view, as raw desire, not as a (potentially flawed) body. In this it is positioned in direct contrast to the crowded, sweaty, foot-sore experience of high street shopping (of which more later). The body haunts the online encounter, but as a set of measurements; its parameters must be known in advance: to be the wrong size is to queer the pitch, to disrupt the fantasy of a pure unmediated cycle of desire and gratification. The body, like desire itself, is 'known': one 'knows' one's comparative size in Missoni and Miu Miu just as one 'knows' one desires to possess a bag, a dress, a Mercedes. To know that I want to possess a Jimmy Choo shoe,

I do not need to know if the shoe fits. What is on offer here is a flattering fantasy of oneself as a subject who wants the right, the most desirable, things: that is, one who desires correctly. This knowledge is perfectly expressed by the term 'savvy', as in 'fashion savvy'. This expression is used to flatter the customer: a kind of street version of savoir faire, it suggests shrewdness, an eye for a good deal, a taste for luxury allied to a canny resistance to bullshit. Savviness is the inverse of passivity, of the kind of bovine narcissistic sensual trance in which it is often assumed women consume the trappings of femininity. Savviness is a convenient means of denying the cycle of commodity fetishism: here desire is a pre-existing known quantity, not constructed or 'manufactured'. Desire is not passive but avid, engaged, vigorous. Indeed it is almost more akin to masculinity than to traditional notions of femininity (and this is why the androgynous swaggering pirate-booted Kate Moss is its ideal symbol: her image is the personification of savviness).

Everywhere there is fashion speak, arcane, extravagant and gloriously allusive: we are told that in the words of the designer, 'the idea is to make leather drape as languidly as a gown and create silhouettes for Dietrich in Sid Vicious leather': To the left of the page there is a glossy ad for Aquascutum featuring the Brazilian supermodel Gisele: below the image, a behind-the-scenes video from the same shoot, shot in grainy black and white, plays on an endless loop accompanied by a raucous guitar soundtrack by the indie punk band Trophy Hearts (and for those of us who remember a time when moving newspapers existed only in fantasy films, there is still a sci-fi glamour about these animated ads, however annoying they may be).[5] The overall image is one of punkish androgyny that is, however, ultimately recuperated as femininity: starting with the 'viciousness' of raw skins, we progress through the androgyny of a Dietrich to the relative safety of normative femininity as sensuous, languid and gowned. Femininity in fashion terms is hence an achievement, a finished state, but one that relies for its impact on its ability to

5 http://www.net-a-porter.com/Content/Magazine/Contents, accessed 28 October 2008.

incorporate edgier, queerer histories. The feminine in fashion is hence inscribed with everything that it is not, with fantasies of Otherness, just as online shopping contains within the culmination of the final click a history of intertextuality, a history of the search.

Unlike the static pages of a women's magazine, the website is constantly moving, shifting, changing, mimicking perhaps the restless changeability of fashion itself. Overall there is a sense of movement, of busyness (indeed of business), that evokes the constant transformations and renunciations of fashion itself. An image of the Rick Owens jacket is accompanied by a text box informing us that 'everyone needs one for fall ... make it your fashion priority'. Reading this, the obvious questions spring to mind: define everyone. Define need. Define priority. But this is beside the point: above all else, this site is knowing; 'need' is used here as it is used throughout the fashion web, in relation high street bargains, haute couture and all points in between: it is a histrionic euphemism for a desire that is neither shameful nor wholly to be celebrated but that is in itself a refusal of (external, culturally imposed) shame. By recasting desire as need, the shopper ridicules an imagined onlooker who, scandalised, cries, 'you don't need that!' Cyber consumption is precisely concerned with the things that are not-needed: it is the apocryphal injunction, 'let them eat cake' re-imagined as intentional self-parody. The fantasy is not so much of possessing the object, as of being one who must possess the object. What is more, the notion of the consumer object as 'necessary' is not confined to the knowing, camp histrionics which can be seen in this editorial. The pages for individual commodities invoke, in a contrastingly austere language, the collective fantasy that the objects on display are simply day-to-day-necessities. This is nowhere more obvious than in the pages dedicated to bags. The 'It Bag' is a recent phenomenon, which probably accounts for much of Net-A-Porter's success. Its rise is contiguous with the period of consumer confidence and rising debt identified above, and has been the object of much despairing (and mock-despairing) commentary in the popular media. In its dispassionate descriptions, Net-A-Porter rises grandly above this debate. So, for example, Marc Jacobs'

'Stam' bag is 'a classic style' which 'would hold all you need for day',[6] the Chloe Bay, first seen in 2005 is described (in 2008) as 'practical ... a classic',[7] and Alexander McQueen's vast red patent python-skin Novak, at just shy of a thousand pounds, is described simply as 'a carryall'.[8] There is some praise for particularly unusual or exclusive styles, but even then the tone is one of genteel restraint with overtones of financial shrewdness: the gold version of the Chloe bag mentioned above, for example, is described as a 'fabulous handbag investment', while the Halston label, relaunched in 2008, features the Zai messenger bag which allows the wearer to 'make a nonchalantly *luxe* statement'.[9] Nonchalance, the idea of shopping not as desire driven by lack but as interest, is central to the fantasy of consumer subjectivity that defines the site.

Virtual Chocolate: The Fantasy Commodity

The pleasure of cyber-consumption, then, derives from a fantasy of deferred gratification, which is simultaneously a deferral of disappointment. In the examples above this desire is focussed on a material object, albeit one that might fail to live up to the complex desires that are invested in it by the consumer. In this section, I turn to the practice of virtual gift-giving in order to explore what happens to this notion of desire when the gift itself is absent. Whilst I have argued that cyberconsumption therefore reveals the extent to which all consumer commodities are 'virtual', there is, however, another form of online commodity: one that does not 'exist' in the sense of a material object. The commodity is at once fetishised and

6 www.net-a-porter.com/product/33938, accessed 8 November 2008.

7 www.net-a-porter.com/product/30468, accessed 8 November 2008.

8 http://www.net-a-porter.com/Shop/Designers/Alexander_McQueen, 8 November 2008.

9 http://www.net-a-porter.com/intl/product/35553?cm_mmc=Datafeed-_-Froogle-_-UK-_-Halston%20Zai%20messenger%20bag, accessed 29 November 2008.

absent, with the result that giving itself becomes over-determined as a performative act through which community is constituted. To desire (rather than to have) a particular commodity hence becomes the shared basis of community.

Virtual gifts are gifts which are exchanged as HTML tags, with a message attached, but without the expectation of sending or receiving a 'real' gift. Although virtual gift-giving has always existed on the Web, it has recently become more popular and widespread as a result of sites like Facebook, which includes a virtual gift programme as part of its user profiles. The idea is to choose a gift which speaks to the recipients' tastes and interests as a means of marking special occasions, celebrations, or day-to-day events, either alongside or as a substitute for actual offline gift exchanges.

There is an obvious connection to be made here between the virtual gift, and Marcel Mauss' notion of the gift economy, an idea which has been much explored in relation to online file-sharing. Like FTP music files, but without their overtones of geek culture (and hence of elitism), the virtual gift conforms to the Mauss' critique of the gift as not 'free', since it demands reciprocation. What is more, like Mauss' gift, the virtual gift is mystically linked to both giver and receiver. For Mauss, the gift is inaliable: it cannot be separated from the giver (1990: 3), and in this sense the giving of gifts transcends a simple transferral of private property from one owner to another. In virtual gifting this is taken one step further: what I give you is not 'the thing itself', since there is no 'thing itself', but rather the performance of a relationship of giving. This allows for a new affective economy of giving where the status of the gift is called into question. It may be permissible to give a virtual birthday present in circumstances where a 'real' present would be considered excessive or otherwise inappropriate. Indeed the giving of a virtual gift may be performative in that it brings into being a relationship of reciprocity between acquaintances. However, this is not to say that virtual gifts are entirely separate either from consumer discourse, or from existing ideas about the relationship between subjects and commodities, as the following example shows.

> Chocolate for comfort by Jonny Bowden, M.A.
>
> [Reader's Question]: I know that eating is often related to your emotions, but even so, I can't stop bingeing on chocolate. In fact, I often justify it by thinking, 'I know I'm only eating because I've had a bad day, but I deserve it.' Any suggestions?[10]

The history of food fetishism in Western culture is seen as early as Brillat-Savarin's famous statement: 'tell me what you eat: I will tell you who you are' (MacClancy 1992). If he is right, then much of online culture would have us believe that 'women' can be summed up by a single foodstuff: chocolate. In online shopping sites, as well as women's sites more generally, chocolate is associated with female desire: to desire chocolate is constitutive of normative female desire. Importantly, it is the desire for chocolate, not necessarily its consumption, that is important: in fact the limiting of chocolate consumption is key to narratives of femininity and female desires as intrinsically linked to the networks of consumption, compulsion and narcissism that constitute normative feminine identity. This is usually expressed through a comic discourse of consumption as addiction: in fact the figure of the 'chocoholic' is closely aligned with that of the 'shopaholic', in that both work to naturalise the notion of the feminine subject as consumer; crucially, as a consumer who is out of control, who has a voracious and overwhelming need to consume and who will literally eat till she is sick and/or hopelessly addicted, as well as shopping until she drops. In this sense, chocolate is the perfect commodity through which to examine fantasies at stake in cyberconsumption. Here, I look at the ways in which 'women's' websites, and sites which sell chocolate online, mobilise notions of comfort (eating/shopping) alongside themes of addiction and compulsion to construct the figure of the cyberconsumer as a subject driven by desire.

10 www.ivillage.co.uk/dietandfitness/wtmngment/snackcrave/qas/0,,236_157930,00.html, accessed 28 November 2008. Ivillage is a site for women, loosely modelled on the format of a mid-market glossy magazine and containing the usual sections on fashion, 'beauty', food, career issues and so on. It is not my intention to discuss the wider implications of such gendered Web spaces here, since these issues have been examined very comprehensively by Nina Wakeford (2000).

The email quoted above, taken from a 'health and fitness' problem page which appears on the women's magazine website Ivillage, typifies this image of the feminine consumer at the mercy of her (pathological) desires. The advice given to the concerned reader by Ivillage's 'expert' Johnny Bowden reinforces this view:

> If you decide not to binge on chocolate, rather than thinking that you're depriving yourself, try seeing it as a gift. In other words, by refusing that binge food, you're actually giving yourself the gift of good health and a leaner, fitter body. Of course, that body isn't going to magically appear tomorrow, and the chocolate is here right now, but think of it as you do frequent-flier miles: Save up those little gifts, and after a while you will have something worthwhile.[11]

What both question and answer have in common is that both show a highly sophisticated approach which is aware of the connections between food and fantasy, and the ways in which these connections are gendered, but is disconnected from any wider political analysis. The way in which the question is posed naturalises a link between desire and eating: the questioner 'knows' that eating is related to the emotions. Yet her query suggests an anxiety relating to the role of consumer, an anxiety that is mirrored in the structure of the question, which consists of two statements of knowing ('I know that eating is often related to your emotions', and 'I know I'm only eating because I've had a bad day'). Her own answer to these problems is presented as a contradiction: 'but … I can't stop bingeing', 'but I deserve it'. As with Net-A-Porter, the subject 'knows'; but here, what she knows is repeatedly called into question. In fact, the statements above do not, in essence, contradict one another; if one were to accept, as the questioner claims to, that eating is a response to an emotional stimulus (rather than simply to hunger), it would be logical to assume that certain emotional states might lead to the consumption of certain foods. Nevertheless, whilst the first sentence implies that emotional eating is a matter of compulsion, by the second sentence the writer has amended her

11 www.ivillage.co.uk/dietandfitness/wtmngment/snackcrave/qas/0,,236_157930,00.html.

position to one of greater control in which she decides to eat chocolate on the grounds that 'I've had a bad day ... I deserve it'.

In other words, there is a shift from 'knowing' that eating is emotional, to suggesting that the act of eating results from a combination of emotional and rational processes. This shift marks a key moment in the shaping of consumer identity, the moment at which the consumer becomes the cyberconsumer. In this case, the woman presents herself as out of control, as 'bingeing'. In other words, she has become aware of herself as the voracious all-consuming Western body evoked by hooks. Unable to stop, she fears that she may eat and eat, even to the point where the thing consumed begins to consume her, distorting her body (and hence, perhaps, destroying the visible signs of her femininity). Crucially, this awareness is affective: in this moment of self-consciousness, the subject feels that she is out of control, that her emotions have got out of hand. Still, she does not address this anxiety simply by ceasing to consume. Rather, she takes two courses of action. The first, which is explicitly stated in her email, is to rationalise her eating by saying to herself, 'I deserve it'. The second, implicit response is to turn to a different, less threatening form of consumption. Seating herself at her computer, she turns to an 'expert' for advice.

Despite Ivillage's expert advice, chocolate is universally presented as hard, even impossible, to resist. Online shops are keen to promote the idea that women's craving for chocolate is both natural and inevitable. In this version of the fantasy, chocolate is rather like love, particularly that idea of 'love' that is associated with traditional, heteronormative femininity. Chocolate Valley, a site which sells chocolate online, typifies this approach. Like the supermarket websites, it too offers the reader the opportunity to consume more than just the commodity itself. Further, whilst Sainsbury's website encourages its users to engage with a fantasy of consuming the 'exotic' Other, Chocolate Valley claims to offer scientific knowledge alongside its more obvious products. Under the heading 'The Science of Chocolate', the site sets out to ask whether women are, in fact, more likely than men to 'crave' chocolate, and whether this corresponds to the sexes' differing attitudes to romantic love. Such a model of 'love' is implicitly heteronormative in that it is grounded in the assumption that love is inextricable from an oppositional model of sexual difference. Further, it works to construct 'woman' as a passive subject who is always craving affection from men, who lack a comparable biological desire for love, with the result that her desire is always partially unsatisfied. It is this dissatisfaction that leads to displacement of the desire for love, which is transformed into a love for chocolate.

This theme is developed in an article headed, 'Feminine Physiology or Cultural Comfort?' The article, which is presented alongside an image of a young, blonde woman eating a bar of chocolate, starts by presenting itself as a kind of literature review of studies about chocolate consumption. Although it begins from a broadly sociological viewpoint, the article quickly turns to pseudoscientific explanations for women's supposed 'cravings' for chocolate:

> Scientific research into chocolate craving and addiction has led to some interesting findings. Any conclusive data remains difficult to pin down since there are so many variables to consider. The data that has been gathered confirms certain chocolate 'myths', but other long held beliefs are being questioned: Some have felt that there is a physiological basis for women to crave chocolate more than men.[12]

The article goes on to state that this 'physiological basis' stems from the presence of phenylethylamine, a substance found in chocolate. It explains that,

> Phenylethylamine is a hormone that affects the body similar to an amphetamine. In theory, it is responsible for our feelings of love when we first make eye contact or hold hands. It also happens to exist in high doses in chocolate.[13]

In other words, the 'physiological basis' for chocolate craving is not physiological at all, since it lies not in the physiology of 'women' themselves, but in the chemical makeup of chocolate, which is said to contain

12 http://www.chocolatevalley.com/choco/site/index.htm, accessed December 2007, since removed.

13 http://www.chocolatevalley.com/choco/site/index.htm, accessed December 2007, since removed.

a 'love chemical' that has an effect on the body similar to that caused by 'falling in love'. It is taken for granted that women are addicted to 'falling in love', which is assumed to be a biological response to the sight of an appropriate (masculine) object to the extent that cultural explanations for this phenomenon are simply disregarded. The site uses the image of a chocolate bar penetrating a female symbol to emphasise the connection between 'women', chocolate and heterosexuality. This image creates a tension within the construction of 'the chocoholic'. Chocolate websites aim to interpolate the consumer into a pleasurable fantasy of the chocolate addict as shameless, sensual and self-indulgent, as a wicked woman. They also present chocolate as an illicit pleasure, for example through the analogy with amphetamine in the article quoted above, and through the use of language associated with illegal drugs more generally; the chocoholic is often portrayed as being in need of a 'fix'. Yet this addiction is always, to some extent, imagined as a performance, a feminine pastiche of more serious addictions to drugs and alcohol. When the performance threatens to become disrupted by a sense of being out of control, as in the letter to a problem page that states 'I can't stop eating chocolate', this fantasy becomes disrupted. This disruption occurs precisely because the consumer has bought into the notion that women are slaves to their biological impulses, that they have biological cravings for love, and that those cravings can be gratified by eating chocolate. Yet what is on offer through sites like Chocolate Valley is not gratification of a physiologically based craving, but the fantasy of having such a craving and hence of aligning oneself with the highly ambiguous figure of the chocoholic. What is given in the case of virtual chocolate is a set of knowledges and ideas about what it means to be attached to a feminine identity. Chocolate comes to stand in for feminine subjectivity, and it is this feminine subjectivity that forms the basis of community.

If, as I have argued, online shopping privileges the fantasies implicit in relations of consumption to a far higher degree than is possible in RL shopping, the chocoholic who shops for her 'fix' online is yet more distanced from the commodity itself, entwined in a complex network of fantasies in which she is both addicted and discriminating, a slave to her desires perhaps, but in full command of the technology which facilitates their gratification. Or, as the text from Gourmet Spot's website suggests, she may be seeking a 'quick fix', but by seeking it on line she is being 'creative', a term suggesting choice and agency.[14] To be 'out of control' is missing the point; the chocoholic may perform helplessness, but to actually feel helpless is to lose her privileged position. It is at this point that she must seek help and, as in the example above, be counselled to practise greater self-control. Hence, failure to take up and to feel comfortable in the privileged role of consumer results in shame, and this shame arises from a fear of becoming excessive. Through the figure of the 'shopaholic', we are constantly reminded that the consumer herself risks being consumed. The constant search for gratification and deferral of that gratification may result in the subject's being consumed by desire itself. This consumption involves a loss of control which Sedgwick calls a 'pathology of the will' (Sedgwick 1994), resulting in addiction. However, this addiction is imagined as an obsession with the commodity (chocolate), but also to shopping itself. Chocolate shopping sites invoke a fantasy of being a particular kind of consumer, that is, a consumer who is always at risk of losing control, yet simultaneously retains agency and privilege. The fantasy of immersive 'clicking' for gratification is identical to that invoked by Net-A-Porter, but here it is imagined as out of control, indeed as pleasurable in that it involves a surrendering of control, a giving in to temptation. In contrast to Net-A-Porter's savvy, fiscally minded connoisseur, the cyber consumer invoked here is willing to surrender: the rhetoric startlingly appropriates the language of accounts of cyber-sex in its insistence on immersion, loss of identity, a willing capitulation that takes the subject to the very edge of helplessness. Crucially, this fantastic narrative of consumption itself is far more important than the acquisition of a particular commodity: indeed, the commodity itself, once purchased, is immediately devoured: one does not have one's chocolate and eat it.

This point is illustrated by a site simply named 'Virtual Chocolate'. In appearance, this site is very similar to Chocolate Valley or Gourmet

14 http://www.gourmetspot.com/features/chocolate.htm, accessed 8 December 2008.

Spot. The design and art direction are almost identical, with photographs of various chocolates displayed on a chocolate-brown background, with headings in a gold italic font which is reminiscent of romantic novels and other 'feminine' products. Indeed, the site also uses a logo reading 'get your fix at Virtual Chocolate', which is almost identical to that shown on the Gourmet Spot site. Like the real chocolate sites, the text uses terms like 'heavenly' and 'luscious' to invoke images of voluptuous self-indulgence, alongside language which suggests addiction. The difference is that, unlike the other sites I read here, Virtual Chocolate does not actually sell chocolate. Instead, the user is asked to choose an image from an online catalogue that exactly mirrors those used by 'real' shopping sites. The user attaches a personal message, and this is then emailed as a gift. Significantly, in spite of the fact that it would be pointless to send virtual chocolate to oneself, the site hails the user as a chocoholic in precisely the same way as the 'real' shopping sites, again suggesting that the user is expected to take pleasure from consuming the text and images of the site itself, from looking; indeed, it states that to do so is to be in 'heaven'. Although the site does state that it is intended only as a source of virtual postcards, everything about its design encourages the user to collude in the fantasy that this is a real shopping site. Significantly, these sites encourage a sense of community greater than that implied by traditional online gift-shops. Whilst the latter construct an unequal relationship between giver and receiver, virtual gifts represent a knowing gesture to a shared understanding of the mores of cyberconsumption. What one gives, here, is a pleasurable acknowledgement of shared fantasies.

Virtual Chocolate is just one of thousands of 'virtual gift' sites on the Web. I would suggest that such sites, read alongside more conventional online shops, provide a significant insight into the relations between fantasy and virtuality, and their relation to practices of consumption. In particular, such a reading works to destabilise the notion of 'shopping' as a direct relationship between a desiring individual, and a commodity. Virtual shopping sites make visible what is implicit in all aspects of consumer culture, though perhaps to a greater degree in online shopping than in 'real life': that there is no 'thing itself' that exists independently of the consumer. To take on the role of consumer is to assume a privileged position which, in the isolated, invisible ideal of online shopping, reduces Otherness to a commodity. The rest of the world becomes a bazaar through which the consumer is able to travel freely, driven by the constant, 'voracious' need to consume. Yet this consumption consists of the consumption of a fantasy, the fantasy of being a (cyber)consumer. In the extreme example of virtual shopping sites, the commodity is not virtual only until the moment it arrives in the post: rather, there is no commodity. For the virtual consumer, fantasy has been privileged to the extent that 'the thing itself' has ceased to matter. The virtual gift negotiates the ambiguities and tensions within consumer culture, doing justice to the desire to be comforted, but also to the guilt and shame that accompany that desire.

Online Shopping and Comfort

The notion of comfort is not restricted to virtual gifting, but is central to the construction of cyberconsumer identity. Above, I have argued that the cyberconsumer is imaged as in need of constant comforting as an escape from the rigours of contemporary life. Here, I want to examine how the notion of comfort has been mobilised in order to present online shopping as an activity which enables the shopper to acknowledge and express desires that would otherwise be forbidden. In particular, we can read comfort alongside narratives of otherness invoked by 'ethnic' food shops. Online supermarkets have appropriated discourses of virtual subjectivity which are imagined through the notion of a 'safe' encounter with the Other. However, in order to define what is Other, it is necessary for consumer websites to interpellate shoppers into an imagined community, to construct a 'sense of belonging'. One of the primary ways in which they do this is by invoking the notion of 'comfort': that is, by suggesting that an encounter with the Other is always haunted by the possibility of danger, but that through online disembodiment, this encounter can be made safe. In order to understand how this works, it is necessary to explore the ways in which RL shopping has been constructed as uncomfortable. Recent debates on the sociology of shopping have indeed stressed the physical and psychological discomforts of high-street shopping. Here, I argue that ads for online shopping have appropriated this notion of discomfort in order to differentiate between online and offline shops. Further, they draw on the themes of liberation associated with virtual reality in order to make the claim that cyberconsumption is superior to other forms of consumer culture: and that they do this by constructing online shopping as an activity that involves getting closer to (and acting out) one's fantasies in a safe environment.

In popular discourse, shopping is imagined in contradictory ways. It is seen as a desirable activity, especially for women (although gay men may also be valued as shopping companions): so much so that it is possible to shop for greetings cards, T-shirts and mugs dedicated to the act of shopping itself, proclaiming 'born to shop', 'shopaholic', and so on. Indeed, the act is so pleasurable it may become addictive, hence the term shopaholic. On the other hand, shopping is hard work; the dedicated shopper may, if she is not careful, end up obeying the imperative to shop 'till you drop'.

According to one e-commerce consultant, the advantages of online shopping are simple. In his account of digital shopping, Julian Markham states that 'most shoppers regard general shopping as a chore', although it is not the act of choosing a product that is viewed in this way. Instead, 'inconvenience' stems from other concerns such as getting to the shops, parking, knowing whether the things one wants are in stock, and the time involved in 'processing' (such as queuing at a checkout) (1998: 110). However, studies of shopping behaviour suggest that women, especially, are likely to view shopping as an enjoyable leisure activity (Campbell 1997, Lunt and Livingstone 1992). Colin Campbell states that women are more likely than men to enjoy 'browsing' and 'shopping around'; although his study does not provide information on consumer attitudes to the less pleasurable realities of RL shopping, both terms are instructive in their evocation of a rather bovine, passive consumer experience. It could be argued, then, that online shopping retains these pleasurable aspects of the shopping experience, whilst omitting the less comfortable elements outlined above. In online shopping sites, the use of the term 'browsing', together with a proliferation of visual imagery and facilities which encourage consumers to compare prices and products, helps to preserve these positive aspects of shopping. The sites construct online shopping as different from its RL equivalent through the notion of comfort. Images of comfort provide a means of distinguishing between the 'inconvenience' and 'discomfort' of 'extraneous' activities like parking and carrying heavy bags, and consumption itself, which is always presented as pleasurable. For example, one shopping directory called comfort.com, based in the town of Comfort, Texas states that, 'It's no surprise so many people come to Comfort to do their shopping, and find it all here! So, take your time, and check us out from the "comfort" of your own home'.[15] As another American-run 'family' shopping site, Oxygen, puts it, 'the best thing about shopping online is you never have to stand on one'.[16] Real shopping is presented as an arduous duty rather than a pleasure: the shopper suffers from sore feet, parking charges, and encounters with rude sales assistants and pushy bargain-hunters. In contrast, the online shopper never has to queue; like a member of the aristocracy, she is encouraged to feel that she is the only person in the store, or that she has been rushed to the front of the queue. A popular British site similarly contrasts the nightmare of high-street shopping with the delights of point-and-click consumer culture:

> With UK Shop Online you can shop from the comfort of your own home, anytime you like, day or night, meaning you will get the most convenient shopping experience possible. Buying online is perfect for the person who hasn't got the time to trek to the shops, stand in queues and travel home again. It takes only a small matter of time to find the product you require and it will be sent in the post straight to your door. Sounds better doesn't it?[17]

15 This site was previously available at www.comfort.com but has since been deleted.

16 http://oxygen.com/family/home/Webshopping101_20011113.jhtml, accessed December 2007, since removed.

17 www.ukshoponline.co.uk, deleted.

EasyEverything Internet cafés capitalise on this idea of shopping from the PC in an advertising campaign which associates online shopping with both fashionable femininity and modernity through the appropriation of catch-phrases from the television comedy series Absolutely Fabulous. One ad has the caption 'Sweetie! Darling! High street shopping is just so 1990s' superimposed over a photo of the bare, high-tech space of the cybercafé, the image being evoked is one of virtual rather than actual travel, despite the fact that cybercafés are generally located in the high street.[18] Whilst the consumer must still travel to the high street in order to access these facilities, the ad suggests an appeal to a naturally feminine indolence that prefers to sit in a comfortable chair and look at goods on the screen, rather than dealing with queues and changing rooms. The Oxygen shopping guide draws on a similar vision of comfort, but one which is to be accessed strictly from one's own home; the page cited above goes on to say that, 'you can shop 365 days a year, 24 hours a day, at your own pace, and in the privacy of your home. No lines, crowds, pushy salespeople, or annoying music blasting in your head. Here are a few tips on how to shop 'til you ... have to stand up!' What is more, Oxygen's image of shopping in one's pyjamas, whilst not gendered in itself, is related specifically to femininity when the site advises its readers that 'since you are in the comfort of your own home, why not shop in your pyjamas, while doing laundry and giving yourself a facial. No one will ever know, you comfortable multi-tasker, you!'[19]

Although the invitation 'shop 'til you have to stand up' suggests that online shopping, too, might involve certain discomforts, these sites do not simply offer a way to avoid queues, sore feet, and so on let alone the discomforts involved in shopping with small children. Indeed, they do not necessarily offer physical relaxation at all; the image of shopping whilst simultaneously doing the laundry and giving oneself a facial suggests that 'comfort', for the feminine subject being invoked here, stems from the reassuring knowledge that the desire to shop need not interfere with

18 www.easyinternetcafe.com/, accessed 10 January 2008.

19 http://oxygen.com/family/home/Webshopping101_20011113.jhtml, accessed December 2007, page removed.

the other daily duties associated with femininity. The message is that she can shop in comfort precisely because she knows that neither the housework nor her appearance need be neglected as a result. Nevertheless, all these images of virtual shopping mobilise images of comfort to suggest that the consumers' sense of comfort and relaxation (and reassurance, an idea I shall look at in greater detail below) allows for a purer experience of consumption than that experienced in RL. What is more, the idea of shopping in comfort involves a fantasy of liberation, of escape from duty, often symbolised by loose clothing. This is exemplified by the iconic 2002 British television commercial for Barclays Bank's online banking service, featuring Robbie Coltrane, which again utilises the image of shopping in one's pyjamas in order to reinforce this point. The advertisement shows the comedian sitting up in bed wearing striped pyjamas and working on a laptop, whilst the voiceover states that 'You can pay your bills in your jimjams – it's a liberating experience I can tell you'.[20]

In this fantasy, cyberconsumption becomes the ultimate shopping experience: it is shopping as liberation, allowing for a direct expression of the consumer's desires. This model of liberation strongly equates freedom with privacy – it is imagined as freedom from the public gaze that is, freedom to look inwards and access one's own desires, which can then be gratified through engagement with technology. Significantly, then, this model of community implies communion with the realm of the symbolic, rather than with (like and unlike) others. In cyberconsumption, the technological apparatus becomes both the thing with which one has communion, and an extension of the self which allows one to be in dialogue with one's deepest fantasies. Other people are removed at every step; for example, as well as boasting of their ability to eliminate crowds and queues, online shopping sites often use the image of a shopping basket or trolley into which the user puts her purchases and, when she is finished shopping, enters her credit card details via a 'checkout'. The imagery differs from that of offline shopping only in that there is no checkout assistant (not

20 Barclays Bank (2002). *Big Bank*. Advertisement directed by Tony Scott for Leagas Delaney.

even a symbolic or virtual one). In many sites this gap is filled, instead, with the image of the symbolic Other (which is presented as an object of desire), as I shall demonstrate. But in order to encounter this Other, the consumer must become liberated from the constraints imposed by the proximity of other bodies as well as her own.

If we look closely at the theme of 'shopping in comfort', several interesting points start to emerge. The first of these is a tension between the term 'comfort', with its suggestion of embodiment (although there is also an association between 'feeling comfortable' mentally and images of safety, which I'll examine in more detail below), and the simultaneous production of online shopping, and consumerism more generally, as an essentially disembodied activity. Perhaps more than any other form of virtual experience, online shopping makes visible the desire to escape embodiment. Such a desire is open to failure insofar as the feminine subject is constructed and defined through images of embodiment, so for example, in the chocolate sites I discuss above, the desire for 'comfort food', for luxury and emotional solace, is troubled by an awareness that eating 'too much' chocolate makes one fat and hence, it is implied, threatens one's femininity. Similarly, whilst the woman reader addressed in the Oxygen shopping guide may be liberated from the trials of real shopping, her liberation does not take the form of becoming disembodied. Rather, she becomes free to spend more time attending to the needs of the body. As Anne Balsamo argues in *Technologies of the Gendered Body*, one effect of virtual reality is precisely that its appeal to discourses of disembodiment allows it to reproduce unchecked highly conservative myths about the body:

> The body may disappear representationally in virtual worlds – indeed, we may go to great lengths to repress it and erase its referential traces – but it does not disappear materially, either in the interface with the VR apparatus or in systems of technological production ... [M]yths about identity, nature and the body are rearticulated with new technologies in ways that ensure that traditional (and occasionally revisionist) narratives about the gendered, race-marked body are socially and technologically reproduced (Balsamo 1996: 15).

In contrast, online shopping does not seek to make the body disappear, since it is concerned with the desire to buy things for the body (clothes, cosmetics, food and so on). It does, however, seek a temporary separation from, or transcendence of the body, hence the appeal to images of 'comfort'. Whilst the self is able to engage directly with its desire for consumption through the technical apparatus, the body is left behind (albeit in conditions of 'comfort', such as relaxing in bed), rather than being experienced as a burden. In 'real' shopping, the needs and sensations of the body are experienced as barriers to the gratification of desire. Online shopping removes these barriers, supposedly allowing the 'real' self – that is, the desiring self – to become detached from the body and to go forth in search of gratification.

The fantasy, then, is not so much of indulging the body as of temporarily transcending it. Sitting perfectly still at the computer screen, dressed in loose-fitting clothing, the online shopper becomes, in this fantasy narrative, representative of pure, free-floating desire. Crucially, though, the body is still present; indeed, the sense of 'comfort' in this scenario is contingent upon the knowledge that the consuming subject is able to return to the body. Indeed, such a return is necessary since the process of shopping always involves buying things 'for' the body. So we can see that the body, far from being repressed or left out, is imagined as the site on which desire originates. In offline high-street shopping, the body is constrained; and when the body becomes physically tired or otherwise restricted, those desires become less visible and hence more difficult to gratify. Therefore, the advertisements cited here should not be read as suggesting that cyberconsumption contains a higher degree of fantasy than RL shopping. Rather, the conditions in which online shopping is ideally carried out (conditions which are similar to those required for yoga and other forms of meditation) allow the elements of fantasy and desire that are always implicit in shopping, to become visible. Hence, this fantasy supposes that online shopping allows for a more authentic experience of consumption in which one's true desires can be understood, and ultimately gratified. Moreover, through an elision of shopping with more basic types of consumption (the body's need for food), the desire to shop itself is presented as a universal and constant feature of Western subjectivity. Online shopping is superior to RL shopping in that it allows the subject to recognise shopping as a basic need, like eating; that is, not as a choice but as a necessity. A further analogy could be made between shopping and sleep. The trope of shopping in pyjamas suggests that the consumer is in a kind of dream state and hence that the fantasies involved in shopping reflect the 'real self': that is, they have a psychic reality that is more authentic, feels more comfortable, than the subject's limited and constrained offline activities.

The nature of this desire, the feminine desire to consume, can be best understood by examining the ways in which the notion of comfort is continually linked to that of privacy. Statements like 'no-one will ever know' suggest that this is a crucial component in fantasies of cyberconsumption, as is a more general avoidance of contact with others in the shape of fellow shoppers, sales assistants, traffic wardens and so on. Thus, online shopping is imagined as private in the sense that one does not have to leave the house, but also in the sense of self-sufficiency. Although online shopping involves a fantasy of having access to the (virtual, exotic) other, as I shall argue in the next section, it also ironically implies a deliberate avoidance of real encounters with actual, embodied others. The online shopper is isolated, solitary. As the examples above show, certain images have become over-determined in discourses of Internet shopping; one of the most striking reiterative images is that of an isolated individual shopping at the dead of night, often in pyjamas, and virtually all the shopping sites and newspaper articles I looked at in the course of my research had something to say about the advantages of twenty-four-hour shopping. The equation of round-the-clock shopping with privacy to produce 'a liberating experience' tells us a great deal about the ways in which Internet shopping comes to be seen as a fantastic activity.

On one level, the commercial for Barclays Bank cited above simply highlights an important material difference between shopping by computer and shopping in the high street, and attempts to present that difference as a definite advantage. Yet it also implies that the ability to shop in the dead of night represents the expression of an innate desire to be free to shop at any time. Hence, shopping is constructed not as an activity one undertakes in order to fulfil one's material needs, but as a matter of impulse, of fleeting desires that demand immediate gratification; or rather, I would suggest that shopping sites construct a binary opposition between desire and need precisely in order to collapse it. For example, online supermarkets position some commodities, such as cleaning products, as 'necessities'. These are then pushed away into the less visible areas of the site, whilst the 'front' pages are dedicated to special offers on branded items, and to those products that are presented as exotic or 'premium' goods. Although the 'necessities' themselves may not be necessary in reality, the distinction is between dull, domestic products and luxuries or self-indulgences. This distinction is then collapsed by the process of persuading the consumer that an element of luxury is necessary if one is to enjoy a satisfactory quality of life. In other words, this process is used to suggest that there is a clear distinction to be made between what we need and what we desire, but that both need and desire must be satisfied. However, this secondary type of 'need' is often presented as slightly transgressive, hence the pyjamas: this is shopping as midnight feast, and is always a slightly wicked experience. Whilst the consumer might 'recognise' a 'need' for luxury, a hierarchy still exists in which the need for chocolate is of a different character than the need for washing-up liquid, for example. The former is presented as frivolous and even shameful.

In her book *Nigella Bites*, the food writer and broadcaster Nigella Lawson describes her late-night shopping sessions in just such terms. In the section entitled, significantly, 'Comfort Food', she says

> I have a bad Amazon habit. You know the 'when the going gets tough, the tough go shopping' line? Well, the not-so-tough get their retail therapy online. Or I do: when I can't sleep I start ordering books. And I comfort myself twice over by telling myself how useful they are, how they really help my work. I offer this recipe, adapted from a book that in itself soothes … bought at about 3 am one unravellingly wakeful night, as proof (Lawson 2001: 47).

Now, Nigella Lawson is, as already noted, a food writer, so recipe books clearly are useful and do help her work. Yet the phrase 'I tell myself' suggests guilt and an attendant need for reassurance and self-justification. This passage reconstructs a mundane activity (that of buying materials for one's work) as transgressive. In the TV show accompanying the book,

Lawson is shown at the end of each episode sneaking into her kitchen in curlers and a dressing-gown to eat leftovers straight from the fridge; this passage constructs online shopping as a similarly self-indulgent and yet necessary ('comforting') act. What is more, online shopping is specifically understood as more effete, more lazy, than real shopping: it is what 'the not-so-tough' do when they are 'unravelling' with stress, yet too enervated even to contemplate a shopping trip (and presumably when food alone does not quite sufficiently gratify one's desire for 'comfort'). Crucially, this quotation suggests that the consumer experiences a tension in which 'retail therapy' is seen simultaneously as a self-conscious act of indulgence (and hence as slightly camp, as the tone of the article suggests), and as a necessity: that is, something one does in order to stop oneself from 'unravelling'. Further, a distinction is made between two different kinds of 'necessity'; the necessity of fulfilling desires and responding to psychological drives is presented as a more authentic and convincing reason for online shopping than the argument that the books 'really help my work'.

Lawson's comments construct online shopping as a self-indulgent activity that threatens to spill over into decadent excess. This view is embedded in the notion of privacy. As the Oxygen article says, the shopper can get on with (presumably more legitimate) activities like housework and facials, and 'nobody need ever know' how much time she has spent browsing the virtual malls. This might indeed be a considerable amount of time. According to Roger Williams, chairman of the Internet market research agency, Claritas, shopping accounts for more time spent online than any other activity. Significantly, most of this time is spent buying food and clothes for oneself, rather than for others. Shopping for clothes is, he claims, the most 'addictive' activity after playing computer games. For example, '[o]f those who buy fashion on the net, 23% shop for clothes online for more than an hour, whilst the quickest activity is buying gifts for family and friends, on which 32% of shoppers spend up to ten minutes' (Williams 2002). Email, in contrast accounts for relatively little time spent online, since it is the second-least time-consuming activity. I am not concerned, here, with the authenticity or otherwise of these figures: what is significant is which accounts of online shopping are circulated in popular culture, and what they tell us about cultural attitudes to cyberconsumption.

It should be clear from these narratives of addiction that while online shopping may be associated with class privilege, this does not quite make for respectability. Rather, as online shopping takes up more and more time, it is all the more likely to be regarded as a private, even a secret activity. This insistence on privacy is embedded in the idea that shopping involves the gratification of deep, perhaps even shameful desires. Online shopping, because it is imagined as giving direct access to the object of desire (and because it allows the shopper to avoid physical effort) is imagined as wholly and unambiguously pleasurable, almost sybaritic, and as such it becomes sexualised. This analogy with sex again reinforces the idea that there is a need for privacy. For example, in the passage by Nigella Lawson (and in the assurance, on sites like Oxygen, that 'nobody need ever know') we can also identify a sense of shame. Online shopping may be a wholly private pleasure, but it is also a shameful one. The shame is a reaction to being caught out, and this is connected to an act of consumption, as well as one of fantasy and pleasure. What is more, I would suggest that this fear of being caught out involves a fantasy of being watched by an invisible other, one which plays on the fears and dangers that may be associated with cyberspace. Whilst online food shops suggest a fantasy of pleasurable, safe contact with the other, however, this fantasy of cyber-surveillance restores a sense of safety through the assurance that the shopper is ultimately in control of the experience. What both fantasies have in common is that they rely for their impact on the frisson of imagined proximity with the other: yet they also work to restore 'comfort' by reassuring the user that this computer-mediated contact is safer, more controllable (and hence ultimately more empowering) than the real thing. Indeed, comfort is restored at the moment when one realises that there is no other 'out there': that the other does not 'really' exist.

Hence, I would propose that gratification is not delayed as such; rather, gratification itself is displaced so that it arises not from having and using the commodity, but from a fantasy of engaging with a wider consumer culture, for example from feeling like a privileged cyber-consumer rather than a high-street shopper. This fantasy is facilitated by the way in which all the shopping sites above 'hail' the user, interpolating her within the role of consumer. This hailing takes the form of a direct first-person address ('makes you think, doesn't it?' 'You comfortable multi-tasker, you!'), or through an informal greeting ('Sweetie! Darling!') which flatters the consumer by appearing to assume that she is familiar with the culture of online shopping. It is by taking on the fantasy identity of cyberconsumer; that the consumer become free to engage in what is presented as one of the key pleasures of online shopping, one in which it differs from 'real' shopping – that is, engagement with the Other.

Eating the Other: 'the exotic' in Online Supermarkets

A central site of this type of encounter is online food shopping. The marketing of food online is marked by what Elspeth Probyn (2000) has termed 'foodism'. For Probyn, foodism refers to the current obsession, in the West, with food as a symbol of difference and social identity. Online, foodism operates through the selling of 'ethnic' foodstuffs which invokes a desire to eat the other, a violent fantasy in which the Internet becomes a kind of global delicatessen in which difference itself, rather than specific foods, is available for consumption. Below, I provide a close reading of British online supermarkets, paying close attention to the ways in which their promotion of 'exotic' foods works alongside the notion of virtuality to construct online shopping as a privileged (and implicitly classed) activity. I suggest a reading that brings together feminist accounts of consumption, drawing on bell hooks' notion of 'Eating the Other' (hooks 1992) together with theories of foodism (Probyn 2000), and commodity racism (McClintock 1995). Such a reading allows for an awareness of the ways in which these sites construct a fantasy of consuming the Other.

According to hooks, Western consumer culture has tended to reduce Otherness to the status of something that can be consumed, and to promote the idea that such a consumption of racial difference can be a source of pleasure. In this view of the relation between difference and consumption, 'ethnicity becomes spice, seasoning that can liven up the dull dish that is mainstream white culture' (1992: 21). This fantasy, which claims that engaging with Otherness can be a source of transgression and liberation, masks a desire to incorporate the Other without compromising one's own privileged position (1992: 23). Clearly, this fantasy of eating the other implies the relation between the consumer and the imagined Other to be one of domination. Probyn has compared the consumer in this sense to both a cannibal and a vampire, a rapacious figure constantly 'hungry for difference' (2000: 81). However, I think that cyberconsumption problematises the use of the term 'hunger'. As I have argued, cyberconsumerism constructs a false distinction between two kinds of need, the need for survival and the need for pleasure. That is, it creates an oppositional distinction between need and desire, but it simultaneously insists that both need and desire must be fulfilled. Here, I would suggest that in foodism, this distinction is overturned altogether, so that the fulfilment of desire is privileged over the fulfilment of physical 'needs'. Crucially, these two different needs then become associated with different kinds of food, so that certain foods are portrayed as a source of pleasure whilst others are not. As a result, online supermarkets relegate some foods to the category of 'necessities', as we shall see; and as a result, these foods are not seen as meriting their own websites. Hence, despite the fact that almost all foods have the potential to give pleasure as well as having nutritional value, a distinction between need and desire is necessary in order to maximise profits, since it allows, 'exotic' or luxurious foods to be heavily promoted: by presenting these foods as objects of desire, they can command greatly increased prices.

'Exotic' foods, then, are presented as a means of gratifying more complex appetites than the mere desire for survival, and consumption is presented as a compulsive activity, in which gratification is constantly deferred. This 'compulsive' quality implies a sense of anxiety. Firstly, as Lury (1996) demonstrates, the act of shopping may itself come to be seen as excessive. Studies of shopping behaviour have demonstrated that the figure of the 'shopaholic', so often mobilised by shopping sites as both humorous and harmless, may mask real experiences of addiction which arise precisely from the normalisation of shopping addiction within popular culture

(Rook and Hoch 1985, Rook and Fisher 1995). In the case of shopping addiction, the consumer herself becomes 'consumed' with desire. Whilst eating the other implies a destructive act, this fantasy is always open to the possibility of the Other's return. Such a return is imagined in terms of a terrible revenge in which the white subject itself is consumed.

The fetishisation of Otherness is necessarily concerned with racial difference. Anne McClintock's use of the term 'commodity racism' is helpful here as a means of understanding the complex networks of desire that characterise cyberconsumerism (McClintock 1995). Although McClintock's argument is concerned with a specific geographical and historical location, much of her analysis is relevant in terms of online consumer culture today. In particular, cyberconsumerism creates particular fetish objects (in this case food) as a means of bringing into being a global culture, albeit one centred on America rather than Europe. Again like the soap ads cited by McClintock, it is concerned with boundaries, although now the dominant fantasy is of boundaries broken down, transgressed, or elided, rather than rigidly policed. Furthermore, the modern, online version of commodity racism, despite its implicit dependence on 'third world' labour, is not concerned with direct oppression of the other, or with justifying any clearly defined colonial project. Rather, it reduces the non-English speaking world to a homogeneous mass vaguely defined as 'ethnic'. Hence, the other is defined as that which 'has' that ethnicity which, according to bell hooks, is offered to the Western consumer as 'a new delight' (1992: 21).

Access to different forms of 'spice', through shopping, is one of the attractions of online consumer culture. Nevertheless, the fantasy of ethnicity as spice is also present in theories of virtual culture. WoN is a loose collective of international feminist activists, including many women working in the 'third world' who discuss their work via an email bulletin board (or 'listserv'). Their objective is to empower women, especially 'third world' and other marginalised women, by bringing them into the developing Internet culture. In doing this, it aims to allow a more diverse range of women's voices to be heard and to intervene in feminist debates, as well as providing technical and practical support. In *Women@Internet* (1999), Wendy Harcourt uses the image of cyberspace as a delicatessen to describe the WoN listserv group on which these discussions are held, and by extension (potentially) the Internet as a whole. She discusses the need to imagine the meeting space as a 'real' place, through 'poetic, personal and political language', and comes up with the image of a delicatessen: 'an image of the corner shop with all the delicious things to see and eat from around the world, a very safe but spicy idea' (1999: 15). This is developed further in a later article:

> We have a 'delicatessen' offered for the tasting by the Women on the Web (WoN). They present the spice of what these new communication technologies offer and the tempting new ways to experience one another, suggesting a new closeness as women (with men) explore and create a cyberculture. Lurking in these new sensations and experiences are the voices warning us to consider carefully that such a mixture of cultures, hopes and visions might well fragment on the tasting. They are housed in a not so congenial structure, and it is uncertain from just where the ingredients come (Harcourt 1999: 219).

The 'we' here is ambiguous: is Harcourt including herself (we have a delicatessen that we offer to you, the reader), or does she rather seek to align herself with the reader (WoN have a delicatessen that they offer to 'us')? Either way, the image of the delicatessen seems at odds with WoN's radical project of putting women's experience back at the centre of analyses of online community, as Kali Tal notes in her review of the book. For Tal, the notion of 'safe spaces' in itself implies a danger that some women will become marginalised in order to create a feeling of safety for the majority. For example, Tal criticises the WoN group's decision to close a discussion on Aboriginal land rights as indicative of an inability to deal with difference:

> There were no Aboriginal women on the listserv but the tension that developed between urban and rural white women was severe enough to disturb the sense of 'safety' and 'community' of list members. In communities that value 'safety' above all, the interests of some women must be sacrificed for the comfort of other women ... [T]his puts 'feeling good' in front of inclusivity, since consensus is rarely achievable in truly diverse groups with genuine (and perhaps irreconcilable) differences. Without a strategy for conflict resolution and with pressure for consensus, 'others' are silenced for the good of 'all' (Tal 2001).

The fear that some women will be silenced in order to construct a 'safe space' is reinforced, for Tal, by Harcourt's use of the delicatessen metaphor, which she calls 'a textbook example of Orientalism' to describe such a space (Tal 2001). This exchange illustrates that the discourse of women's relationship with new technology as primarily one of consumption is powerful and pervasive. In the following section, I look more closely at the ways in which discourses of cyberconsumption mobilise certain cultural myths about race, class and gender, and how these fantasies naturalise the desire to appropriate the other. Taking my lead from the debate between Harcourt and Tal, my argument explores these themes in relation to 'ethnic' foods to examine how the online purchase of spice is imagined in terms of an 'authentic', but safe, encounter with an exotic other.

The Global Bazaar

The anxieties surrounding shopping as a whole, and online shopping in particular, are clearly related to class as well as gender. The women's magazine and shopping site Handbag addresses the question of class directly in its description of the 'typical' user:

> She is likely to be ABC1, and either married or living with a partner in the home she owns. In her spare time (of which there is little!), she enjoys the cinema and reading magazines – particularly the women's and home improvements titles. There'll be a bottle of good quality wine in her weekly shop, and she is constantly on the search for a good book. As a voracious shopper, she purchases by mail order and online.[21]

In other words, the 'typical' user is a middle-class heterosexual woman whose identity is defined almost entirely in terms of consumption.

21 www.handbag.com/About-us/v1, accessed 28 November 2008.

Again, the image is one of greed: like Net-A-Porter woman, Handbag woman is 'voracious', driven by an insatiable desire to shop, to devour everything that is 'out there'. Hence, online shopping is, by implication, the answer to one of her most fundamental needs, the need to pack in as much shopping time as possible. In this fantasy, the conditions of cyberspace are used to create the illusion that shopping itself is an activity unbounded by geographical or bodily constraints. Further, virtual shopping creates the impression that everything is accessible. This fantasy of being able to buy absolutely anything recalls the myth of with upper-class (and perhaps *nouveau riche*) privilege associated with 'exclusive' department stores such as Harrods, which prided itself on being able to provide anything its customers asked for, however obscure.

In the virtual supermarket the illusion of unlimited travel is compromised by a need to explain how food is actually delivered to the consumer's home. Supermarkets are keen to emphasise the fact that individual customers' orders are hand-picked, and then delivered in a van (the image of the van, especially, recurs on almost every page of Sainsbury's' home shopping site). The fetishisation of this icon of class privilege gives an impression of exclusivity, which is carried over into reassurances of the authenticity of particular foods; the sites are careful to evoke the upper-middle-class ideal of having one's food delivered by tradesmen, and just as keen to distance themselves from the (decidedly working-class) phenomenon of catalogue shopping. The notion of class distinction is apparent in the fantasy of shopping in comfort, since middle-class Western subjectivity is precisely that which is at-home in the role of consumer, and in relations of consumption which involve being waited on rather than serving oneself. This privileged subjectivity is linked to a similar differentiation between bodies; the privilege body is capable of consumption, of taking-in. Hence, 'comfort' suggests both racial and class privilege. Seated comfortably in front of her computer screen, the Western consumer is able both to travel freely, and to remain fixed. Whilst she may temporarily transcend the limits of the corporeal to travel in cyberspace looking for new forms of otherness, she does not expect to interact with real people and places. Otherness is simply the fantasy that makes certain kinds of food desirable. The fantasy of travel is ultimately closed off by the fact that food is brought to the consumer.

Although all virtual supermarkets and shopping malls sell a wide range of food and other household goods, many of the sites I looked at in the course of my research contained large amounts of advertising, especially for new products, or more expensive products such as ready-prepared meals. That is to say, although shopping for groceries online is not necessarily a fantastic activity, these sites encourage their customers to spend more by 'buying into' a form of online shopping which is fantastic rather than simply instrumental. Customers are encouraged to engage with the online store as a starting-point for virtual travel, rather than simply as a more convenient way to shop. In this sense, the advent of the virtual supermarket marks a radical move away from the traditional image of supermarkets, which have previously presented themselves as a strictly functional and cost-effective place to shop (Bowlby 1997: 96). The idea of 'shopping in comfort' outlined above sets out the conditions in which this engagement takes place; once the consumer feels comfortable, she can transcend the limits of her body and go on a virtual journey whose pleasures stem from a (mediated) encounter with Otherness, in the form of spicy foods.

One such online supermarket is Sainsbury's, which devotes a whole section of its website to regional foods from different countries, particularly its Oriental and Regional Italian ranges. The homepage for the former draws on images of virtual travel, as well as the real-life benefits of having food delivered; users are encouraged to click on links to pages representing different geographical regions, but the sense of world travel is contradicted by the ubiquitous image of the white delivery van and the reminder to 'order your Oriental food – from Sainsbury's to you'. The site emphasises themes of exploration and discovery; the headline, displayed against a background of the sun setting behind back-lit pagodas, with Chinese lanterns and banners in the foreground, reads 'Discover New Flavours of the Orient', and the text states that the range consists of 'authentic' foods, 'many of which are first to Sainsbury's!' The food is presented as both authentic and, crucially as representative of regional difference, as the following passage shows:

> Sainsbury's re-labelled Oriental range contains easy-to-prepare dishes and ingredients from seven countries from around the Orient. From the four regions of China, as well as food from Japan, Singapore, Thailand, Malaysia, Vietnam and Indonesia – all authentically prepared dishes and ingredients typical of the region.[22]

Here, the emphasis on authenticity is significant, since it suggests that what Sainsbury's is selling here is difference rather than Otherness. This is crucial; to return to hooks, commodity culture is violent in that it positions white Western culture as the norm, whilst grouping all other ethnic groups together as Other. The process of Othering thus denies specificity. By making distinctions between the regional cuisines of seven different countries, and by insisting that the dishes are authentically prepared, the site avoids accusations of grouping all 'spicy' foods together. This implies that the consumer is being invited to learn more about the lived experience of people from different cultures, and also flatters the consumer by reassuring her that her interest in those cultures is more informed and less ignorant than that of other shoppers. In doing so it invokes an image of cosmopolitanism, in which the user is made to feel like a virtual traveller in a multicultural world, and hence to avoid any anxiety that might stem from feeling her engagement with other cultures to be exploitative or racist. Indeed, the site is different from 'real' Sainsbury's stores in that it is harder for users to ignore this fantasy of virtual travel; all customers are addressed as though they thought of the foods on offer as 'different' and 'exotic', and no attempt is made to address those who might want to buy those foods precisely because they are familiar.

Sainsbury's use of 'world cuisine' as a symbol of the 'multicultural' and 'cosmopolitan' is widespread in consumer culture (see Cook and Crang 1996). This would seem to offer a more positive reading of consumer culture's engagement with difference, one which contradicts William

22 www.sainsburys.co.uk/food/mealideas/foodforyourmood/oriental_flavours/, accessed 28 November 2008.

O'Barr's view that otherness in advertising serves to reinforce existing boundaries between people of different ethnicities, rather than to challenge them (O'Barr 1994). However, as Daniel Miller has noted, there has been some debate as to whether cosmopolitanism in taste 'is relevant to a cosmopolitanism expressed in tolerant or positive attitudes to peoples of varied or plural origin' (2001: 114, and see Cheah and Robins 1998). What is more, cosmopolitanism is a problematic model for thinking through issues of multiculturalism, since 'tolerant' or 'positive' attitudes in themselves do not necessarily have any effect on the realities of consumer culture, which may remain materially exploitative. I think the notion of the 'cosmopolitan' is itself fantastic, in that it is mobilised in order to create the idea of a non-exploitative engagement with, rather than a violent incorporation of the other, which satisfies the Western consumer's need for reassurance (indeed, for comfort) in the face of the anxiety that her desire for otherness may indeed be racist.

For example, in the case of the Sainsbury's site, the notion of cosmopolitanism is invoked in order to distinguish between the site's customers and other, less well-informed (and hence, perhaps, more 'racist') consumers. This recalls Pierre Bourdieu's argument, in *Distinction*, that consumers use consumption as a means of distinguishing themselves from others (Bourdieu 1984), although in this sense 'the other' is a lower-class Westerner rather than an inhabitant of the 'Oriental' cultures whose foods are for sale on the site. As well as reassuring the user that she is a cosmopolitan and non-racist consumer, then, the term 'authentic' serves another purpose in that it creates a distinction between middle-class and working-class consumers. As Miller argues, Western attitudes to 'foreign' food are often as constitutive of class relations within Western culture, as of relations between ethnic groups. According to Miller, middle-class shoppers 'manipulate' the ethnicity of food as a means of securing social prestige, and distinguishing themselves from the working class:

> There may be considerable prestige attached to making sure one's recipe for palm oil stew is 'authentically' West African and carried out to the letter, or if South Asian 'curry' has become part of working-class food, then middle-class emphasis will be on the precise distinctions between the regional cuisines of Maharashtra and Tamil Nadu (Miller 2001: 117).

Whilst working-class culture absorbs dishes like curry sauce and Vindaloo, which it sees as 'British', Miller says that middle-class consumers distance themselves from this culture by continually moving on to new, ever more authentic foods (2001: 117–18). Sainsbury's website, with its reiteration of 'authenticity' alongside notions of discovery and 'the new', continues this process. But the virtual shop is different from other sites of consumption in that it draws on notions of virtual travel to promote the fantasy that the user can actually come into contact with the other culture. By clicking on the link for China or Japan, the consumer is made to feel that she is able to cross continents at the click of a mouse. Hence, the site works to create a fantasy of engaging with those sites of Otherness that are associated with the desirable notion of 'authenticity' (e.g. 'the Orient'), whilst creating boundaries which exclude the less desirable, working-class Other.

These distinctions are problematised, then, by a reading that sees 'authenticity' as a fantasy. In particular, the claim that foods are 'authentically prepared' does not stand up to close scrutiny. Although the Oriental range includes some fresh ingredients such as Chinese salad leaves, the range consists mostly of mass-produced, ready-made meals.[23] What is more, the emphasis on the regionality of particular foods is largely cosmetic; although the store's range of Chinese ready-meals is divided up according to the four traditional regions of Chinese cuisine, each of the other six countries listed above constitutes a single region. The design of the site further undermines the notion of regionalism; click on the caption 'regional food' at the top right of the screen, and a drop-down

23 This section has now been removed from Sainsbury's website at www.sainsburys.com, perhaps in response to changes in Sainsbury's Oriental food ranges. However it should be noted that the supermarket recently had to apologise over one of its television commercials, also for the Oriental range, which featured the celebrity chef Jamie Oliver speaking in a caricatured 'Chinese' accent, after it was criticised by an ITC report on racism in advertising (http://www.brandrepublic.com/News/15817/Sainsbury-apologises-oriental-Jamie-Oliver-ad/: accessed 8 December 2008). The accusation of racism, and the potential damage to the brand that it implies, is perhaps another explanation for the disappearance of some of the materials I discuss here.

menu appears listing just two regions. The first is Chinese, and the second groups together Japanese, Singaporean and Thai cuisines. Each of these links takes the user to a single page with a paragraph on each country's (or in the case of China, each of the four regions') cooking, together with images which continue the Orientalist clichés seen on the site's homepage together with a scattering of facts about each country, headed 'did you know?'. So, for example, the section on Japan tells us that 'the Japanese have the longest life span of any nation on Earth', suggesting perhaps that we, as Western consumers, might increase our longevity by eating Sainsbury's Japanese foods; and the page on China includes the information that 'more people live in Shanghai than in the whole of Australia!' although the page devotes only one short paragraph to describing the food of Shanghai. By classifying such vast areas as 'regions', the site constructs 'the Orient' as a fantastic location (and again closes off the possibility of addressing Japanese or Chinese users, to whom these 'facts' might seem irrelevant or absurd), a process which is further implied by the omission of other south-east Asian countries whose cuisine is less familiar to British consumers. Whilst the site makes considerable claims to recognition of authentic difference and variety, the use of the term 'Orient' denies any such differentiation.

The fantasy being constructed here, which presents food shopping as a safe means of encountering the Other, can also be seen in non-virtual shopping environments, including the 'Oriental' sections of 'real' Sainsbury's supermarkets. Yet virtual shopping is different in two ways. The first, outlined in detail in the previous section, is that by linking Orientalist fantasies to the notion of 'shopping in comfort', cyberconsumption foregrounds fantasy in such a way that the liberated consumer, transcending the limitations of the flesh, is assumed to be in touch with her desires, her appetites for difference, to a far greater degree than ordinary shoppers. In this, online shopping is different from the process of Eating the Other that bell hooks describes. Hooks states that when race and ethnicity are reduced to the status of commodities, 'the culture of specific groups, as well as the bodies of individuals, can be seen as constituting a symbolic playground', where members of dominant groups 'affirm their power-over in intimate relations with the Other' (1992: 23). Whilst the question, 'what can't I buy' certainly works to portray the Web as a playground, one in which the consumer is free to try on new identities (including that of cyberconsumer), this fantasy works precisely because it is not intimate. Online, one does not come into contact with the Other; rather, the self is privileged to such an extent that everything else becomes Other; what the consumer experiences is their own desires, which are assumed to be embodied in a stereotypical fantasy of 'the Orient'. Online shopping is hence a 'safer' and more 'comfortable' means of acting out the desire for the Other because it does not expose the consumer to accusations of racism, nor does it involve the 'dangers' of real-life travel. Protected by the screen, and spared the sight of the Other's body, the cyberconsumer does not even experience her power-over as such. Whilst the spectacle of difference might still arouse feelings of power, the user is encouraged to internalise this power and to experience it as personal empowerment, rather than power over others.

Online shopping works to amplify a sense of affective attachment and intensity through the consumer's relationship both to the commodity itself, and to a fantasy of the self-as-consumer. The relation between consumer and product is fraught with tensions and anxieties that stem from the inescapable links between the disembodied act of consumption, and the materiality of the commodity itself which often takes the form of 'something for the body' – clothes, cosmetics or food. However, through an appeal to 'safety', cyberconsumption also becomes about protecting the body: that is, the body is left behind not only to avoid the indignities of queuing or battling for parking spaces, but also to protect it from more sinister assaults. In the following, and final, section, I examine how fantasies of safety overturn the narratives of desire for the Other invoked in the websites cited above, to suggest the logical outcome of such fantasies – that is, the fear that the other, uncontrollable after all, might return to destroy the subject.

Shopping for National Security

What all the websites I have read have to offer is 'retail therapy', or, more exactly, the idea of retail as therapy, offering shopping as an antidote to the discomforts and dangers of life in the twenty-first century. The cyber-consumer is presented as an empowered subject, whose agency lies precisely in her ability to live with the lack of agency implied in the need to shop. Although the notion of shopping in comfort and safety suggests anxiety, implying that one was not comfortable or safe before, it also offers the hope of transcendence. The cyber-consumer, unlike her counterparts on the high street, is imagined as having escaped; she is supposed to feel utterly safe and at ease, as though she has come through a difficult course of therapy and is now at ease with herself. This privileged position comes about through a higher form of consumption, one which has a healing power superior to that of mere shopping, and involves a more-complex and multi-layered consumption: that is, consumption of texts, technologies and fantasies, as well as commodities. Whilst fantasy is also a feature of RL shopping, cyberconsumption is imagined as opening up the possibility for a purer and more authentic experience of consumption because it allows for transcendence of the body.

Why, then, does the consumer still feel unsafe? As I have shown, the over-determination of the terms 'safety' and 'comfort' suggests an implicit fear of danger and discomfort. Partly, this arises from an implicit failure of the transcendence promised by cyberconsumption; that is, following Allucquère Roseanne Stone's notion of the virtual subject, the cyber-consumer may temporarily take on a privileged point of view, but 'there is always a body attached' (1991: 111). This body may be situated in the home, or in an EasyEverything cybercafé, neither of which are unproblematically safe and comfortable spaces. The boundaries of 'home' may be breached by burglars or violent criminals, or violence may emanate from within the home itself. Similarly, whilst online malls may allow the fearful consumer to shop without going out into the streets at the risk of becoming a victim of terrorism (or 'street crime', its British equivalent in terms of popular fears), the commodities themselves arrive in the mail, as do anthrax parcels, letter bombs, and fire; the letterbox itself may be the conduit through which desired commodities and communications arrive, or it may be a point of weakness, letting the outside in.

Soon after the terrorist attacks of September 11 2001, urban myths began to circulate on the Internet, suggesting that further attacks were imminent. One email, which achieved particularly wide circulation, insisted that these attacks would take place in shopping malls on Halloween, 31 October 2001.[24] Partly as a result of this and similar messages, and partly because of the reduced 'consumer confidence' that follows any such disaster, newspapers reported that fewer people were going shopping: a survey carried out in late September found that 'confidence among British consumers had plunged to its lowest since the previous recession 10 years ago', whilst the IMF said that in America, a recession was 'a done deal' as a result of a similar slump (Thornton 2001). 'Disaster shopping' and 'disaster cooking', that is, tips on how to stockpile food to survive earthquakes and other natural disasters, were already a feature of some online shopping guides, especially in the United States; after September 11, these sites also began to instruct users on how to survive terrorist attack. At the same time, some online shopping sites were quick to present Internet shopping as a safer alternative to leaving the house in search of provisions. What is more, online shopping became constructed as a form of patriotism; the virtual consumer was urged not only to store food and other essentials, but also to continue to buy consumer goods as part of a civic duty to help prevent a recession. Shopping, so often viewed as a frivolous way to waste time, hence became a respectable way of exercising citizenship. As a result, the Internet became a crucial means of performing consumer citizenship.

This brings me to the final version of the slogan: 'shopping in the safety of your own home'. Historically, questions of safety have been constructed as especially relevant to women, whose movement outside the home is assumed to be limited despite feminist research suggesting that

24 The full text of this email is reproduced at the Urban Legends Page: http://www.snopes2.com/rumors/mallrisk.htm.

women are far more likely to encounter violence within the home than outside it. As a result, the idea of 'shopping in your pyjamas' as 'liberating' has a deeper resonance for women, who might feel unsafe leaving the house after dark, being confined instead to the domestic sphere. If Western woman's identity as a citizen is associated with her power as a consumer, then, the ability to shop at night might seem to offer a breaking down of the boundaries between these clearly delineated spheres, appearing to allow women to exercise their citizenship more freely and to resist confinement in the home. Such a fantasy is potentially dangerous, though, not only because it does nothing to ensure women's safety if they do venture outside, but also because one is supposed to shop for things for the body and things for the home, probably objects one has read about in fashion and 'home improvement' magazines.

Moreover, it is not only individual safety that is at stake here. According to online shopping malls such as Delamez Unlimited, online shopping is specifically associated with fears about national security in the wake of September 11. Alongside links to stereotypical women's interest stories (including an interview with Oprah Winfrey), the online shopping mall's homepage displays an American flag with the tag line, 'During this time when safety is a concern, doesn't it make sense to shop online?' The blurb for another article entitled 'Older, Wiser and More Anxious', reproduced from *Time* magazine, says that 'stress over world events is affecting the elderly. So have you emailed your grandparents today?'[25] Ironically, the article goes on to list the factors causing this stress, one of which is 'isolation'. The solution implicitly offered by the site is to stay indoors, but to keep in touch with friends and family via email, and with society as a whole by shopping, which becomes, here, both an assertion of citizenship and a demonstration of personal freedom. Again, this model of consumer citizenship is linked to a specifically American world-view, with the rest of the world portrayed as Other; either the world of the exotic which is laid open for consumption (the delicatessen metaphor),

25 Dickinson, A. (2001) 'Older, Wiser and More Anxious', *Time*, Monday 1 December, available at http://www.time.com/time/magazine/article/0,9171,1001360,00.html, accessed 8 December 2008.

or as the source of danger, a threat to civilisation (which is equated with consumer culture). Cyberconsumption hence becomes not only a means of fulfilling one's personal fantasies, but also the process by which the national community is held together in an emergency.

In the previous two chapters, I traced the conflicting narratives which construct the Web as a space in which it is possible to 'find oneself', either through erasure of the physical body or, paradoxically, by allowing a space in which to make oneself visible. These issues are not generally considered relevant to the culture of online shopping, which is generally understood in purely instrumental terms, either as a simply a more 'convenient' way of carrying out a routine activity, or as a cynical tool by which big business hopes to annexe the contested spaces of the Internet. Yet, as I have shown, online shopping and banking sites draw upon precisely those narratives of self-discovery, liberation and belonging outlined in the previous two chapters to construct a powerful fantasy figure – that of the cyberconsumer. If shopping is seen as a civic duty, as I have argued, the cyberconsumer is constructed as enjoying a privileged form of consumer citizenship. In this, online consumer culture capitalises on precisely that sense of isolation which critics fear will lead to increasing alienation and estrangement as the popularity of the Internet continues to rise. Yet the isolation of the online shopper is never imagined as such, since online shopping sites employ imagery associated with virtual travel to suggest that consumers might go anywhere, and engage with any culture they like. This engagement is presented as liberating, in a way which draws on a misreading of early radical narratives of virtual existence which, unlike online shopping, imagined cyberspace as pleasurable and important precisely to the extent that it was not safe or comfortable. In the culture of online consumption, in contrast, notions of comfort and safety are overstated (indeed, the fantasy that one is comfortable and safe is one of the things being consumed by the cyberconsumer), as the means by which one frees oneself to transcend the body and engage with one's deepest desires, desires which, it is implied, can always be gratified by some form of consumption.

According to this vision of the consumer as desiring subject, who transcends the body only in order to buy things for the body, narratives of cyberconsumption unwittingly confirm bell hooks' notion of the privileged subject as that which sees itself as neutral, yet it seeks encounters with Otherness as a means of adding 'spice' to the 'dull dish' that is its own existence (hooks 1992: 21). Online consumer culture takes this further, encouraging the consumer to see herself, during the act of consumption, as more neutral, to see the taking-on of a neutral point of view as one of the special privileges associated with online shopping. This neutral point of view is privileged in that it allows the user to situate herself as universal consumer, as that which is able to take in. Transcending the body (which is left behind in, but importantly is not abandoned but rather left in comfort), the online consumer is reduced to a restless, desiring, virtual presence, a ghost in the machine, whilst the rest of the world becomes a bazaar in which Otherness is commodified and displayed for her pleasure.

Despite its constant reiteration, the fantasy of becoming a cyberconsumer is constantly in danger of being disrupted; the constant reassurance that one is comfortable and safe opens up the possibility for discomfort and danger. Indeed, in the 'disaster shopping' sites I read in the previous section, danger is always assumed as the motivation for shopping online. Hypertext itself carries the possibility of encountering less docile Others than those who appear, neatly packaged and ripe for incorporation, on commercial websites, proving that the Web can be used for purposes which are intended to be transgressive and threatening, as well as for those that are soothing and comforting. Whilst commercial interests use the Web as a convenient and safe space in which to encounter the Other (however illusory that safety might be), the Web's very accessibility means that it is open to being used by others as a space through which to become visible, to speak. In the next chapter, I explore how one online community has used the Web in precisely this way, refusing the separation of mind and body that is implicit in cyberconsumption, and examine what is at stake in such a refusal by focussing on the consequences for that community.

CHAPTER 5

Pro-Ana: Writing the Virtual Body

'Pro-ana' and 'pro-mia' are the names given to personal homepages that deal with the experience of living with an eating disorder. These sites are published on the Web by young anorexic women who see eating disorders as an identity position, rather than as a disease. The image of an emaciated female body with the head cropped is typical of representations of the body in pro-ana. These images are usually presented as pictures of the site author's own body (the heads are left off to protect the author's identity, since many of these, often very young women are running these sites without the knowledge of their families and peers). Despite the strategy of removing the head, the body is not detached from the subject; since many of the sites contain diaries, poetry and other highly personal material alongside representations of the author's body, the effect is to imply that body and subjectivity are inseparable. It is through sharing this view of subjectivity that pro-ana authors come to see themselves as members of a community.

In other words, these sites construct a community that is rooted in anorexic embodiment. The anorexic body, the body shown in these pictures, is the basis of the community, that is, the body is what members of the community 'have in common', both as an ideal, and as lived experience. In pro-ana, the community itself is rooted in the corporeal, and a sense of belonging derives from a sense of coming into contact with other bodies which are both like (one's own), and different (from what is seen as the norm). Being located on the Web means that they are easily accessed by search engines, and can be accessed freely without the need to negotiate security channels. However, it also makes them vulnerable to censorship, especially by large corporate ISPs, as we shall see. My point here, though, is that that pro-ana sites make the anorexic body visible in two ways: firstly by exploiting the possibilities of the medium to produce highly visual sites incorporating photographs and colourful graphics, and secondly by reaching a very wide potential audience. Moreover, as I noted in Chapter 1, early feminist responses to digital culture focussed on the question of whether the visual content of much of the Web consisted of 'normative' images of femininity (Wise 1997). Whilst the question of what constitutes a normative image is debatable (and while studies of the Web have emphasised the ways in which it challenges a 'media effects' model of celebrity culture, making new forms of participation possible; see for example Stefanoni et al. 2008), there is no doubt that pro-ana is hypertextually 'linked in' to a network of feminine imagery centring on images of fashion and celebrity culture. As a result it constantly juxtaposes images of 'marginal' anorexic bodies alongside 'normal' bodies (which may themselves be extremely thin) such that, as Karen Dias notes, 'if the models and celebrities were not familiar to us, it would be very difficult to discern between the "deviant" bodies of the anorexics and the "normal" and "acceptable" bodies of the models' (2003: 6). This is highly significant in the context of a media culture which opposes, not just thin and fat, but the 'in balance' and the 'out of balance', with 'balance' defined increasingly narrowly (Ferreday 2008).

Pro-ana is thus seen as resisting an externally imposed separation between the ideal celebrity body, and the abject body of the anorexic. In this, it can be read as a radical misuse of the notion of community. Pro-ana proposes an intercorporeal relationship between thin bodies: a community of the very thin which cuts across the rhetoric of divide and rule which characterises popular appropriations of feminist discourse. In this chapter I want to suggest that the great outpouring of hostility to pro-ana that we have seen in recent years, and are still seeing, is an attempt to wrench apart this intercorporeal bond. It is unsurprising that it should be the Internet that constitutes the theatre for this radically unsettling performance of community. It is possible to read one of the best theoretical accounts of anorexic subjectivity as a claim that the anorexic body is imagined as always already virtual.

The dialogue between Gilles Deleuze and the journalist Claire Parnet contains only a brief section on anorexia, though the figure of the anorexic weaves in and out of the text, for example in their returning to the question of whether Virginia Woolf's *Orlando*, with its fluid temporal and elemental shifts, required Woolf's anorexia for its genesis (2007: 37). Anorexia hence becomes linked with both writing and affect: after all, 'one only writes through love' (38). As Isabelle Meuret elegantly summarises, for Deleuze, 'writing and anorexia are two sides of the same coin' (2008: 80). For Deleuze and Parnet moreover, anorexia is a 'political system' a manifesto recording a desire 'to escape from the norms of consumption, in order not to be an object of consumption oneself' (2007: 67).

For Deleuze, the anorexic body is thus what he and Felix Guattari call a body without organs (1972, 1987). It is not my intention here to give an overview of Deleuzian theory, but it is worth noting that although interpretations of the body without organs differ, it can be read as a way of seeing the body in terms of its potential: that is, as virtual (Massumi 2002: 106). The anorexic occupies a paradoxical position, defying the logic of consumption, embodying at once life and death or, as Deleuze and Parnet put it, 'fullness' and 'the void' (2007: 110). Anorexic subjectivity is hence unintelligible to medicine, which reduces everything 'to the level of a neuro-organic or symbolic code ("lack, lack")' (2007: 111). This reduction of anorexic subjectivity to a model of desire based on lack is, I would argue, what lies at the heart of the objections to pro-ana that I am about to describe. Anorexia is imagined as a linear progression of becoming thin that begins in, but then pathologically diverges from, the desire to achieve an ideal feminine appearance. The (normal, healthy) desire to 'look good' is imagined as becoming fatally conflated with a desire for thinness which has its own inescapable linear trajectory (i.e. towards death). Such a view of anorexia as a moving-towards a final destination refuses to acknowledge the power of the anorexic as a boundary figure, a figure in tension between life and death. Further, this view constitutes a turning-away from the power of anorexic subjectivity as a site of resistance to consumer identity. If, as I argued in the previous chapter, shopping has become both a central focus of ideas about virtuality and desire, and one of the primary means by which citizenship is performatively constituted, then the figure of the anorexic as she-who-does-not-consumer is potentially a powerfully unsettling emblem of resistance.

I do not wish to claim, here, that pro-ana is inherently subversive, for to do so would simply be to reproduce the logic that calls for its censorship on the grounds that pro-ana authors are a danger to themselves and others. What I am suggesting is that both pro-ana and anti-pro-ana narratives share a fantasy of pro-ana as resistant, albeit in different ways. In thinking through the ways in which pro-ana functions at the level of fantasy, we need to keep in mind Sara Ahmed and Jackie Stacey's comments on the re-imagining of bodies. Following their argument, we can see that through fantasy the body is re-imaged and re-lived, 'but the possibilities for the re-imagining and re-living are not endless, or a matter of choice' (Ahmed and Stacey 2001: 9). Whilst pro-ana threatens the view of anorexia as Other since it disrupts the view that it is always possible to 'tell the difference' between anorexic and 'ideal' bodies, this is not to claim that such a threat is always intentional. Nevertheless, there is a subversive power in pro-ana's concern with the areas in which the dividing line is thinnest, in its implication that the level of body obsession and thinness associated with normative femininity is not so different from, and certainly not in opposition to, anorexia itself.

This disruption occurs on the sites themselves, in the form of so-called 'thinspiration' pages. These pages, which are a feature of most pro-ana sites, show pictures of famously thin actresses and models. These bodies are offered for consumption by the pro-ana community, as 'triggers' or 'thinspiration'; by looking at them, the anorexic reader is meant to inspire herself to ever greater feats of self-denial. This practice has occasionally provoked responses from the stars themselves; for example, Zoe Brennan quotes 'a spokesman for [the supermodel] Jodie Kidd' who says, 'Jodie will feel very, very upset about this. The dreadful thing about websites like this is that we have no control over them using her image, so there's absolutely nothing we can do' (Brennan 2001). Kidd herself is absent, here: the 'we' who defend her 'image' are the image-makers: there is no 'self' to be protected, only the sacred image under threat from the unknown and unknowable cyberspace Other. Kidd-as-image is hence imagined as under attack in much the same way as the canon, the notion of authorship itself, comes under attack from the threatening multiplicity and heteroglossia of online authorship.

Brennan's article claims that the picture of Kidd, on an unnamed site, had been doctored so that the model looked 'like a concentration camp victim'. Certainly, Kidd is a popular subject of thinspiration pictures: one site, Xtremity, has an entire gallery of images taken from magazines and other websites, under the heading, 'Jodie Kidd, although she has put on weight recently, is the embodiment of anorexic strength and purity'. The images do include one rather shocking, but very obviously computer-generated image that is captioned as such. Otherwise, they consist of a great many more pictures which are also widely available on fan sites, and in which she is indeed extremely thin.[1] This is not to deny that the images may already have been retouched professionally. What I find interesting (although I do not know for certain that this is the website which caused Kidd's 'people' such consternation) is firstly the fact that one very obviously altered photograph is used to deny the realism of the other images on display, and secondly the assumption that certain practices, such as retouching, and using pictures of models for inspiration whilst dieting, are normal in some hands, but become dangerous, obsessive and pathological in others.

I would like to focus, here, on this question of retouching since I think it highlights some key ways in which pro-ana sites differ from other images and stories about the anorexic body. The difference, here, has to do with relations of power, specifically with the question of who decides which images are authentic and which are false. In other media, such as women's magazines, the relation of looking is fundamentally hierarchical. The slender body is handed down as ideal, and the (female) reader is expected to aspire to transform her own body in order to conform to that ideal. It is widely accepted, however, that the ideal body is not natural but

1 www.xtremity-journal.oopage.com/photo4.html, accessed 8 December 2008. Although Kidd subsequently gained weight and reinvented herself as a television celebrity in the BBC series *Strictly Come Dancing*, she remains an important figure for pro-ana, not least for being the first model to be dismissed from a catwalk show for being too thin. Kidd's changing weight is documented on the lifestyle website Female First: www.xtremity-journal.oopage.com/photo4.html, accessed 8 December 2008.

constructed. The model's body is subjected to the discipline of diet and exercise, pasted with theatrical make-up, and extensively retouched before being made available for consumption. However, the advent of desktop publishing packages such as Photoshop, together with the highly visual style of the Web in contrast with early Unix-based Internet applications, has made it much easier to alter images, and to distribute the results.

The juxtaposition of famously thin bodies with anonymous, faceless anorexic women calls into question the normality of those bodies. More precisely, it highlights the potential for disgust which, it has been argued, is always implied by Western culture's obsessive, fascinated desire to look at the feminine body. Indeed, the notion of disgust is inextricably entwined in feminist discussions of practices of looking: a theme which emerges as early as Laura Mulvey's declaration that disgust is 'the last resort', final outcome of Western culture's preoccupation with the to-be-looked-at-ness of the female body. Mulvey's discussion of the work of Cindy Sherman's photographs of entrails drew attention to the pervasive cultural status of disgust as the limit of pleasure, 'the end of the road, the secret bodily fluids that the cosmetic is designed to conceal'. Disgust is the borderline at which 'the topography of exterior/interior is exhausted' (cited in Probyn 2000: 127).

Thinspiration photographs aim to transgress the boundaries of the body (the bones visible as barely contained within, or emerging out of, the toned and tanned flesh); however, by claiming that the body of the actress or model is like that of the anorexic, they also call into question the relationship between image and practice and, by extension, public and private. The implication is that, though an appeal to a sense of shared praxis, the pro-ana community is able to reach out and claim famous women as members. Whilst mainstream culture may present some extremely thin bodies as ideal, then, pro-ana claims that in private they are no different from the headless torsos that characterise its own visual economy. The implication is that women like Kidd may be engaging in practices such as bingeing and vomiting, and that the combination of these practices together with a celebratory attitude to the resulting thin body, they are always already pro-ana.

However, this fantasy of a global community of pro-anorexics exists alongside a more hierarchical view in which models like Jodie Kidd represent the zenith of pro-ana identity through achieving a peak of thinness to which pro-ana authors aspire. This brings us to a fantasy that is of central importance in pro-ana communities: that of perfecting the body.

'My Differing Views': Being Other, Not-Being Meat

> Before You Enter Please Take Note!
>
> This site was created to express *my differing views* of my bulimia and eating disorders in general ...[2] (emphasis added)

Above, I have argued that the online community may be constituted through the exclusion of all bodies but especially that of certain bodies that are imagined as unspeakable. In this it works differently from normative femininity, which is constituted as a community whose boundaries exclude excessive and pathological bodies, particularly those that are seen as either too fat or too thin. Hence, the moral panic surrounding pro-ana websites represents an attempt to police the boundaries of this community; the shape of the community itself is constituted through the recognition of some bodies as abject, and the subsequent relegation of those bodies to the margins. The anorexic is constructed as other, a construction that suggests the impossibility of speaking from the position of the anorexic body. Anorexic bodies are thus constructed as unspeakable bodies. The quotation above illustrates this dilemma. The author's views are her own, but she can only imagine her own point of view as one that 'differs'. The writer states that her point of view is 'different'; this notion of anorexia as different from the norm is so deeply ingrained that there is no need to explain the nature of this difference. Like the anorexic body,

2 blessmebulimia.fabpage.com/, site deleted.

her text is imagined as embodying the quality of difference; difference (from the norm) is assumed to be an extension of the 'visible difference' that is written on the anorexic body.

Partly, this difference arises from a sense of shared fantasies that would be unacceptable in mainstream society, especially the fantasy of achieving perfection through thinness. For example, the Anorexic Nation web page reviews other pro-ana sites in these terms: '[t]here are times I look at these pro-ana sites over and over and feel ill ... don't get me wrong but it's a good ill feeling, like you never want to eat again.' Anorexic Nation has been singled out in particular as disgusting and dangerous. The image on its front page is indeed shocking. It shows the torso of an extremely emaciated young woman, cropped so that only the bottom part of the chin is visible, and dressed in jeans and a cut-off T-shirt. The image is reproduced to give three identical torsos arranged side by side, and in the most recent version the T-shirts have been digitally altered so that one reads 'perfection', the second 'starvation', and the third 'emaciation'. Below this image is the caption 'Love Not What You Are, But What You May Become'.[3]

Perhaps the most striking aspect of this and other images on pro-ana sites is that the bodies on display are always headless. As I have noted, there is a practical reason for this, since many authors need to preserve their anonymity from parents and peers. Like anorexia itself, authorship of these sites is often described as a secret activity. However, the effect of this proliferation of headless bodies is a dehumanising one. On the Anorexic Nation homepage, the line of identical, faceless torsos is suggestive of meat; the extremely prominent bones suggest an economy of abjection in which the boundaries between inside and outside have become unstable.

3 Anorexic Nation has been deleted so often as to make accurate citation almost impossible, but a current iteration of a site operating under the same name and using some of the same text and images can be found at http://nafella.com/naflogger/?CultureVulture/Anorexic_NationIdiotic_Thinspirations. See Ferreday 2003 for more on this site.

> She has always appeared, first and foremost, as a starving woman. A woman close to death, she brings us the deathly woman. Her ability to carry death so vividly while still alive fascinated one doctor as early as 1689, who commented that his patient was 'like a skeleton only clad with skin' (Spignesi 1983: 8).

However, for Spignesi, the anorexic woman is not, first and foremost, a dying woman but rather 'a woman very much alive and active who brings us death', a living corpse, or a 'being-beyond-the-world' (1983: 8). The pro-ana writers echo this macabre yet romantic language. The perfectibility of the body, where perfection is identified with death, is a recurring theme.

In cyberculture, the naming of the human body as 'meat' originated with William Gibson's proclamation, in the cyberpunk novel *Neuromancer*, that 'the body is meat' (cited in Stone 1991: 112). As critics have pointed out, the widespread dissemination of this metaphor has been used to promote a culture of transcendence which reproduces a dualistic and conservative ideology of transcendence, which echoes both Cartesian and Christian notions of subjectivity (Lupton 1996, Morse 1994, Penny 1994). This dualism is widely understood to be problematic in that it tends to become hierarchical, with the body viewed as inferior to the mind or inner self. It is taken for granted that the term 'meat' is derogatory, and is used as a weapon in the battle to cast off the physical body.

In *Carnal Appetites*, Elspeth Probyn tracks the relationship between 'flesh' and 'meat' in Western literature (2000). In order to illustrate the uneasiness of this relationship, she cites Angela Carter's comment, in *The Sadeian Woman*, that, 'The word "fleisch," in German, provokes me to an involuntary shudder. In the English language, we make a fine distinction between flesh, which is usually alive and typically human; and meat, which is dead, inert, animal and intended for consumption' (Carter 1979, cited in Probyn 2000: 71). Cyberculture seeks to deconstruct this distinction, suggesting that the two are too close for comfort. However, this is not to say that cyberculture sees the body as 'just' meat, in opposition to the mind. This view dominated early studies of online culture and embodiment, and I think, is still highly relevant to popular narratives of online experience. For example, Thomas Foster argues that in cyberpunk novels, 'the possibilities of cyborg existence seem reduced to a radical devaluation of organic bodies, usually referred to as "the meat"', an attitude he calls 'post-biological' (Foster 1999: 215). Furthermore, he argues that this view of the body is inherently conservative and represents a refusal of the radical possibilities offered by cyborg identity:

> Cyberpunk texts often appear to reproduce the mind/body split that characterises much of Western philosophy and culture, rather than replacing such dualistic and dialectical habits of thought with models of hybridity and partial perspectives, as Haraway proposes. This fiction typically seems structured around two dichotomous alternatives: either imprisonment within a contingent bodily existence as a 'meat puppet' or becoming a 'robopath' whose fondest wish is to transcend the body by replacing it with mechanical prosthesis, or to dispense with the body entirely by downloading consciousness into computer networks ... (Foster 1999: 215).

This analysis seems to resonate, for example, with ongoing fantasies about the ways in which digital technologies might allow 'us' to transcend death. This analysis is convincing in terms of pro-ana, but limited in that it ignores the violence implicit in the term 'meat' itself (as opposed to the more neutral term 'flesh'). As I have noted, the headless bodies on display in pro-ana site, with their prominent bones, are often posed in such a way as to suggest meat, and their slogans play with the idea that the body becomes perfected only at the moment of death. This is the crucial difference between 'flesh' and 'meat': meat is by definition both dead, and capable of being eaten.

It should be obvious, then, that this denial of the corporeal has much in common with the anorexic culture of purification through self-denial; as Susan Bordo argues, the preoccupation with slimness in Western culture also has its roots in Christian traditions of fasting. Historically, she reminds us that:

> [Other] cultures have dieted. Aristocratic Greek culture made a science of the regulation of food intake, as a road to self-mastery and the practice of moderation in all things. Fasting, aimed at spiritual purification and domination of the flesh, was an important part of the repertoire of Christian practice in the middle ages. These forms of diet can clearly be viewed as instruments for the development of a 'self' – whether an 'inner' self, for the Christians, or a public self, for the Greeks

– constructed as an area in which the deepest possibilities for human excellence may be realised (Bordo 1992: 185).

In popular culture, she goes on to argue, preoccupation with the body underwent a shift away from its spiritual roots, becoming 'a project in service of body rather than soul' (Bordo 1993: 185), a shift which, I think, has been to some extent reversed since the advent of virtual reality. In virtual worlds, the desire to become disembodied is closely linked with the dream of becoming immortal. Both the fantasy of becoming cyborg, and that of uploading consciousness, are theorised as supreme acts of transcendence; in one, the flesh is replaced (piece by piece, or all at once) by a superior technological body; in the latter, it is to be dispensed with altogether.

The fantasy of transcending the 'meat' arises from a fear that the relationship with the other, imagined as one of consumption, may become reversed: that one may become the thing consumed. Consumption itself, in the form of shopping or eating, may become a consuming obsession, as may the relationship with technology as Other: the stereotyped hacker is one who sits wasted at his computer terminal, surrounded by fast-food containers, sometimes forgetting to eat for days at a time. This fantasy is implicitly raced and gendered; as Vivian Sobchak has argued, the image of 'beating the meat', suggesting male masturbation, itself ironically implies the impossibility of transcending the physical body (1995). Similarly, pro-ana writers speak of a desire to become nothing but bones and spirit. The sexual implications of 'meat' are not lost on Jaoi, who is the author of a pro-mia page and for whom the statement 'men like women with a bit of meat on their bones', which she says she hears frequently, is a trigger which inspires her to take pride in her anorexic identity.[4] However, bones are still part of the body, and the bony, anorexic body must be displayed precisely in order to demonstrate the anorexic subject's difference from the desirable, 'meaty' bodies of pornography. For Jaoi, anorexia becomes a means of resisting a heteronormative

4 http://jaoii.lunarpages.com, accessed December 2007, now deleted.

culture in which women's bodies are determined by cultural notions of 'what men like'.

It is this display of the anorexic body that separates pro-ana from the fantasy of transcending the body-as-meat. Fantasies of unmarked belonging have positioned the body as unspeakable, as well as unfit to be seen. This is especially true of 'marked' bodies, which are positioned as particularly threatening since they contradict the view of online belonging as unmarked by inequality and prejudice. In the case of pro-ana, the anorexic body has been positioned as marked by mental illness as well as by gender, and through such a reading, pro-ana communities have come to be read as subversive. In the next section, I examine how a community of concerned readers has been imagined in order to address the need to expel pro-ana sites from the online community. I argue that, whilst hostile accounts of pro-ana draw on discourses of caring and concern, they also share a desire to position these sites as abject.

Unspeakable Bodies: Anorexia and Abjection

So far, I have looked at the ways in which pro-ana constructs a sense of community through a sense of shared embodiment, and especially through shared fantasies of bodily perfection. Here, I turn to some of the articles criticising pro-ana that have appeared in recent years (Atkins 2002, Brennan 2001, Brown 2001, George 2002, Dwyer-Hogg 2001, Kidman 2001, Reaves 2001) in order to examine in the ways in which pro-ana sites and their critics provide an insight into the relationship between the virtual community and the body. By focusing first of all on the moral panics that has surrounded such sites since they first came to the attention of the press in 1999, and the subsequent censorship of some of those sites, I shall explore the ways in which some bodies are positioned as dangerous and subversive.

Above, I noted that pro-ana communities are fragile, existing within a wider Internet community which constantly threatens expulsion. In this section, I discuss the ways in which both feminist and non-feminist observers have attempted to re-position anorexic women as outsiders. By drawing on Julia Kristeva's theories of abjection, I shall go on to suggest that the public outcry surrounding pro-ana communities represents an appeal to censorship as a means by which outsiders might be 'ejected beyond the scope of the possible, the tolerable, the thinkable' (1982: 1) in order to re-instate the notion of consensus through the suppression of some forms of difference. In previous chapters, I introduced the notion of 'deletion' as a means of thinking through the small acts of erasure by which racially marked and gendered selves are sacrificed for the benefit of the online community as a whole. Here, I examine what happens when anorexic women refuse to participate in this process of deletion, arguing that censorship of pro-ana sites can be read as the virtual performance of a desire to eradicate abject bodies from the real world. This approach highlights the contradictions inherent in mainstream Western culture's attempt to maintain its obsession with body image, whilst continuing to exclude, vilify and marginalise those who are imagined as having 'gone too far'.

One characteristic shared by most of the reactions to pro-ana is a strong affective dimension; all the articles cited above refer to their authors' being moved by pro-ana websites. However, the dominant emotion is not sympathy or concern for the young women involved, but disgust. Commentators write of this disgust in highly embodied terms; confronted with the spectacle of the anorexic body, they recoil in shock, becoming sick to the stomach. An article in *Time* magazine refers to the 'ick factor' of seeing anorexic bodies (Reaves 2001). The *Mail on Sunday* says that 'the images are shocking, the words horrific', and describes the sites as 'gruesome' and 'sinister' (Brennan 2001). There was also a parallel outcry from the Internet community. The reaction of one woman, posted in her blog, is typical in its sense of a visceral reaction to the sites:

> To find out that pro-anorexia websites even exist not only shocked me but it outright disgusted me … it actually made me sick to my stomach thinking about

> all the young girls and women logging onto these sites looking for support from fellow anorexics promoting the eating disorder.[5]

However, this reading goes on to imply that it is not only the 'thought' of pro-ana that provokes disgust. Rather, there is often slippage between disgust at the content of the sites, and disgust at the anorexic body, which is expressed through revulsion at the images displayed on the sites. Another website, Plastic Halo, reproduces a photograph from one pro-ana site (onto which the author has superimposed the caption 'DON'T KILL YOURSELF TO LIVE'). The text, taken from her online journal, describes a reaction of shock and outrage at discovering pro-ana, and compares anorexics to 'confused little children ... [who] think they're making a stand and coming together to form this community of anorexics', whereas, in fact, anorexics are to be pitied because they do not know how disgusting their bodies are. For example, she says, 'the most disgusting external thing about being anorexic is that you grow extra hair in weird areas because your body can no longer keep itself warm'.[6] Similarly, Reaves states that the images are the most shocking aspects of the sites: 'on many sites are pictures. Pictures of women starving themselves that are so horrific they cause the average person's stomach to knot up with disgust' (2001). This recalls Elspeth Probyn's summary of the expected reaction to images of anorexic bodies: '[n]o doubt about it, these bodies are pitched to make us gag and turn away' (2000: 126).

Pro-ana is not only seen as disgusting, however; it is also widely imagined as dangerous; or rather, perhaps, disgust gives way to a desire to see the disgusting object removed, and this drive to delete, to censor, becomes re-imagined as a desire to protect vulnerable others (women, children) from danger.[7] It is interesting to note that commentary in the

5 http://www.wlu.ca/~wwwws/faculty/mtoye/100b/classbook/horyn.htm, accessed December 2007, since deleted.

6 Accessed December 2007: again, this site has now been deleted. Also note that this site is apparently unrelated to the current blog of the same name.

7 As Lisa Agustin has pointed out, this rhetoric of protection has traditionally been used to justify the expulsion of particular subjects beyond the boundaries of the community: as she says, 'circus sideshow performers, transgender artists, beggars

mainstream press generally assumes that pro-ana material is rendered more dangerous precisely because of its location in cyberspace. Indeed, the article from *Time* cited above, goes on to blame pro-ana exclusively for the increasing numbers of pre-adolescents developing the disease:

> Researchers have noted a marked increase of cases in the eight to 11-year-old age range over the past five years ... Kids in that age range (perhaps not coincidentally) are also spending more and more time in front of computers, educators note, a trend that leaves them especially susceptible to the proliferation of pro-anorexia sites (Reaves 2001).

One of the ways in which the sites promote anorexia, as Reaves points out, is by displaying pictures of emaciated actresses and models as 'inspiration'. Yet her argument fails to explain how a culture which continually produces and disseminates such images might itself share some of the responsibility. Instead, the writers of pro-ana sites are positioned as scapegoats. The act of copying and pasting images from mainstream culture is thus re-figured such that responsibility for the images themselves is displaced onto the pro-ana community. This economy of blame works to re-instate a dualistic model in which a clear dividing line exists between 'normal' feminine obsession with the body, as promoted in sites of respectable journalism; and the excessive, pathological body obsession of the anorexic. In other words, it attempts to resolve the ambiguities suggested by pro-ana pages, particularly in relation to notions of responsibility, by identifying pro-ana with the category of the abject.

As I have shown, the rhetoric of disembodiment, which has characterised theories of virtual reality, sits uneasily alongside the constant

... and children who break dance in the street, when found in a "nice" residential neighbourhood, will be quickly moved on' (1999: 153). This attitude, she says has extended into the policing of cyberspace, where it is assumed that members of marginal groups should not be 'given' access to new technologies (and further that 'they' do not want access). However, she points out that travellers and sex workers, to name just two groups, have benefited from online networking. Thus, she concludes, '[It] is imperative not to project our own desires and assumptions onto others ... how do "we" know what "they" want?' (1999: 152–3).

reproduction of highly conservative images of the female body on the Internet. Here, however, it is the representation of the wrong kind of body that is seen as disgusting, as uncanny. In mainstream culture, for example in women's magazines, any degree of thinness short of anorexia is presented as normal, whilst anorexia itself is marginal. When anorexic bodies threaten to cross the boundary and become visible, they are experienced as threatening, as in the case of 'size zero' celebrities who are constantly portrayed as occupying a boundary position (Ferreday 2008). In tabloid accounts of these women, their thinness is imagined as having reached the point at which viewers become 'uncomfortable', that is, where normative femininity is threatened by the incursion of the sick, anorexic body. As Elspeth Probyn points out in her account of her own childhood experience of anorexia, the anorexic body is precisely that which cannot be represented for fear of inspiring disgust:[8]

> Like many, I spent much of my childhood feeling disgusting. However, any evidence of that time is scant. Of the series of photographs that document my childhood, there is an absence that occurs about the time that I was severely anorexic ... why or how could such a sight be documented? (Probyn 2000: 125)

The extremely thin body is precisely that which cannot be documented; its force is such that it evokes an instant reaction of disgust, making the reader 'gag and turn away' (Probyn 2000: 126). Whilst Probyn is referring, here, to images in a magazine, I think the mechanisms of

8 As Probyn's account shows, this disgust does not only come from outside: self-disgust is also a major factor in her account of anorexia, and it is certainly true that pro-ana sites often reproduce this narrative of self-loathing. However, it is important to note that critiques of pro-ana have not, as a whole, drawn attention to this aspect of the phenomenon, perhaps because this would threaten to push out or make redundant the critic's own disgust. In any case, it is not my purpose here to speculate about the formation of the anorexic subject as such, and I am particularly concerned that my reading not fall into the trap of assuming that these sites give me, as an outsider, an insight into 'how it really feels' to be anorexic. Rather, I am interested in exploring the ways in which certain subjectivities might experience a sense of belonging in cyberspace, and how these belongings trouble the idealistic notions of online community I have discussed.

disgust she describes are heightened by the conditions of cyberspace, particularly in relation to the fantasies of mind/body separation that virtual culture implies. Whilst I concur with Probyn's argument that anorexic bodies are less likely to be considered appropriate for display, I think the location of pro-ana on the Web has tended to problematise the process by which the anorexic body causes the onlooker to turn away. Whilst 'disgust' implies a movement of repulsion, a recoiling, hypertext implies repeated clicking to access a proliferation of similar images. All the articles I cited above reproduce lists of quotes from several pro-ana Web pages, often uncredited, which are typically run together in order to evoke the sheer volume of such sites 'out there'. And yet, these hypertextual journeys through the pro-ana community always begin with a search engine, that is, with a non-anorexic subject deliberately seeking out the websites in question. Having read about them, one sets out to look for images of the anorexic body, to see them for oneself. Having found them, it is implied, one wants more, more and more moments of disgusted recognition underwritten by a sense of outrage which is presented as cumulative and constantly mounting.

Similarly, the anorexic reader is presented as constantly wanting more; indeed, many critics point to the sheer volume of sites (and hence their potentially limitless potential to gratify this desire, a gratification which is, however, endlessly deferred) as one of the key elements that make them so dangerous. Although pro-ana sites are imagined to produce very different affective responses in anorexic and non-anorexic readers, both are presented as wanting more, more images, more encounters with the anorexic body. These shocking manifestations, materialising one by one on the computer desktop (that is, on the user's home ground) become monstrous through proliferation. Attempts to censor pro-ana sites (apart from making my job as a researcher very difficult, and I shall address this problem in greater detail) have increased this fear; as fast as one head of the hydra is severed, it seems, more and more appear. I think, then, that these websites problematise Probyn's notion that the anorexic body makes the reader 'gag, then turn away'. Such a turning away, rather, always implies an inevitable turning back, or a turning towards new images, in the quest to define the boundaries of the self in opposition to the monstrous, abject anorexic subject.

This moment of disgust, then, can be read as defining the moment at which the boundaries of the 'healthy' body are threatened by an encounter with the anorexic body. Specifically, the term 'disgust' itself, meaning 'unpleasant to the taste', suggests a failure of oral incorporation. If the encounter with the other suggests a desire to 'eat the other', as I suggested in the previous chapter, the moment at which the healthy body becomes 'sick to the stomach' is precisely the moment at which this incorporation fails. By producing a physical sensation of revulsion (the 'ick factor'), the anorexic body breaks down the distinction between the healthy subject (in whom the Cartesian division between mind and flesh is taken for granted), and the other, who is always seen as purely corporeal. This is not to claim that the non-anorexic subject is unaware of her body (indeed, the comparison between one's own normal body, and the abject images onscreen, is a crucial element in these online encounters). Rather, the distinction is between the normal subject, whose body is fixed in its proper place, and the pathological, abject anorexic for whom the boundaries between body and subjectivity are blurred.

Historically, medical science has attempted to resolve this threat by assimilating the anorexic body back into the healthy body of the community. However, it has tried to accomplish this by focussing on the anorexic body, and the practices associated with the condition itself. It has been left to feminist commentators such as Susan Bordo to suggest that eating disorders exist on a continuum with other forms of bodily discipline, that 'preoccupation with fat, diet, and slenderness are not abnormal', are indeed a logical response to the double bind of consumer capitalism (1992: 186). For Angelyn Spignesi, the drive to 'cure' anorexics is precisely a reaction to the ambiguities implied by the anorexic body. Spignesi argues that the medical profession has been fascinated by anorexia precisely because of the undecideability of the anorexic body. She imagines the anorexic as a 'female of borders', especially in relation to gender: 'we have to look twice when she appears: female without curves, male with long hair? Researchers comment on her third-sex attributes

– that she steps outside of each gender.' The anorexic is hence associated with 'duplicity and ambiguity'. She continues:

> Strange mystery lady of the borders – you are difficult to live with, you shake us, make us groundless. Gone are the traditional and useful guides to what is feminine. Your doctors urgently try to carry or translate you back to conventional, natural existence. Your duplicity and borderline nature unnerve us, bring about a change in us. Wherever we grasp, you disappear; whatever we categorise, you modify ... As an inhabitant of borderlines she can serve the double nature of upper- and underworld perspectives and perhaps initiate us into the underworld. Does this 'lady of borders' have a ritual for such an initiation? (Spignesi 1983: 15–16)

Spignesi's account implies that the anorexic body is understood as problematic because it seems to speak back to the doctors, to subvert their view of 'natural existence'. This is clearly problematic; eating disorders, after all, have the highest rate of mortality for any psychiatric condition, a fact which ought to moderate any enthusiastic claims that pro-ana sites are unproblematically subversive or transgressive. However, I have included this account because it identifies a crucial component in the drive to censor pro-ana websites; that is, the failure of medical science to position the anorexic body as object. This refusal to be reduced to the status of object, more than the absence of curves, is what marks the anorexic body as unfeminine. Pro-ana websites repeatedly perform this refusal of object status despite the fact that their content, with its emphasis on constant surveillance and discipline of the body, might send a contradictory message, one which is all about the subordination of the body (and indeed, one in which the 'perfect' anorexic body becomes, for the anorexic reader, an object of desire). For the non-anorexic reader, however, the authors of these sites, and the bodies on display, become positioned as abject.

In *Powers of Horror: an Essay on Abjection*, Julia Kristeva writes that 'the abject is not an object facing me, which I name or imagine ... the abject has only one quality of the object – that of being opposed to I' (1982: 1). The notion of an 'object' which one can 'name or imagine' (e.g. the anorexic body as an object of pity and/or medical scrutiny) works to reinforce the boundary between self and other; it is through this process that 'I' comes into being as a clearly defined self, with clear boundaries. The object may be the focus of fantasy, of desire, but it is always experienced as other (although, as I argue in the previous chapter, this dualistic model of self/other is always in danger of becoming unstable, and hence gives rise to anxiety). In contrast, the abject causes revulsion; it comes into being through bodily encounters with 'the improper/unclean':

> Loathing an item of food, a piece of filth, waste, or dung. The spasms and vomiting that protect me. The repugnance, the retching that thrusts me to the side and turns me away from defilement, sewage, and muck. The shame of compromise, of being in the middle of treachery. The fascinated start that leads me toward and separates me from them (Kristeva 1982: 2).

Again, the abject, like Probyn's anorexic bodies is imagined as that which makes one 'gag and turn away'. Indeed, for Kristeva, 'food loathing is perhaps the most elementary and most archaic form of abjection'. Already, then, we can see that 'food loathing' exists on many levels in the reactions to pro-ana sites cited above, and in the practices of anorexia itself. I shall explore this issue of 'food loathing' in greater details below, when I turn to the content of the websites. First, however, I want to examine what implications Kristeva's theory of abjection might have for virtual bodies.

According to Kristeva, abjection refers to a bodily encounter that threatens to destroy the boundaries between self and other. 'Disgust', like desire, requires proximity to an object. Statements like 'the sight of these anorexic bodies makes me sick to my stomach', describes the moment at which the 'healthy' subject encounters the anorexic body, and is sickened by it. In the case of anorexia, the process of abjection, of writing the other's body as abject (and hence as unclean, filthy) becomes visible precisely because the onlooker's behaviour is almost a parody of the practices of anorexia: anorexics are disgusting (that is, they cause a disgust that is akin to 'food loathing') because they refuse food. Hence we can see the process by which the anorexic body threatens the boundary between self and other; crucially, the subject's revulsion at the sight of the other can only be expressed (indeed, can only be imagined) on the other's terms. This,

I think, speaks directly to Kristeva's claim that the abject 'simultaneously beseeches and pulverises the subject' (1982: 4).

However, I also need to be aware that the encounter in question is not, in fact, a bodily encounter. The commentator has not 'seen' the authors of any of these sites. Whilst it is true that many pro-ana sites display pictures of anorexic bodies, we do not always know whether they are in fact those of the sites' authors. Could they perhaps have been downloaded from another site, like most of the other graphics (buttons, headers and so on) people use to customise their homepages? Are they retouched to look thinner (or less thin?) Indeed, how do 'we' know, given the culture of multiple and shifting identities that has been a recurring theme in studies of cyberculture, that these sites are (always) authored by 'real' anorexics?

Similarly, the moment of disgust is communicated to me as a reader after the fact. Like the anorexic identities produced by the pro-ana sites, such a moment comes into being through language and through the use of familiar imagery, as well as through a fantasy image of the journalist as a dispassionate witness whose only desire is to warn and protect. Indeed, in cyberspace the encounter with the abject is re-positioned as fantasy. The Web page presents a hyper-real, fantastical and idealised account of anorexic experience. This is seen by a journalist, who reports this experience of seeing in such a way as to evoke a real (i.e. non-virtual) confrontation. This is implicit in the quotation '[they] actually make me sick to my stomach'; the affective response, sickness, becomes over-determined in an attempt to convince the reader and to provoke her, in turn, to a similar reaction of shock, horror and disgust.

As we have seen, such a reaction is produced again and again. Pro-ana sites are imagined as constantly provoking the same reaction over and over, for as long as the reader feels compelled to keep clicking on links between different sites. One is given the impression that this might go on forever, for just as the pro-ana community 'reaches out' of the screen to incorporate 'normal' women, so it has the power to compel the viewer to look at more and more 'disgusting' images. The only way to bring this process to a close is to ensure that some of the links are broken, so that the hypertext journey becomes disrupted and the reader cannot find any more sites. In the next section, I look at the ways in which this has been brought about, as a result of censorship.

Censorship: the Deletion of Pro-ana

> Battling an Internet giant
>
> According to ANAD, Yahoo! hosts by far the most pro-anorexia sites of any Web portal ... On July 26, citing Yahoo!'s ability to take down any site they choose, as well as the company's self-described commitment to the safety of adolescents and children, ANAD asked Terry Semel, the portal's CEO, to remove the pro-anorexia sites from its server. 'The fact is that most people who become anorexic first experience symptoms before they are eighteen,' says ANAD vice president Christopher Athas. 'Yahoo! claims to be interested in the health and welfare of children? Here's a good chance to prove it.'
>
> The response surprised even ANAD. By Monday, July 30th, 21 of Yahoo!'s estimated 115 pro-anorexia sites had been taken down. While no one at ANAD is willing to link the action directly to their letter of complaint, organisation leaders sent off a note thanking Semel for his quick action.
>
> Yahoo! sees things a bit differently. 'The removal of the sites was definitely not a reaction to the ANAD request,' a company spokesperson said Tuesday. She went on to explain the 'long-standing terms of service' at Yahoo!, and outlined the consequences for anyone who violates them (which pro-anorexic sites certainly seem to do). 'Content with the sole purpose of creating harm or inciting hate is brought to our attention, we evaluate it, and in extreme cases, remove it, as that is a violation of our terms of service.'[9]

In contrast with the open disgust expressed by the Internet community, the press attitude to pro-ana has been characterised by an often uneasy combination of (understandable) concern for the health of the young women involved, and irritation at their obtuseness, their apparent

9 This article is no longer displayed on the ANAD website, but can be found at www.time.com/time/health/article/0,8599,169660,00.html, accessed 28 November 2008.

inability to see how irresponsible they are being. In the extract above, which is taken from the *Time* article (Reaves 2001), a tension emerges between the need to protect anorexics, who are seen as vulnerable and childlike (that is, as objects of pity, concern and so on), and the continuing desire to vilify the pro-ana authors. In order to manage the implicit contradictions here, a kind of parent-child relationship emerges in which the anorexic reader is positioned as a child in need of protection by some higher moral authority (a responsibility which is laid at the door of service providers and search engine programmers), yet the authors themselves are positioned sometimes as vulnerable, and sometimes as abject and monstrous. The image is that of a bad mother who does not care about the safety of children, and who provides damaging, poisonous propaganda in the guise of nurturing 'support'. The only real support, it is implied, would be to refer anorexics to a higher, usually medical authority; as George (2002) states, 'in this realm, "support" or "advice" doesn't mean referrals to doctor's care or tips for recovery'. To suggest that providing a forum for young women and men to discuss the fantasies they associate with anorexia does constitute support is unthinkable, akin to admitting that one comes from this sinister, other realm.[10] Crucially, the pro-censorship argument rests on the assumption that pro-ana sites aim to recruit young women and to make them become anorexic. It therefore assumes that these sites are not, as they claim, by and for anorexics, rather that their accessible position, and the fact that they do not usually require members to register, makes them available to, and capable of endangering, a far wider audience.

It is this need to re-position the pro-ana authors as wilful seducers of innocent children that lies behind the headline 'battling an Internet giant'. The account reproduced above is hardly that of a plucky charity battling an insensitive corporation. Indeed, faced with the press outcry

10 In fact, this is not true; whilst pro-ana is openly critical of the notion of 'cure', many pro-ana sites do appropriate medical discourse, and some provide information on recovery and self-help, with links to relevant sites. For example, AnorexiAngel's links page includes sections on recovery, nutrition and health (http://www.geocities. com/anorexiangel/links.htm).

over pro-ana and lobbying from ANAD, Yahoo! seems to have acted with indecent haste to delete pro-ana homepages from its server, despite the fact that its terms of service explicitly warn users that 'by using the Service, you may be exposed to Content that is offensive, indecent or objectionable. Under no circumstances will Yahoo! be liable in any way for any Content ...' This might be understandable if Yahoo! took a particularly strict line on potentially offensive content. It does not. Its directory of approved sites includes, for example, an 'Adult Movies' channel including 749 sites in the category of 'Porn Stars'.[11] These sites, as the spokeswoman for Yahoo! makes clear, were censored not on grounds of obscenity, but as an example – indeed, an 'extreme example' – of 'content with the sole purpose of creating harm or inciting hate'.[12] This has been widely reported as an indictment of pro-ana sites as a new form of hate speech. However, no such clause exists in Yahoo!'s Conditions of Service. As I have already noted, this document makes it clear that Yahoo! cannot prevent websites containing material that some readers may find offensive. However, it goes on to add that websites will be deleted if they violate certain rules. In this case, the rules Yahoo! believes, or claims to believe, were violated by the 115 deleted homepages appear to be section a. and b. of the Conditions of Service. These are as follows:

> You agree to not use the Service to:
>
> a. Upload, post, email, transmit or otherwise make available any Content that is unlawful, harmful, threatening, abusive, harassing, tortious, defamatory, vulgar, obscene, libellous, invasive of another's privacy, hateful, or racially, ethnically or otherwise objectionable;
> b. Harm minors in any way.[13]

11 It is not my intention either to suggest a similarity between pro-ana and pornography or to argue that pornography should be censored. Rather, I want to point out that service providers come under constant pressure from religious groups, and some feminist groups, to remove pornographic content from their servers, but consistently refuse to do so on the grounds that this would compromise their commitment to free speech.

12 info.yahoo.com/legal/us/yahoo/utos/, accessed 28 November 2008.

13 info.yahoo.com/legal/us/yahoo/utos/, accessed 28 November 2008.

Clearly, there is some contradiction between these clauses, neither of which appears particularly relevant to any of the pro-ana homepages I have seen in the course of my research, and their interpretation as 'material with the sole purpose of creating harm or inciting hate'. The language of this clause seems more accurately to describe the rantings of Westboro Baptist Church, described in Chapter 2, than genuinely speaking to the content of pro-ana web pages. Further, it is unclear just who is the victim, who is being incited to hate whom. Perhaps the author is imagined as producing 'hate speech' against her readers' innocent bodies; but the image invoked here is rather a paradoxical one of hate speech against the self. To inhabit anorexic subjectivity is to hate the body, to refuse the false position of body-love that is demanded of women in Western society (ironically, as a sop to popular media's endless reproduction of imagery that, whilst 'prettier', is widely held to promote self-hatred). We may hate ourselves, but only as long as our self-hatred remains within the limit and as long as it fulfils its purpose as a stimulus to further consumption. That is, we must imagine ourselves as lacking in order to attempt to compensate for that lack through consumption. The anorexic, by definition non-consuming, complete in herself, endlessly absorbed in her own body and the connection between that body and others, defies this logic of desire as lack. The self-hatred demanded by consumer culture becomes projected onto pro-ana as hated Other precisely in order to deny the continuum between 'normal' feminine subjectivity, and pathology. Pro-ana image and text are therefore positioned as hate speech, as the first step on a trajectory of hate that ends with the body 'looking like a concentration camp victim', as Brennan has it, the journalistic shorthand invoking the atrocities of the Holocaust as the unanswerable final proof of pro-ana's position beyond the limit. Significantly, this statement absolutely refuses the possibility of a community of anorexics sharing information and support. Like the news articles cited above, it implies that there are only two types of reader. The first is the healthy reader; her natural reaction is one of disgust, or in this case offence or objection (both of which might be read as the result of fixing the moment of disgust, of bringing disgust into the realm of law). When a number of healthy readers see these sites, the repetition of these moments of disgust results in the formation of a community of disgust, which positions itself as a majority voice representing the Internet community 'as a whole', as if such a formulation were possible. The pro-anorexic is hence positioned once again as abject; all that remains is to cast her out, to delete the offending sites (and hence, by implication, the offending point of view).

The second type of fantasy reader is the vulnerable girl or young woman who is at risk of contracting anorexia through reading pro-ana material. This fantasy figure is crucial since she allows the violence of deletion to be re-presented as resulting from a desire to protect the innocent. These victims are always imagined as isolated, and the constant slippage between presenting these victims as women, and as minors, helps to deny that they have the right to free speech. It is impossible for them to be imagined as forming a community; there is only 'the' community (healthy readers), and then there are isolated victims (looking for a sense of belonging, but in all the wrong places). Pro-ana websites, however, are seen as intolerable in that they destabilise the 'natural' power relation between the community which seeks to protect, and the feminine subject who, individualised and infantilised, is always constructed as a potential victim and hence as the object of protection.

Conclusion

In this chapter, I have argued that pro-ana websites problematise existing views of eating disorders. For Susan Bordo, eating disorders represent the inevitable outcome of a society which positions the feminine body as unruly, and demands that it be subjected to constant surveillance and discipline (1992: 164). Following from this point of view, we might read pro-ana sites rather pessimistically, as yet another place where technology becomes the vehicle for mastery over 'less rule-y' elements (Sophia, cited in Wise 1997: 181). By bringing together fantasies of domination through technology with an existing culture of disciplining the body, it is possible to see how pro-ana sites might indeed be read as highly problematic.

To be sure, pro-ana websites do put forward fantasies of achieving 'perfection' through the discipline of the body. However, this is not the whole story, as I have demonstrated. By allowing anorexic subjects to speak for themselves, pro-ana sites provide an insight into the ways in which their accounts of anorexia problematise some aspects of the Foucauldian approach taken by Bordo, as well as confirming others. Further, the reactions to pro-ana cited in this chapter justify censorship precisely on the grounds that pro-ana communities are unruly. The newspaper articles make clear that the sites are guilty of exceeding the boundaries imposed by a medical model of eating disorders which positions anorexic subjects as isolated 'patients'. In other words, however disciplined the anorexic body may be, it is not supposed to be visible; it becomes excessive the moment it is made visible, although this excessiveness takes different forms according to who is looking. For the non-anorexic, it takes the form of disgust, causing a desire to vomit. For the anorexic or potentially anorexic viewer (and as we have seen, this argument positions all young women as potential anorexics), the sight of an anorexic body is seen as provoking an insatiable desire to become like the image by 'starving for perfection' (Anorexic Nation). This perfection is not simply beauty, but self-sufficiency, a life-in-death which is inherently virtual, embodying a boundary position which defies the pervasive notion of consumption as a self-cure for desire which is, nonetheless, endlessly deferred.

Whilst it would be absurd to claim that websites celebrating anorexia are subversive, I have demonstrated that pro-ana communities have been widely read as subverting particular sets of values. I have suggested that it is this view of pro-ana as subversive, as much as concern for the 'victims' of anorexia, that has motivated the media to call for their censorship. The tension between concern and censure can be seen, for example, in the confused language that positions the authors of the sites simultaneously as victims, and villains. Further, I have shown that pro-ana communities have been positioned as subversive in three different ways. Firstly, they have been in the context of mainstream heterosexual culture, as a result of their insistence that iconic figures like Jodie Kidd properly belong to the anorexic community. Secondly, by encouraging sufferers to talk about their condition, they disrupt the medical model of anorexia, and as such they challenge the distinction between the public and the private. Thirdly, and most significantly for the purposes of my argument, the sites are constructed as acting in opposition to the pervasive fantasy of an online community founded on shared neo-liberal principles.

This fantasy of community suggests that online belonging is achieved through small acts of self-erasure that allow the community to come into being. Pro-ana has been read as deliberately refusing the work of self-erasure. Indeed, this refusal is doubly visible, since self-erasure is a crucial part of the work demanded by sufferers of 'mental illness' in society as a whole. By attempting to build a community precisely through representing and speaking about minds and bodies that have been positioned as abject, pro-ana websites perform a model of community which explicitly refuses the project of becoming unmarked. Whilst I am not claiming that the articles cited in this chapter do not express genuine concern for anorexics, I have proposed that that concern masks the more troubling elements I describe here. Although pro-ana still exists, it is now more scattered and more secretive. It is much more difficult to find avowedly pro-ana homepages, yet the mood of disgust that I am about to describe persists: on Facebook, for example, 'anti-ana' groups outnumber pro-ana groups by three to one, and the term itself is more likely to be used by objectors (one group which allowed 'recovering' pro-anas to join, and which like many of its homepage counterparts, has now disappeared, was aptly named 'the Secret Skinny Society'). Indeed, it seems as though the ana body has become increasingly spectral: a fantasy figure, half faded from sight, which exists only in the febrile imagination of the ever-growing concern industry which continues to feed on, and even to exceed pro-ana itself. In this sense, the story of pro-ana and its detractors brings my argument full circle. In Chapter 2, I began by outlining the argument that self-erasure is necessary if one is to feel at-home in online communities. In this chapter, I have shown the consequences for communities that are seen as opposing this view of what the online belonging should involve. When such an embodied community makes itself visible beyond its intended audience, in this case anorexics, it becomes vulnerable. In this case, the result is that if communities and their members refuse to erase problematic or troubling aspects of their embodied experiences, erasure will be imposed from outside. The critic of pro-ana, reading the site in order to feel disgusted, recalls Lucie Armitt's subject who reads a ghost story 'in order to be disturbed, but [anticipating] being disturbed in a particular manner' (1996: 35). The process of reading and shutting down these sites of fantastic subjectivity hence mirrors the processes of fantasy itself which, as Armitt reminds us, quoting Jackson, is to '[supply] a vicarious fulfilment of desire and [neutralise] an urge towards transgression' (1996: 35). By opening up a space in which it is possible to gaze upon the hated Other, pro-ana sites give the reader the pleasure of distinction, of knowing who she is through knowing who she is not, but this pleasure is haunted by the terror that one is oneself 'like' the bodies on display. In order to close down this moment of identification – imagined as a moment of gagging, of becoming-Other through bodily practice – the threat must be removed, the fantasy of transgression of bodily boundaries re-covered. The different between pro-ana and fantasy fiction is that real selves, real communities are at stake here. The process of resisting erasure (as in the formation of 'secret societies' that are at once private and public) hence becomes central to the work of the community. The subject who refuses self-erasure must continually be engaged in the act of constructing the self: it is only through continual, repeated acts of self-making that erasure can be resisted.

AFTERWORD

Full Circle

Having ended on a rather pessimistic note, I want, briefly, to think again. It is neat to think of censorship as an ending, but endings are always artificial. The previous chapter ended with a disappearance, both literal and figurative: anorexic bodies are imagined as disappearing bodies, but they are also bodies that are made to disappear from the online text. The facts, however, are much messier. Sites do reappear, often many times over, and what is hidden in this process of erasure and return is the history of labour, of migrating from one server to another, reprogramming, reproduction, that underpins those reappearances. So I want to think now about things that return. I want to think through returns as a way of reflecting critically on the argument of this book, and to reflect on the ways in which my analysis of online and offline textual materials might build on existing debates on community, belonging and identity within studies of online media, and in feminist theory and cultural studies more generally. What does a model of fantastic community and identity make possible for studies of the relation between the virtual and the real? In keeping with the exploratory approach of *Online Belongings*, this conclusion, rather than proposing a simplistic answer to this question, examines the ways in which my case studies work to challenge historic notions of 'the virtual', asking how the debate might be opened up by a model that pays attention to the role of fantasy in producing offline, as well as online identities.

Since this is, in part, a book about affect, I had better confess to some strong feelings of my own. I have always detested writing conclusions. However great my interest in a project, the act of sitting down the final page or closing few paragraphs has always instilled in me a deep resistance. I am not claiming to be special: I know that I am not alone in this, and that for all academics there are moments in the writing process when marking, cooking, even cleaning suddenly take on a kind of shimmering glamour: what was the object of aversion becomes the focus of intense interest. Faced with the greater horror of closure, of breaking the attachment to the nearly-born text, the mere affectless absorption commonly known as boredom holds a far lesser dread.

When I was a student, a mentor who shared my hatred of endings told me two things: firstly, that what is necessary is to draw a circle around your material; and secondly, when you have said everything that you want to say for the time being, stop. And in writing this it occurred to me that it is perhaps this telling and retelling itself that is both my downfall, here, and my only possible hope: that my project in this book, however imperfectly realised, has something to do with this impossibility of making a conclusion, this resistance to the work of 'summing up'.

For one thing, my experience in researching and writing this book has shown me that stories do not end. It seems that this is especially true, in the most literal sense, of stories on and about cyberspace. In the introduction, I wrote that there is a certain dominant view of cyberculture as a moving target, impossible to pin down. Yet it seems that there are particular stories about cyberculture that do not change, however different the technologies being discussed may seem. Instead they are told and retold: like the urban myths that have found a new, online oral tradition through which to circulate, they circulate and re-circulate through new networks, new avenues of communication. There have been times, writing this book that I have suffered anxieties about the age, and hence the relevance of the source material. I need not have worried. For practically every newspaper article in this book, however ancient in Internet terms, there has been a counterpart in the last few months, almost to the point that I have felt haunted: at times the similarity between, say, the Lock and Pascoe article cited in Chapter 2, and a scare story about Second Life in my Sunday newspaper, has seemed uncannily serendipitous. Recent articles and television shows about pro-ana, meanwhile, have continued to reproduce exactly the dominant discourse I describe in Chapter 5. The popular media continue to reproduce stories which emphasise the terrors and dangers of anonymity and invoke fears of the strange, the exotic, just as though the early vision of cyberspace as a virtual playground of unmarked immersion in fantasy identities had in fact been achieved, as if the personal pages I discuss in Chapter 3 had not come vastly to outnumber text-based communities, as though MUDs were not closing all over the internet and the Web had not become inextricably rooted in our everyday lives.

I am uncomfortably aware that this seems pessimistic, but it is not intended to. My argument here has not simply been concerned with the ways in which 'inequalities' from everyday life are reproduced online: instead, I have been concerned with the mutually constitutive nature of online and offline life. What is at stake in the network of complex and shifting interrelationships between these two categories is the idea, or fantasy, of the virtual: of what is, or ought to be, possible. This is as true of cyberculture studies itself, with its ambivalent longing for a sense of 'the canon' as of the online personae, the networks of personal profiles, homepages, self-writing and email conversations that carry the hopes we have of new relationships, new selves, new lives. Cyberculture studies, as well as popular narratives of digital culture, seem always to be holding out for a revolution, when 'the new' is always already with us, in the shape of small everyday acts of connection. The recycling and repetition of offline experience is hence inescapable and also hopeful. As Butler has shown us, it is in the possibility, however slim, of old signifiers being 'repeated with a difference' (Butler 1990, 1993), and not in grand utopian narratives, that the hope of change really lies. 'The virtual' can hence be seen not as something that happens through a particular technological apparatus, but of as a way of thinking through our investment of what is possible, what new possibilities are inherent in selves, communities and experiences, and particularly how this intersects with the possibilities for connection afforded by digital technologies.

Nevertheless, it is clear from their very repetition that stories of newness, whether expressed as utopian longing or dystopian fear and loathing, are important to us. The idea of 'the new' is clearly the object of intense and deep attachment, and it is the purpose of cultural theory above all to pay attention to those stories that keep being recycled. Why are we so interested in the notion of transcendence, despite our supposed incredulity towards metanarratives? Perhaps the continuing interest in utopian and dystopian visions is simply a gesturing towards the affirmative, a means of implicitly refusing cynicism. To be sure, we need to pay attention to the oppressive outcomes of moral panics around technology: but we might read, in the larger pattern of repetition of narrative of newness, a hopefulness. In this book, I have reflected on the ways in which what has been termed the increasing 'embeddedness' of online media in day-to-day life (Bakardjieva 2005, Lally 2002) works to destabilise the notion of a discrete 'virtual' existence, often in challenging and surprising ways. I have examined the complex ways in which online sites of identity production negotiate the continuities and discontinuities between texts and day-to-day existence, between online and offline lived experience, and between 'real' and fantasy productions of the self. I have paid attention to a few of the many ways in which users become attached to online communities through the textual production of emotion, as well as to the ways in which the body 'returns' in online spaces. As I have suggested in Chapter 2, feminist critiques of what were seen as the patriarchal narratives of early cyberculture studies were, understandably, particularly critical of the metaphors of mastery and colonisation that often structured those stories. But this suspicion of utopian narratives does not mean that such stories ought never to have been told. If, as I have argued, it is the finger poised over the delete key, the internalisation of a sense of oneself as unspeakable, that threatens to silence some voices before they can be heard, then feminist cyberculture studies must not simply perform an inversion in which other stories, other voices, are deleted before they can be told. We need instead to do justice to the powerfulness of utopia as a vessel that carries ideas about what is possible, about the virtuality of lived experience. As Lucie Armitt tells us, quoting Lee Khana, the utopian is 'not, finally, any one place or time, but the capacity to see fresh' (1996: 183). As this book suggests, feminist theory might want to reflect on the irony inherent in a notion of 'seeing afresh' which simultaneously repeats old stories. But we might also want to reflect on the ways in which our own hopes and desires are also articulated with the possibilities that digital culture offers. In particular, we might want to question the idea the virtual as a playground in which anything is possible and focus instead on the performativity of online life. Participation in cyberculture is structured by tiny movements – 'clicks' – which make up pathways of affect and disaffection. The pattern of clicks may add up to the repetition of old stories, old codes, but each click also carries the promise that what is repeated may be repeated with a difference.

Central to this notion of the online performative is the question of what it means to belong. Belongings need not be solely the preserve of those spaces of which 'we' approve, instead they can arise in the most unpromising of circumstances. So, for example, it is exasperating to read yet another paean by a female journalist to the joys of online shopping: but by reading through affect, it is also possible to recognise in such a celebration of feminine identity not simply a pathetic lack, a willingness to become a cultural dope, but also a possibility of pleasure, of joy, in belonging to a community brought together not by proximity, necessarily, nor through any radical cause but through a sense of a shared sensuality, of joy. The one need not negate the other: indeed, if online belongings teach 'us' anything, it is that multiple and often contradictory identities, subject positions, spaces can be occupied simultaneously. Theory already 'knows' this, of course, but the very accessibility of online lives demonstrates the extent to which theory is not an isolated activity but is already 'being done', and not always in the way that we expect. As Sadie Plant has argued, 'All new media ... have an extraordinary ability to rewire the people who are using them' (1997: 143–4).

To 'draw a circle' around my argument, then, is simultaneously to acknowledge that like the Web, theory is never complete: it is constantly in the process of being made and remade, torn, patched, woven and rewoven. The Web is not a site of escape, but of returning. I have argued that the Internet continues to shape and be shaped by everyday lives, and this is not a failure of some cosmic other potential, always missed, always mourned: this is its potential, although mourning is also an intrinsic part of the story. And this has brought me full circle, to Plant's vision of digital culture as an endless weaving, through which there is always the possibility, though not the promise, of becoming rewired.

Bibliography

Agustin, L. (1999). They Speak, but Who Listens? In Harcourt, W. (ed.), *Women @ Internet*. London and New York NY: Zed Books, 149–55.

Ahmed, S. (1998). *Differences that Matter: Postmodernism and Feminist Theory*. Cambridge: Cambridge University Press.

Ahmed, S. (1999). Phantasies of Becoming (The Other). *European Journal of Cultural Studies*. 2 (1), 47–63.

Ahmed, S. (2002). Communities that Feel: Intensity, Difference and Attachment. In Larreta, E.R. (ed.), *Identity and Difference in a Global Era*. Rio de Janeiro: UNESCO, pp. 414–48.

Ahmed, S. (2004). *The Cultural Politics of Emotion*. Edinburgh: Edinburgh University Press.

Ahmed, S. and Stacey, J. (2001). Introduction: Dermographies. In Ahmed, S. and Stacey, J. (eds), *Thinking Through the Skin*. London and New York NY: Routledge, pp. 1–18.

Anderson, B. (1991). *Imagined Communities: Reflections on the Origin and Spread of Nationalism*. London: Verso.

Armitt, L. (1996). *Theorizing the Fantastic*. London and New York NY: Arnold.

Arnold, J. and Miller, H. (1999). Gender and Web Home Pages. Paper presented at CAL99 Virtuality in Education Conference, The Institute of Education, London.

Arnold, J. and Miller, H. (2000). Same Old Gender Plot? Women Academics Identities on the Web. http://ess.ntu.ac.uk/miller/cyberpsych/gendplot.htm [16 October 2002].

Atkins, L. (2002). It's Better to be Thin and Dead than Fat and Living. *The Guardian*, 23 July. http://www.guardian.co.uk/health/story/0,3605,761598,00.html

Auerbach, N. (1995). *Our Vampires, Ourselves.* London: University of Chicago Press.

Bakardjieva, M. (2005). *Internet Society – the Internet in Everyday Life.* London: Sage Publications.

Bakhtin, M. (1981). *The Dialogic Imagination: Four Essays.* Trans. C. Emerson and M. Holquist. Austin TX: University of Texas Press.

Balsamo, A. (1996). *Technologies of the Gendered Body.* Durham NC: Duke University Press.

Baudrillard, J. (1981). *Simulacra and Simulation*, New York: Semiotext(e).

Bell, D. (2000). Cybercultures Reader: A User's Guide. In Bell, D. and Kennedy, B. (eds), *The Cybercultures Reader.* London and New York NY: Routledge, pp. 1–12.

Bell, V. (1999). Performativity and Belonging: An Introduction. In Bell, V. (ed.), *Performativity and Belonging.* London, Thousand Oaks CA and New Delhi: Sage, pp. 1–10.

Blanchard, A.L. and Markus, M.L. (2002). Sense of Virtual Community. Paper given at the 35th Hawaii International Conference on System Sciences.

Bordo, S. (1993). *Unbearable Weight: Feminism, Western Culture and the Body.* Berkeley CA: University of California Press.

Bourdieu, P. (1984). *Distinction: a Social Critique of the Judgement of Taste.* Trans. R. Nice. London: Routledge and Kegan Paul.

Bowlby, R. (1997). Supermarket Futures. In Falk, P. and Campbell, C. (eds), *The Shopping Experience.* London, Thousand Oaks CA and New Delhi: Sage, pp. 92–110.

Bowlby, R. (2000). *Carried Away.* London: Faber and Faber.

Brennan, Z. (2001). Websites that Prey on Eating Disorders. *Mail on Sunday*, 12 January.

Bromberg, H. (1996). Are MUDs Communities? Identity, Belonging and Consciousness in Virtual Worlds. In Shields, R. (ed.), *Cultures of Internet.* London, Thousand Oaks CA and New Delhi: Sage, pp. 143–52.

Brown, J. (2001). The Winner Dies. *Salon.* dir.salon.com/story/mwt/feature/2001/07/23/pro_ana/, accessed 10 December 2008.

Bruckman, A. (1997). Programming for Fun: MUDs as a Context for Collaborative Learning, ftp://ftp.media.mit.edu/pub/asb/papers/necc94.ps, accessed 10 December 2008.

Butler, J. (1990). *Gender Trouble.* London and New York NY: Routledge.

Butler, J. (1993). *Bodies that Matter: on the Discursive Limits of 'Sex'.* London and New York NY: Routledge.

Campbell, C. (1997). Shopping, Pleasure and the Sex War. In Falk, P. and Campbell, C. (eds), *The Shopping Experience.* London, Thousand Oaks CA and New Delhi: Sage, pp. 166–76.

Campbell, J. and Rew, A. (1999). *Identity and Affect.* London: Pluto Press.

Carey, J.W. (1989). *Communication as Culture: Essays on Media and Society.* Boston MA: Unwin Hyman.

Carter, A. (1979). *The Sadeian Woman.* London: Virago Press.

Chandler, D. (1998). Personal Home Pages and the Construction of Identities on the Web. Aberystwyth University. http://www.aber.ac.uk/media/Documents/short/webident.html, accessed 10 December 2008.

Cheah, P. and Robins, B. (1998). *Cosmopolitics: Thinking and Feeling Beyond the Nation.* Minneapolis MN: University of Minnesota Press.

Clough, P.T. and O'Malley Halley, J. (2007). *The Affective Turn,* Durham, Duke University Press.

Cobb, J. (1998). *Cybergrace.* New York: Crown.

Cobb. M. (2006). *God Hates Fags: The Rhetorics of Religious Violence.* New York NY: New York University Press.

Cook, I. and Crang, P. (1996). The World on a Plate: Culinary Culture, Displacement and Geographical Knowledge. *Journal of Material Culture* (1) 1, 131–53.

Cronin, A.M. (2000). *Advertising and Consumer Citizenship.* London and New York NY: Routledge.

Cross, R. (1996). Cybergette: Sadie Plant, *21C,* 3 (95), 17–19.

Cvetkovich, A (1992). *Mixed Feelings: Feminism, Mass Culture, and Victorian Sensationalism*. New Brunswick NJ: Rutgers University Press.

Davies, E. (2004). Survival of the Smartest. *The Times*, 8 November. http://women.timesonline.co.uk/tol/life_and_style/women/fashion/article503680.ece

Dean, J. (1999a). Virtually Regulated: New Technologies and Social Control – Introduction. *Signs* 24 (4), 1067–8.

Dean, J. (1999b). Virtual Fears. *Signs* 24 (4), 1069–78.

Dean, J. (2006). Blogging Theory. *Bad Subjects* 75. http://bad.eserver.org/issues/2006/75/dean.htm, accessed 10 December 2008.

Deleuze, G. and Guattari, F. (1972). *Anti-Œdipus: Capitalism and Schizophrenia Vol. I.* Trans. R. Hurley, M. Seem and H.R. Lane. London and New York NY: Continuum.

Deleuze, G. and Guattari, F. (1987). *A Thousand Plateaus: Capitalism and Schizophrenia Vol. II.* Trans. B. Massumi. Minneapolis MA: University of Minnesota Press.

Deleuze, G. and Parnet, C. (2007). *Dialogues II.* New York NY: Columbia University Press.

Derrida, J. (1994). *Given Time I: Counterfeit Money*. Trans. P. Kamuf. Chicago IL and London: University of Chicago Press.

Dias, K. (2003). The Ana Sanctuary: Women's Pro-Ana Narratives in Cyberspace. *Journal of International Women's Studies* 4 (2).

Dibbell, J. (1993). A Rape in Cyberspace: or How an Evil Clown, a Trickster Spirit, Two Wizards, and a Cast Of Dozens Turned a Database into a Society. *Village Voice*, 21 December, 36–42.

Dibbell, J. (1998). *My Tiny Life: Crime and Passion in a Virtual World*. London: Fourth Estate.

Diken, B. (1998). *Strangers, Ambivalence and Social Theory*. Aldershot: Ashgate.

Doheny-Farina, S. (1996). *The Wired Neighbourhood*. New Haven CT and London: Yale University Press.

Dwyer-Hogg, C. (2001). How Eating Disorders are Being Promoted on the Net. *Independent*, 2 August.

Dyer, R. (1988). Children of the Night: Vampirism as Homosexuality/Homosexuality as Vampirism. In Radstone, S. (ed.), *Sweet Dreams: Sexuality, Gender, and Popular Fiction*. London: Lawrence and Wishart, pp. 47–73.

Eidson, S. (n/d). Starving for Perfection. http://www.lunarpages.com/jaoi/articles/art2#0.html, accessed 10 December 2008.

Erickson, T. (1996). The World Wide Web as Social Hypertext. Advanced Technology Group: Apple Computers Inc. http://www.pliant.org/personal/Tom_Erickson/SocialHypertext.html, accessed 10 December 2008.

Fanon, F. (1970). *Black Skin, White Masks*. London: Paladin.

Featherstone, M. and Burrows, R. (1995). Cultures of Technological Embodiment: An Introduction. In Featherstone, M. and Burrows, R. (eds), *Cyberspace, Cyber-bodies, Cyberpunk: Cultures of Technological Embodiment*. London: Sage, pp. 1–20.

Ferreday, D. (2008). Beyond the Fourth Wall: Reading, Passing and Intervention in Internet Research, Comment and Criticism section on New Methodologies in Feminist Research. *Feminist Media Studies* 8 (1), 85–99.

Ferreday, D. and Lock, S. (2007). Computer Crossdressing: Queering the Virtual Subject. In O'Riordan, K. and Philips, D.J. (eds), *Queer Online: Media Technology and Sexuality*. Oxford and Bern: Peter Lang, 155–74.

Fonow, M. and Cook, J. (1991). *Beyond Methodology: Feminist Scholarship as Lived Research*. Bloomington and Indianapolis IN: Indiana University Press.

Fortier, A.M. (1999). Re-Membering Places and the Performance of Belonging(s). In Bell, V. (ed.), *Performativity and Belonging*. London, Thousand Oaks CA and New Delhi: Sage, pp. 41–64.

Foster, T. (1999). Meat Puppets or Robopaths? Cyberpunk and the Question of Embodiment. In Wolmark, J. (ed.), *Cybersexualities*. Edinburgh: Edinburgh University Press, pp. 208–29.

Franklin, S., Lury, C. and Stacey, J. (2000). *Global Nature, Global Culture*. London, Thousand Oaks CA and New Delhi: Sage.

Freud, S. (1991). *The Interpretation of Dreams*. London: Penguin.

Garber, M. (1992). *Vested Interests: Cross-Dressing and Cultural Anxiety*. London and New York NY: Routledge.

Gatens, M. (1996). *Imaginary Bodies: Ethics, Power and Corporeality*. London and New York NY: Routledge.

Gauntlett, D. (2000). Web Studies: A User's Guide. In Gauntlett, D. (ed.), *Web Studies*. London: Arnold, pp. 2–18.

George, L. (2002). Nurturing an Anorexia Obsession. *Los Angeles Times*, 12 February.

Gere, C. (2002). *Digital Culture*. London: Reaktion Books.

Gould, P. (1991). Dynamic structures of geographic space. In Brunn, S.D. and Leinbach, T.R. (eds), *Collapsing Space and Time: Geographic Aspects of Communications and Information*. London: HarperCollins, pp. 3–30.

Hall, S. (1994). Cultural Identity and Diaspora. In Williams, P. and Chrisman, L. (eds), *Colonial Discourse & Postcolonial Theory: A Reader*. London: Harvester Wheatsheaf, pp. 392–403.

Haraway, D. (1991). *Simians, Cyborgs and Women*. London: Free Association Press.

Haraway, D. (1995). Cyborgs and Symbionts: Living Together in the New World Order. In Hables Gray, C., Figueroa-Arriera, H.J. and Mentor, S. (eds), *The Cyborg Handbook*. London and New York NY: Routledge, pp.xi–xx.

Haraway, D. (1997). *Modest witness @ second_millenium_femaleMan_meets_OncoMouse : Feminism and Technoscience*. London and New York NY: Routledge.

Harcourt, W. (1999). Cyborg Melody: an introduction to Women on the Net. In Harcourt, W. (ed.), *Women@Internet*. London: Zed Books, pp. 1–20.

Harris, D. (1985). The Kitschification of AIDS. In *The Rise and Fall of Gay Culture*. New York NY: Hyperion.

Hayles, N.K. (1993). The Seductions of Cyberspace. In Andermatt Conley, V. (ed.), *Rethinking Technologies*. Minneapolis MN: Minnesota University Press, pp. 173–90.

Hayles, N.K. (2000). The Condition of Virtuality. In Lunenfeld, P. (ed.), *The Digital Dialectic*. Cambridge MA: MIT Press, pp. 69–94.

Hayles, N.K. (1999). *How We Became Posthuman: Virtual Bodies in Cybernetics, Literature, and Informatics*. Chicago IL: University of Chicago Press.

Healy, D. (1997). Cyberspace and Place: the Internet as Middle Landscape on the Electronic Frontier. In Porter, D. (ed.), *Internet Culture*. London and New York NY: Routledge, 55–68.

Hill, S. (2002). Profile: David Silver strikes cybergold. *University Week* 19 (23). University of Washington. http://depts.washington.edu/uweek/archives/2002.04.APR_18/news_d.html, accessed 10 December 2008.

Hine, C. (1998). Virtual Ethnography. Paper given at IRISS conference, Bristol, 25–27 March.

Holmes, D. (1997). Introduction. In Holmes, D. (ed.), *Virtual Politics: Identity and Community in Cyberspace*. London: Sage, pp. 1–25.

hooks, b. (1992). *Black Looks: Race and Representation*. Turnaround Press.

Jackson, R. (1981). *Fantasy: the Literature of Subversion*. London and New York NY: Routledge.

Jarman, D. (1995). *Derek Jarman's Garden*, London: Overlook Press.

Jones, S.G. (1995). Understanding community in the information age. In Jones, S.G. (ed.), *Cybersociety: Computer-mediated Communication and Community*. London, Thousand Oaks CA and New Delhi: Sage, pp. 10–35.

Jones, S.G. (1997). The Internet and its Social Landscape. In Jones, S.G. (ed.), *Virtual Culture*. London, Thousand Oaks CA and New Delhi: Sage 7–35.

Kidman, A. (2001). Starved of Revenue. *Australian IT*, 27 September.

Kristeva, J. (1982). *Powers of Horror: an Essay on Abjection*. New York NY: Columbia University Press.

Lally, E. (2002). *At Home With Computers*. London and New York NY: Berg.

LaPlanche, J. and Pontalis, J.B. (1986). Fantasy and the Origins of Sexuality. In Bergin, V., Donal, J. and Kaplan, C. (eds), *Formations of Fantasy*. London and New York NY: Methuen, pp. 5–34.

Lawson, N. (2001). *Nigella Bites*. London: Chatto & Windus.

Lemos, A. (1996). The Labyrinth of Minitel. In Shields, R. (ed.), *Cultures of Internet*. London, Thousand Oaks CA and New Delhi: Sage, pp. 33–48.

Locke, J. and Pascoe, E. (2000). Can A Sense of Community Flourish in Cyberspace? *Guardian*, 11 March.

Lorde, A. (1984). *Sister Outsider*. New York NY: The Crossing Press.

Lunt, P.K. and Livingstone, S.M. (1992). *Mass Consumption and Personal Identity*. Buckingham: Open University Press.

Lupton, D. (1996). *Food, the Body and the Self.* London, Thousand Oaks CA and New Delhi: Sage.

Lury, C. (1996). *Consumer Culture*. Oxford: Blackwell.

MacClancy, J. (1992). *Consuming Culture*. London: Chapmans.

McClintock, A. (1995). *Imperial Leather*. London and New York NY: Routledge.

McMillan, D.W. and Chavis, D.M. (1986). Sense of community: A definition and theory. *Journal of Community Psychology* 14 (1), 6–23.

Markham, A. (1998). *Life Online*. New York NY: Sage.

Markham, J.E. (1998). *The Future of Shopping*. London: MacMillan.

Massumi, B. (2002). *Parables for the Virtual*. Durham NC: Duke University Press.

Mauss, M. (1990). *The Gift: forms and functions of exchange in archaic societies*. London and New York NY: Routledge.

Medhurst, A. (1998). Shop till you(r connection) drop(s): Producing and consuming e-commerce. Paper given at Language, Identity and New Technologies Conference, University of Westminster, 7 November.

Merleau-Ponty, M. (1964). *The Visible and the Invisible*. Trans. A. Lingis. Evanston IL: Northwestern University Press.

Meuret, I. (2008). Writing Size Zero: Figuring Anorexia in Contemporary World Literatures. In Twohig, P.L. and Kalitzkus, V. (eds), *Social Studies of Health, Illness and Disease*. Amsterdam and New York NY: Rodopi, pp. 75–94.

Miller, D. (1997). Could Shopping Ever Really Matter? In Falk, P. and Campbell, C. (eds), *The Shopping Experience*. London, Thousand Oaks CA and New Delhi: Sage, pp. 31–55.

Miller, D. and Slater, D. (2000). *The Internet: an Ethnographic Approach.* New York NY: Berg.

Miller, D. (2001). *The Dialectics of Shopping.* Chicago IL and London: University of Chicago Press.

Miller, H. (1995). The Presentation of Self in Electronic Life: Goffman on the Internet. Paper presented at Embodied Knowledge and Virtual Space Conference, Goldsmiths College. www.isr.uci.edu/~jpd/classes/ics234cw04/miller.pdf, accessed 10 December 2008.

Miller, H. (1999). The Hypertext Home: Images and Metaphors of Home on World Wide Web Home Pages. Paper presented at the Design History Society Home and Away Conference, Nottingham Trent University. ess.ntu.ac.uk/miller/cyberpsych/goffman., accessed 10 December 2008.

Milne, E. (2000). Vicious Circles: Metaphor and the Historiography of Cyberspace. *Social Semiotics*, 10–1, 99–108.

Mitchell, W.J. (1999). *E-topia.* Cambridge MA and London: MIT Press.

Mitra, A. (1997). Virtual Commonality: Looking for India on the Internet. In Jones, S.G. (ed.), *Virtual Culture.* London, Thousand Oaks CA and New Delhi: Sage, pp. 55–79.

More, T. (1974). *Utopia.* London: Everyman.

Morley, D. and Robins, K. (1995). *Spaces of Identity.* London and New York NY: Routledge.

Morse, M. (1994). What do Cyborgs Eat? Oral Logic in an Information Society. *Discourse* 16 (3): 86–123.

Moser, M.A. (1996). *Immersed in Technology: Art and Virtual Environments.* Cambridge MA: MIT Press.

Nakamura, L. (1995). Race In/for Cyberspace: Identity Tourism and Racial Passing on the Internet. *Works and Days* 25/26, 13 (1–2), 181–93.

Nakamura, L. (2007a). Cultural Difference, Theory, and Cyberculture Studies: A Case of Mutual Repulsion. In Silver, D. and Massanari, A. (eds), *Critical Cyberculture Studies.* New York NY: New York University Press, pp. 29–36.

Nakamura, L. (2007b). *Digitizing Race: Visual Cultures of the Internet.* Minneapolis MN: University of Minnesota Press.

Nava, M. (1992). *Changing Cultures*. London, Thousand Oaks CA and New Delhi: Sage.

Nixon, N. (1999). Cyberpunk: Preparing the Ground for Revolution or Keeping the Boys Satisfied? In Wolmark, J. (ed.), *Cybersexualities*. Edinburgh: Edinburgh University Press, pp. 191–207.

Noble, D.F. (1997). *The Religion of Technology*. London: Penguin.

Nunes, M. (1997). What is Cyberspace? The Internet and Virtuality. In Holmes, D. (ed.), *Virtual Politics: Identity and Communication in Cyberspace*. London: Sage, pp. 163–78.

O'Barr, W.M. (1994). *Culture and the Ad: Exploring Otherness in the World of Advertising*. Boulder CO: Westview Press.

O'Riordan, K. and Philips, D.J. (eds) (2007). *Queer Online: Media Technology and Sexuality*. New York NY: Peter Lang.

Pearce, L. (1994). *Reading Dialogics*. London: Edward Arnold.

Pearce, L. (1995). Finding a Place from which to Write: the Methodology of Feminist Textual Practice. In Skeggs, B. (ed.), *Feminist Cultural Theory: Process and Production*. Manchester: Manchester University Press, pp. 81–96.

Penny, S. (1994). Virtual Reality as the Completion of the Enlightenment Project. In Bender, G. and Druckrey, T. (eds), *Culture on the Brink*. San Francisco CA: Bay Press, pp. 231–48.

Personal Home Page Institute (1996). *The First World Wide Web Personal Home Page Survey*. Philadelphia, University of Pennsylvania. http://www.nicoladoering.de/Hogrefe/buten/www.asc.upenn.edu/usr/sbuten/survey1.htm, accessed 10 December 2008.

Persram, N. (1997). *In My Father's House are Many Mansions: The Nation and Postcolonial Desire*. In Mirza, H. (ed.), *Black British Feminism*, London: Routledge, pp. 205–15.

Plant, S. (1997). *Zeroes and Ones*. London: Fourth Estate.

Poppe, E. (1998). Forward to the Past: Is a Hypertext a Text? – Some Provisory Notes and Reflections. *Iris* 25, 39–43.

Porter, J.E. (1999). Liberal individualism and Internet policy: A Communitarian critique. In Hawisher, G.E. and Selfe, C.L. (eds), *Passions, Pedagogies, and 21st-Century Technologies*. Logan UT: Utah State University Press, pp. 231–48.

Poster, M. (1995). Postmodern Virtualities. In Featherstone, M. and Burrows, R. (eds), *Cyberspace, Cyberbodies, Cyberpunk*. London, Thousand Oaks CA and New Delhi: Sage, pp. 79–95.

Probyn, E. (1993). *Sexing the Self: Gendered Positions in Cultural Studies*. London and New York NY: Routledge.

Probyn, E. (1996). *Outside Belongings*. London and New York NY: Routledge.

Probyn, E. (2000). *Carnal Appetites: Food Sex Identities*. London and New York NY: Routledge.

Quinby, L. (1999). Virile-Reality: from Armageddon to Viagra. *Signs* 24 (4), 1079–87.

Reaves, J. (2001). Anorexia Goes High Tech. *Time*, 31 July.

Reinharz, S. (1992). *Feminist Methods in Social Research*. Oxford: Oxford University Press.

Rheingold, H. (1993). *The Virtual Community: Homesteading on the Electronic Frontier*. http://www.well.com/www/hlr/vcbook/index.html, accessed 10 December 2008.

Rheingold, H. (2000). Community Development in the Cybersociety of the Future. In Gauntlett, D. (ed.), *Web Studies*. London: Arnold, pp. 170–8.

Riley, D. (2002). *Impersonal Passions: Language as Affect*. Durham NC: Duke University Press.

Roberts, L.D., Smith, L.M. and Pollock, C. (1996). MOOing Till the Cows Come Home: The search for sense of community in virtual environments. Paper given at the 6th National Australian and New-Zealand community Psychology Conference, Toodyay, Western Australia.

Robins, K. and Webster, F. (1999). *Times of the Technoculture*. London and New York NY: Routledge.

Rook, D.W. and Fisher, R.J. (1995). Normative influence on impulsive buying behaviour. *Journal of Consumer Research* 22, 305–13.

Rook, D.W. and Hoch, S.J. (1985). Consuming Impulses. In Holbrook, M.B. and Hirschman, E.C. (eds), *Advances in Consumer Research* XII, 23–7.

Rothstein, E. (1995). Hell is Other People's Web Pages. *New York Times*, archived at http://www.xent.com/FoRK-archive/spring96/0249.html, accessed 10 December 2008.

Rucker, R. (1992). *Mondo 2000: A User's Guide to the New Edge*. London: Thames and Hudson.

Said, E. (1978). *Orientalism*. London: Routledge and Kegan Paul.

Sedgwick, E.K. (1994). *Tendencies*. London and New York NY: Routledge.

Sedgwick, E.K. and Frank, A. (1996). *Shame and its Sisters: A Silvan Tomkins Reader*. Durham NC: Duke University Press.

Sedgwick, E.K. and Frank, A. (2003). *Touching Feeling: Affect, Pedagogy, Performativity*. Durham NC: Duke University Press.

Seidler, V. (1998). Embodied Knowledge and Virtual Space. In Wood, J. (ed.), *The Virtual Embodied: Presence/Practice/ Technology*. New York NY: Routledge, pp. 15–29.

Serfaty, Vivien (2003). The Mirror and the Veil: An Overview of American Online Diaries and Blogs. *Amsterdam Monographs in American Studies* 11. Amsterdam and New York NY: Rodopi.

Shaw, D.F. (1997). Gay Men and Computer Communication: a Discourse of Sex and Identity in Cyberspace. In Jones, S.G. (ed.), *Virtual Culture*. London, Thousand Oaks CA and New Delhi: Sage, pp. 133–45.

Silver, D. (2004). Internet/Cyberculture/Digital Culture/New Media/ Fill-in-the-blank studies. *New Media and Society* 6 (1), 55–64.

Silver, D. (2006). Introduction: Where is Internet Studies. In Silver, D., Massanari, A. and Jones, S.G. (eds), *Critical Cyberculture Studies*. New York NY: New York University Press, pp. 1–14.

Skeggs, B. (1995). Theorising, Ethics and Representation in Feminist Ethnography. In Skeggs, B. (ed.), *Feminist Cultural Theory: Process and Production*. Manchester: Manchester University Press, pp. 190–207.

Smith, J. and Balka, E. (1988). Chatting on a Feminist Computer Network. In Kramarae, C. (ed.), Technology and *Women's Voices: Keeping in Touch*. New York NY and London: Routledge and Kegan Paul, pp. 82–97.

Smith, W. and Kelemen, M. (1999). Virtual Dreams, Imagined Communities. www.le.ac.uk/ulmc/doc/9912.pdf, accessed 10 July 2006.

Sobchak, V. (1995). Beating the Meat/Surviving the Text, or How to Get Out of this Century Alive. In Featherstone, M. and Burrows, R. (eds), *Cyberspace/Bodies/Punk: Cultures of Technological Embodiment*. London, Thousand Oaks CA and New Delhi: Sage, pp. 205–13.

Sophia, Z. (1992). Virtual Corporeality: a Feminist View. *Australian Feminist Studies* 15, 11–24.

Sophia, Z. (1998). The Mythic Machine: Gendered Irrationalities and Computer Culture. In Bromley, H. and Apple, M. (eds), *Education/Technology/Power: Educational Computing as a Social Practice*. Albany NY: State University of New York Press, pp. 29–51.

Spender, D. (1995). *Nattering on the Net: Women, Power, and Cyberspace*. Melbourne: Spinifex Press.

Spignesi, A. (1983). *Starving Women: A Psychology of Anorexia and Bulimia*. Dallas TX: Spring Publications.

Springgay, S. (2003). Cloth as intercorporeality: Touch, fantasy, and performance and the construction of body knowledge. *International Journal of Education and the Arts* 4 (5).

Stallybrass, P. and White, A. (1986). *The Politics and Poetics of Transgression*. London: Methuen.

Stanley, L. and Wise, S. (1990). *Feminist Praxis*. London and New York NY: Routledge.

Star, S.L. (1995). *The Cultures of Computing*. Oxford: Blackwell, pp. 30–46.

Star, S.L. (1996). From Hestia to Home Page: Feminism and the Concept of Home in Cyberspace. In Lykke, N. and Braidotti, R. (eds), *Between Monsters, Goddesses and Cyborgs: Feminist Confrontations with Science, Medicine and Cyberspace*. London: Zed Books, pp. 30–46.

Stefanoni, M., Lackaf, D. and Rosen, D. (2008). We're All Celebrities Now: Reality Television, Web 2.0, and Mediated Identities. *Proceedings of the nineteenth ACM conference on Hypertext and hypermedia*. Pittsburgh PA, 107–12.

Steinfield, C. and Whitten, P. (1999). Community level socio-economic impacts of electronic commerce. *Journal of Computer Mediated Communication* 5 (2).

Sterne, J. (2006). The Historiography of Cyberculture. In Silver, D. and Massanari, A. (eds), *Critical Cyberculture Studies*. New York NY: New York University Press, pp. 17–28.

Stoll, C. (1995). *Silicon Snake Oil: Second Thoughts on the Information Highway*. New York NY: Doubleday.

Stone, A.R. (1991). Will the Real Body Please Stand Up? Boundary Stories about Virtual Cultures. In Benedikt, M. (ed.), *Cyberspace: First Steps*. Cambridge MA: MIT Press, pp. 81–118.

Stone, A.R. (1993). What Vampires Know: Transsubjection and Transgender in Cyberspace. gender.eserver.org/what-vampires-know.txt, accessed 10 December 2008.

Stone, A.R. (1995). *The War of Desire and Technology at the Close of the Mechanical Age*. Cambridge MA: MIT Press.

Stratton, J. (1997). Cyberspace and the Globalisation of Culture. In Porter, D. (ed.), *Internet Culture*. London and New York NY: Routledge, 253–75.

Sturken, M. (1997). *Tangled Memories: The Vietnam War, The AIDS Epidemic, and the Politics of Remembering*. Berkeley CA: University of California Press.

Tal, K. (2001). Book of the Month. *Resource Centre for Cyberculture Studies*. http://www.com.washington.edu/rccs/books/harcourt/index5.html, accessed 10 December 2008.

Talbott, S.L. (1995). *The Future Does Not Compute: Transcending the Machines in Our Midst*. Sebastopol CA: O'Reilly.

Thornton, P. (2001). Terror Attacks are Tipping World Economy into Recession. *Independent*, 27 September.

Tomkins, S. (1962). *Affect, Imagery, Consciousness*. New York NY: Springer.

Turkle, S. (1984). *The Second Self*. New York NY: Simon and Schuster.

Turkle, S. (1988). Computational Reticence: Why Women Fear the Intimate Machine. In Kramarae, C. (ed.), *Technology and Women's*

Voices: Keeping in Touch. New York NY and London: Routledge and Kegan Paul, pp. 365–80.

Turkle, S. (1995). *Life on the Screen: Identity in the Age of the Internet*. New York NY: Simon and Schuster.

Ulmer, G. (1994). *Heuretics: The Logic of Invention*. Baltimore MA: Johns Hopkins University Press.

Vincent, F. (2002). An evaluation of Freud's contribution to our understanding of gender difference, accessed 10 December 2008.

Wakeford, N. (2000). Handbag.com and other sites of real queerness on the net. http://virtualsociety.sbs.ox.ac.uk/events/pvwakeford.htm, accessed 10 December 2008.

Wertheim, M. (1999). *The Pearly Gates of Cyberspace: a History of Space from Dante to the Internet*. London: Virago Press.

Wilbur, S.P. (2000). An Archaeology of Cyberspace: Virtuality, Community, Identity. In Bell, D. and Kennedy, B.M. (eds), *The Cybercultures Reader*. New York NY: Routledge, pp. 45–55.

Wilding, F. (1998). Where is the Feminism in Cyberfeminism? *Paradoxa* 1 (2), 6–13.

Williams, R. (2002). Use it Up, Wear it Out. *Guardian*, 3 January.

Wise, P. (1997). Always Already Virtual: Feminist Politics in Cyberspace. In Holmes, D. (ed.), *Virtual Politics: Identity and Community in Cyberspace*. London: Sage, pp. 179–96.

Wisker, G. (1998). If Looks Could Kill: Contemporary Women's Vampire Fictions. In Pearce, L. and Wisker, G. (eds), *Fatal Attractions: Re-scripting the Romance in Contemporary Literature and Film*. London: Pluto Press.

Wissinger, E. (2007). Always on Display: Affective Production in the Modelling Industry. In Ticineto Clough, P. and Halley, J. (eds), *The Affective Turn: Theorising the Social*. Durham NC: Duke University Press, pp. 321–60.

Wood, A.F. and Smith, M.J. (2005). *Online Communication*. London and New York NY: Routledge.

Young, C. (1998). A Kinder, Gentler Glossary for Net Neophytes – and Others. http://www.grouchy.com, accessed 1 November 2006.

Zaleski, J. (1997). *The Soul of Cyberspace*. San Francisco: Harper.

Žižek, S. (1998). The Cyberspace Real: Cyberspace Between Perversion and Trauma. http://www.egs.edu/faculty/Žižek/Žižek-the-cyberspace-real.html, accessed 17 November 2008.

Žižek, S. (2008). The Interpassive Subject. http://www.egs.edu/faculty/Žižek/Žižek-the-interpassive-subject.html, accessed 1 December 2007.

Index